Managing Tourism in Cities

Managing Tourism in Cities

POLICY, PROCESS AND PRACTICE

Edited by

DUNCAN TYLER
YVONNE GUERRIER and
MARTIN ROBERTSON

JOHN WILEY & SONS
Chichester · New York · Weinheim · Brisbane · Singapore · Toronto

Other Wiley Editorial Offices

John Wiley & Sons, Inc., 605 Third Avenue,
New York, NY 10158-0012, USA

WILEY-VCH Verlag GmbH, Pappelallee 3,
D-69469 Weinheim, Germany

Jacaranda Wiley Ltd, 33 Park Road, Milton,
Queensland 4064, Australia

John Wiley & Sons (Canada) Ltd, 22 Worcester Road,
Rexdale, Ontario M9W 1L1, Canada

John Wiley & Sons (Asia) Pte Ltd, 2 Clementi Loop #02-01,
Jin Xing Distripark, Singapore 129809

Library of Congress Cataloging-in-Publication Data

Tyler, Duncan.
     Managing tourism in cities : policy, process, and practice / Duncan
Tyler, Yvonne Guerrier and Martin Robertson.
          p.   cm.
     Includes bibliographical references and index.
     ISBN 0-471-98315-2
     1. Tourist trade.   2. Cities and towns.   I. Robertson, Martin.
II. Guerrier, Yvonne.   III. Title.
G155.A1T888   1998
338.4'791—dc21   98–5756
                                                                          CIP

British Library Cataloguing in Publication Data

A catalogue record for this book is available from the British Library

ISBN 0-471-98315-2

Typeset in 10/12pt Times from authors' disks by Dorwyn Ltd, Rowlands Castle, Hants
Printed and bound in Great Britain by Bookcraft (Bath) Ltd, Midsomer Norton, Somerset.
This book is printed on acid-free paper responsibly manufactured from sustainable forestry, in which at least two trees are planted for each one used for paper production.

Contents

List of contributors

Gary Akehurst is Professor of Marketing at the University of Portsmouth Business School (UK). He has a first degree in economics, a masters in management, and a PhD in marketing. Previously he was with the Greene Belfield-Smith Division of Deloitte & Touche Consulting Group, during which time he led a team which prepared the tourism plan for the government of Albania (funded by the European Bank of Reconstruction and Development) and a review of EU member states' tourism policies for the British government's Department of Employment. He is founding Editor of the *Service Industries Journal*, the first academic journal devoted to the study of the service sector.

Jan van der Borg is a researcher at the University of Venice and Assistant Professor at the Department of Regional Economics at the Erasmus University, Rotterdam. His writings concern the economics and management of tourism in general, and of tourism in urban environments in particular. Moreover, he has advised, among others, UNESCO, the European Commission and the Council of Europe on issues regarding tourism in heritage cities.

Belinda Dodson is a Lecturer in the Department of Environmental and Geographical Science at the University of Cape Town. She joined the department in 1990 having obtained her PhD in Geography from Cambridge University, which focused on the socio-economic impact of minor flood-control projects in Bangladesh. Her broader teaching and research interests include cultural geography, development geography and human–environment relations, especially issues of environment and development in the developing world. Together with Darryll Kilian she has been researching the redevelopment of Cape Town's waterfront, practically since its inception. Her other current research interest is the history of soil conservation in South Africa.

Katie Evans is a Senior Lecturer in Tourism Management at the University of Derby, UK. She is course Leader of the MA in Tourism Management and co-Director of the Tourism Research Group. She completed her MBA at Nottingham Trent University while teaching undergraduate and postgraduate tourism courses. She has travelled independently in South-east Asia, followed by time spent working for both tour operators and travel agents. Initial research interests and publications were focused on development issues in the Gambia and current research includes resource management issues at World Heritage Sites.

Yvonne Guerrier is Professor of Hotel Management at South Bank University, London. Her main research focus is in the field of human resource management and organisational behaviour, especially in the hospitality and tourism sector. She is author of some 40 academic articles in these areas. However, she has an interest in the way people respond to their environment and was editor-in-chief of the Wiley book *Values and the Environment: a social science perspective.*

C. Michael Hall is Professor of Tourism at The Centre for Tourism, School of Business and Government, University of Otago, Dunedin, New Zealand. His major interests include tourism planning and development, public policy, regional development, environmental history, heritage management, special interest tourism, and wine tourism. Specific regional interests include Australia, Canada, New Zealand, the Pacific Rim, northern Europe and the polar regions.

Howard L. Hughes is Professor of Tourism Management at Manchester Metropolitan University, UK. He is author of a specialist economics textbook and of over thirty published papers on aspects of the hotel and tourism industries. He is currently engaged in a research project examining the entertainment–vacation link. Other research interests include: urban tourism and hallmark events; the government–tourism relationship; holidays for disadvantaged and marginalised groups.

Habibullah Khan, PhD (New South Wales), is a Senior Lecturer in the Department of Economics and Statistics at the National University of Singapore. His research areas include socio-economic analysis of development, economics of tourism, industrial policy, and marine resource economics. He has published in various international journals and has undertaken consultancy with the World Bank, ESCAP, and the UNCRD in these subject areas.

Darryll Kilian is an environmental manager with the Environmental Evaluation Unit at the University of Cape Town, working on a range of impact assessment, research and policy-related projects. As an environmental management practitioner located within an academic institution, he combines consulting activities with postgraduate teaching and training. He has been involved in a three-year research project assessing the socio-economic implications of waterfront revitalisation in Cape Town. Presently, he is researching issues related to leisure, urban change and social transformation in the post-apartheid South African city.

Trevor Mules is Associate Professor within the Graduate School of Management at Griffith University, Queensland, Australia. He is a PhD in economics and has published and researched widely in the area of economic impacts of tourism, especially major event tourism. He led a team of researchers investigating the economic impacts of the inaugural Formula One Grand Prix in Adelaide in 1985, and the 1990 Adelaide Arts Festival. He developed forecasts of economic impacts for Adelaide's bid to host the 1998 Commonwealth Games, and was part of a team working with KPMG Management Consultants which developed forecasts of the economic impacts of the 2000 Sydney Olympic Games.

Martin Robertson is a Lecturer in Tourism Management at South Bank University. His first degree was in Politics and Modern History and he has an MA in Leisure Policy and Practice from Heriot-Watt University, Edinburgh. He specialises in event management and the social science of leisure and urban tourism and was the coordinator of the original conference 'The Urban Environment: Tourism' upon which this volume has drawn for some of its inspiration.

Myra Shackley is Professor of Culture Resource Management and Head of the Centre for Tourism and Visitor Management at Nottingham Trent University. Her major research interests lie in the utilisation of cultural and natural resources for tourism, particularly related to visitor management issues. Most of her work is carried out in the developing world with recent fieldwork-based projects in Mali, Guyana, India, Namibia and Nepal. Her most recent book *Wildlife Tourism* (Thomson International Business Press, 1997) has received favourable reviews, and she is currently editing a volume of case studies examining visitor management at World Heritage Sites (Butterworth-Heinemann, 1998).

John Tunbridge is Associate Professor of Geography at Carleton University in Ottawa. He has published on heritage issues and related tourism, particularly in urban and waterfront contexts, for over twenty years. He has a further longstanding interest in Southern Africa, particularly with respect to heritage tourism.

Duncan Tyler is Senior Lecturer in Tourism Management at South Bank University, London. His first degree is in Environmental Sciences (major environmental policy) and his Masters in Urban and Regional Studies (specialism Leisure and Tourism). His research interests range from ecotourism to urban development, with a focus on policy development. He worked for ten years as a consultant in environmental, tourism and leisure fields before joining the university. He is researching his PhD on influences on national and local tourism policy development within the UK.

Introduction: policy, process and practice in urban tourism

DUNCAN TYLER

Urban tourism has, as a field of academic enquiry, been addressed only in recent years. As a result, much writing to date has been involved in the description of supply and demand and assessment of current trends. This, as befits an emerging field, has concentrated on the exploration of factual demand and supply statistics (Law, 1993, 1996) and the nature of existing strategies and administrative structures (van den Berg, van der Borg and van der Meer, 1995). If the field of urban tourism is to progress, however, it must begin to inquire into the nature of the changes in urban economies and governance that tourism is part of. Page (1995 : 3) considers it 'apparent that major gaps exist in our understanding of the processes contributing to tourism . . . and the way it functions in different environments, particularly urban areas'. It is the aim of this book to explore these processes, in relation to case studies taken from major or emerging tourism cities around the world.

This book has its origins in several events taking place at South Bank University in mid-1994. At this time the university had just established an undergraduate degree in tourism management, and a research focus was being sought by the new team. Being based in that part of inner London, Southwark, which was just about to take off as London's new city-centre destination, an urban focus was the obvious choice. At the same time, the London Borough of Southwark (see Chapter 3) had just appointed their first Tourism Officer who was looking to learn, from the experience of other cities across the world, about the issues that may arise from their impending tourism development. The university agreed to invest some of its management training money in a conference to aid the aims of the team, the local authority and others interested in the subject.

The conference 'The Urban Environment: Tourism' took place in September 1995 at the university. Thirty-eight papers were presented covering a wide range of political, social, cultural, environmental, product development, visitor management and strategic development issues (see the Appendix for a full list). One might view these papers as a rather eclectic mix (Bramwell, 1997), but at a time when Law (1993) was the only true text on the subject, and others were debating whether such a beast as urban tourism existed, as an exploratory conference it was felt to be successful.

As Bramwell (1997) discussed, the main thread, emphasised by van der Borg's (1995) keynote speech, was that cities must determine their carrying capacities before committing to development, even if this limit seems a long way off when the immediate need is often for economic restructuring and employment creation. It appeared to us that there was a need to explore the political and management processes buried under the carrying capacity issue, i.e. who decides what type of tourism? How much tourism should be allowed? Should tourism be developed at all? If so how can one manage the change from a Fordist to a post-Fordist urban economy? Will tourism development change the residents' views of their cities? How far is tourism development a national or a local issue?

Given these types of questions and our interest in process it was decided to produce this volume based around a few core papers from the conference, supported by specially commissioned papers that explore these issues. We have not directly addressed the 'city marketing' theme as, first, this is discussed elsewhere (Ashworth and Voogd, 1990), and, second, the major issues for city tourism are often not how to sell their product but how to manage the product and its development to the benefit of local residents and industry players. It is this issue which occupies us in this volume.

The chapters have been collated around four themes. These are: *Policy and Planning*, *Visitor Management*, *Perception of Space*, and *Events Management*. Each section has its own introduction, so it is not the place here to discuss the content of each chapter, but it is clear from recurring themes which cross the section boundaries that the management of tourism in cities is a convoluted, iterative and political process with many dimensions.

Carrying capacity limits are explicitly discussed in the chapters by Khan, van der Borg, Tyler, Shackley and Evans, considering such aspects as politicians' fear of tourist crowding, the loss of identity of heritage areas, loss of city functions from the centre, and clashes of interest between the tourism industry, residents and international agencies. Some solutions are explored including the use of new technology and sales techniques, regional perspectives to city tourism development, analysing, as Gunn (1993) does, the city in a wider geographical context, visitor flow management and, above all, consultation processes.

Underlying the carrying capacity issues is who decides what type of *tourism policy* is acceptable. Again this theme is present in all the sections, but is concentrated upon in Section I where Hall explores the nature of top-down planning, Tyler a more pluralist form, Akehurst a bottom-up process and Khan an economic or 'governed economy' approach. Elsewhere, Dodson and Kilian explore the incremental process of development decision making and Evans the differing needs of internationally designated areas and the residential requirements of the city's population. What these case studies clearly show is that policy decisions must be made within the cultural, political and social environment of the city. Prescriptive models, as Hall discusses, are of little relevance to policy making practice in reality.

Holloway, in his paper to the conference (see Appendix), was concerned that the *visitors' perceptions* of the city should be taken into account when developing the product to ensure that the visitor understands the city and feels secure. Section III explores these issues in relation to heritage (Evans) and redeveloped city areas (Dodson and Kilian). Hughes takes a different view, not so much of tourist perceptions but looking at the appropriation and commoditisation of space by the tourism industry, a theme also picked up by Dodson and Kilian. Tunbridge, and Dodson and Kilian also highlight issues of residents' perception of tourist areas, with Hughes also considering this in the context of the culture of the city.

A theme that runs through nearly every chapter is that of the effect of urban processes and administrative structures on the development and management of the city tourism product. In his challenging paper, Ashworth (1992) considered that urban tourism exists if the city is either shaping or is shaped by tourism; the existence of tourism in a city as a geographic concept was little reason for its continued study as a separate field. Law (1993) considered that urban tourism should also be characterised by the whole of the city tourism product creating an experience larger than the sum of the parts.

In this book we see that the urban *processes* of local politics (Hall, and Tyler), regeneration structures (Hall, Tyler, Dodson and Kilian, Akehurst), the role of the city in the state or national scene (Mules, Tyler, Hall, Khan, Robertson and Guer-rier), city jurisdiction issues (Hall, Tyler, Dodson and Kilian, Tunbridge, Shackley), city development cycles (Tyler, Dodson and Kilian) and international pressure (Evans and Shackley) all determine the nature of the urban tourism product. Thus it is the intrinsic nature of urban governance that shapes the city along with com-moditisation of the city which is shaped by tourism.

The role of the public sector is also much emphasised. Mules discusses the catalytic role of the state in coordinating events, Hall and Tyler consider the public sector role in the speed and nature of product development, Khan in the direction of future strategy and Dodson and Kilian in the role as regeneration leaders.

These themes permeate the case studies, and are supported by relevant theory. This later part is important, for as Hughes (1997 : 180) states in his review of Law (1996):

> It remains for Law or others to position this [urban tourism] material more firmly in theories of development, location, spatial transformation etc and start the process of synthesising it into something that might approach paradigms of urban tourism.

We do not claim to have achieved all that Hughes asks for here, indeed it would not be possible in one volume such as this, but it is hoped that we have begun to apply theories of urban development and processes of change management to the field of urban tourism, that others may pick up on and develop further.

References

Ashworth, G.J. (1992) 'Is there an urban tourism?', *Tourism Recreation Research*, 17, 2, 3–8.
Ashworth, G.J. and Voogd, H. (1990) *Selling the City*, London: Belhaven.
Bramwell, W. (1997) 'Managing urban tourism numbers', *Annals of Tourism Research*, 24, 1, 248.
Gunn, C. (1993) *Tourism Planning: Basics, Concepts and Cases*, New York: Taylor and Francis.
Hughes, H. (1997) 'Book review: Tourism in Major Cities, Law, C. (ed.)', *Journal of Vacation Marketing*, 3, 2, 180.
Laws, C. (1993) *Urban Tourism: Attracting Visitors to Large Cities*, London: Mansell.

Law, C. (ed.) (1996) *Tourism in Major Cities*, London: International Thomson Business Press.

Page, S. (1995) *Urban Tourism*, London: Routledge.

van den Berg, L., van der Berg, J. and van der Meer, J. (1995) *Urban Tourism Performance and Strategies In Eight European Cities*, Aldershot: Avebury.

van der Borg, J. (1995) 'The future of urban tourism: a synthesis', paper presented to *The Urban Environment: Tourism Conference*. South Bank University, London.

Section I
Policy and planning

Introduction

Much of what we call tourism planning now is more akin to policy development and analysis. Most of the major decisions which shape the nature of tourism development are not undertaken by planners *per se* but by politicians and interested parties. It is politicians and other influencers who shape the objectives from which plans are born, it is these same players who, very often, shape the nature of public participation, and it is the political and social values of a society which can eventually lead to the acceptance or not of the process and end products of plans (see Hall and Jenkins, 1995).

In this section we move the debate on planning for urban tourism, away from merely describing a tourism planning process as a series of rational, prescriptive steps (Gunn, 1993; Inskeep, 1991) to consider how the political, social and cultural processes of cities affect the way in which real-life decisions are made about the future of their tourism industries. This section looks at the processes that cities, and sub-city areas, have followed in adopting their plans and strategies.

This socio-political approach to planning does not negate the basic planning process, as described by Cooper *et al.* (1993). However, it takes a much closer look at the very early stages that shape the nature of that process in any given destination. The basic planning process begins with a set of planning objectives, and then, through a series of analyses (including demand and supply and options assessment), develops a plan to suit an area. A feedback loop links the final plan to the objectives, thus acting as a monitoring tool.

The academic emphasis has traditionally concentrated either on the analyses and end product elements of the process (Gunn, 1993; Inskeep, 1991; Pearce, 1989; WTO, 1994) or on public participation models (Murphy, 1985). Here, we have instead chosen to look at the influence of the city planners and politicians, and the political and social influences on the tourism planning process, particularly when setting the objectives or developing the processes of implementation. It is, after all, the objectives that direct the rest of the planning process, and the implementation process that ensures that a product (whether locally acceptable or not) actually gets developed; but it is the analysis of these and, hence the role of tourism in the wider urban economy, that is often overlooked.

The case studies in this section have been chosen to demonstrate that planning is more than a technical process, and that, although urban areas may show a certain amount of repetition of product types (heritage and cultural attractions, conference and convention centres, festival shopping, and events) the planning process under-taken to establish these or other products are shaped by the social and political conditions of the particular city or sub-city area rather than the nature of the product.

Early in the first chapter, Hall reviews the academic tourism planning literature, setting the scene for the rest of the section. He follows this with an analysis of how Darling Harbour, Sydney, was developed, using a top-down model where urban managers and politicians imposed upon a city a planning solution; a process justi-fied on the greater, state-wide need and time constraints. However, he questions the type of end-product that such a planning process produces, and calls for more local consultation in order for the city's tourism product to be relevant to all city residents rather than be dominated by a middle-class elite.

Following on, Akehurst discusses the practicalities and political imperatives that are required to be considered when developing a new tourism product in the urban setting. He takes his case study from Poland in eastern Europe, where the word 'planning' has centralist connotations and where people have not had to take deci-sions within a market economy for the past fifty years. He demonstrates the need to consult widely and to get the local community to 'own' the plan and the ideas within it. However, he is also quite emphatic that no matter what process one follows, there are certain elements that have to be included within the plan in order to realise the benefits that tourism can offer. Having said this, he clearly states the need not to impose an outside will and knowledge onto a community, but to let ideas and com-mitment evolve throughout the planning process.

Tyler, in Chapter 3, explores how a tourism policy has evolved, over twenty years, within an inner London borough, charting the myriad influences that helped turn a very tourism-sceptical borough into one of London's most successful destina-tions in attracting inward investment. It is clear that far from a rational process of tourism market analysis and options development persuading decision makers of the benefits of tourism, it was changes in the economic, social and political environ-ment that led to tourism becoming an acceptable part of the regeneration solution of the borough.

In Chapter 4, Khan considers how a tourism product has been planned over the past 15 years within a governed-market economy. In particular, he investigates what happens when a city-state, Singapore, realises that its carrying capacity has been or is being reached. Conventional planning may seek to manipulate the mar-ket to attract higher-value tourism, or to develop products that have a higher social and environmental carrying capacity. However, the social and political nature of Singapore's governed-market economy seeks to continue to reap the economic benefits of tourism development not only through product improvement but also by extending its influence outside the city-state boundaries and seeking to become a leader in regional tourism promotion and development, working in a competitively cooperative environment with its neighbours.

The cases show, therefore, that it is the process by which objectives and pro-grammes are identified (which is governed by the social, cultural and political environment), that are as important as, if not more than, the actual plan and recommendations themselves. While recommendations and development options can change over time with market conditions and tourist trends, the basic fundamental beliefs of a society, its goodwill, political and social acceptance and willingness to implement are less flexible beasts and need to be carefully nurtured if the final results are to lead to acceptable developments.

References

Cooper, C., Fletcher, J., Gilbert, D. and Wanhill, S. (1993) *Tourism: Principles and Practice*, London: Pitman.
Gunn, C.A. (1993) *Tourism Planning: Basics, Concepts, Cases*, Washington, DC: Taylor and Francis.
Hall, C.M. and Jenkins J.M. (1995) *Tourism and Public Policy*, London: Routledge.
Inskeep, E. (1991) *Tourism Planning: An Integrated and Sustainable Approach*, New York: Van Nostrand Rheinhold.
Murphy, P (1985) *Tourism: A Community Approach*, New York/London: Routledge.
Pearce, D. (1989) *Tourist Development* (2nd edn), Harlow: Longman Scientific & Technical.
World Tourism Organisation (1994) *National and Regional Tourism Planning*, London: Routledge.

1 The politics of decision making and top-down planning: Darling Harbour, Sydney

C. MICHAEL HALL

> ... the question arises as to whether or not there should be some form of public life or culture, accessible to all local citizens of the city; and if so, how this can be stimulated by local policies. This last question is particularly relevant in local politics. Is the city a product to be sold on the tourism market and/or as a location in which to invest money? Or is a city a place to live, where people can express themselves, even if it is in terms of resistance to, rather than rejoicing in, the dominant culture? (Bramham *et al.*, 1989 : 4).

CHAPTER SUMMARY

Mega-events have played a major role in the growth of tourism in Australia and are a major tool with which to encourage urban redevelopment and re-imaging. A case study of the redevelopment of Darling Harbour, Sydney, is provided. This indicates that the hosting of a mega-event leads to fast-track planning in which public participation is negligible and which also leads to the development of new middle-class urban leisure spaces.

Introduction

Tourism is an increasingly important component of the Australian economy, generating an estimated 10.48% of GDP in 1996 and accounting for 11.52% of employment (World Travel & Tourism Council, 1996). Long seen as only a 'bit part' or 'minor' industry in terms of national development, tourism has now assumed centre-stage as a major source of foreign income and overseas investment and as a key component in regional development strategies (Hall, 1995, 1998; Hall, Jenkins and Kearsley, 1997; Jenkins and Hall, 1997). Several complex reasons for the change of attitude towards tourism by politicians, bureaucrats, business and the public can be put forward and include:

Managing Tourism in Cities. Edited by D. Tyler, Y. Guerrier and M. Robertson.
Copyright © 1998 John Wiley & Sons Ltd.

- Recent major recessions
- Increasing concerns over foreign debt since the late 1970s. International tourism in particular is seen as a mechanism to help boost exports incomes
- Economic deregulation and the impacts of globalisation which have affected 'traditional' employment in the agricultural and manufacturing sectors. Tourism is seen as a 'sunrise' industry that is labour-intensive and which offers the potential to be a substantial source of employment
- Australia becoming a significant destination for international travellers in both global and regional terms (Hall, Jenkins and Kearsley, 1997).

Tourism planning, and related areas such as policy making, have been little studied in Australia (Craik, 1991; Hall, 1995; Hall, Jenkins and Kearsley, 1997) to the detriment of a comprehensive understanding of the supply-side of tourism, the formulation of government policy and the nature of public–private partnerships. One of the key components in the development of tourism in Australia since the early 1980s has been the hosting of mega-events including:

- The 1982 Commonwealth Games in Brisbane, Queensland
- The Australian Formula One Grand Prix held in Adelaide, South Australia, from 1985 to 1995
- The hosting of the 1986–7 Americas' Cup Defence in Fremantle, Western Australia
- The 1988 Australian Bicentennary which celebrated the 200th anniversary of the landing of the first fleet in Sydney
- The 1988 World's Fair held in Brisbane as a focal point for the Bicentennary celebrations (see Chapter 11 of this volume).

In the 1990s mega-events have continued to be a key facet of Australian urban tourism development through the successful bid of Sydney for the 2000 Summer Olympic Games and the shift of the Australian Formula One Grand Prix from Adelaide to Melbourne in 1996. The purpose of this chapter is to examine the planning dimensions of the interrelationships between the hosting of mega-events and the development of Darling Harbour, particularly with respect to their influence on urban tourism planning and decision making in Sydney. The chapter will first examine some of the key themes that emerge from the tourism planning and mega-event literature. It will then provide an overview of the development of Darling Harbour. Finally, the chapter will discuss the implications of the case study for our understanding of urban tourism planning processes.

Tourism planning

Planning for tourism has traditionally focused on land-use zoning, site development, accommodation and building regulations, the density of tourist development, the presentation of cultural, historical and natural tourism features, and the provision of infrastructure including roads and sewerage. However, in recent years, tourism planning has adapted and expanded to include environmental and sociocultural concerns, and the need to promote economic development at local, regional and national scales (Pearce, 1989).

The diverse nature of the tourism industry has meant that tourism planning has been difficult to define and grasp conceptually and, therefore, coordination of the various elements of the tourism product has been extremely difficult to achieve. Yet, somewhat paradoxically, it is the very nature of the industry, particularly the way in which local communities, their culture and lifestyles, and the environment are part of the tourist product, which makes planning so important (Murphy, 1985). As Gunn (1977 : 85) observed, because of the fragmented growth of the tourism industry 'the overall planning of the total tourism system is long overdue . . . there is no overall policy, philosophy or coordinating force that brings the many pieces of tourism into harmony and assures their continued harmonious function'. Moreover, planning is rarely exclusively devoted to tourism *per se*. Planning for tourism tends to be an amalgam of economic, socio-political and environmental considerations reflecting the diversity of the factors which influence, and are affected by, tourism development (Heely, 1981).

What is planning?

Veal (1992 : 3) stated that 'planning can be seen as the process of deciding'. However, the tourism planning process is not just about *deciding* what is to be provided in the future. It is very much more complex than that. Chadwick's (1971) response to 'what is planning?' is far more relevant. Chadwick states 'that planning is a process, a process of human thought and action based upon that thought – in point of fact, forethought, thought for the future – nothing more or less than this is planning, which is a very general human activity' (p.24). Hall's explanation of what planning should do further supports Chadwick's case: 'it [planning] should aim to provide a resource for democratic and informed decision-making. This is all planning can legitimately do, and all it can pretend to do. Properly understood, this is the real message of the systems revolution in planning and its aftermath' (Hall, 1982 : 303). Therefore, planning is only one part of an overall 'planning–decision–action' process. Further, various activities in that process may be difficult to isolate as the planning process and other activities involve such things as bargaining and negotiation, compromise, coercion, interests, values, choice, and, of course, politics (Hall and Jenkins, 1995).

The focus and methods of tourism planning have not remained constant and have evolved to meet the new demands which have been placed on the tourism industry (Getz, 1987; Hall and Jenkins, 1995). Getz (1987) identified four broad traditions or approaches to tourism planning: 'boosterism', an economic/industry-oriented approach, a physical/spatial approach, and a community-oriented approach which emphasises the role that the destination community plays in the tourism experience. As Getz (1987 : 5) noted, 'the four traditions are not mutually exclusive, nor are they necessarily sequential. Nevertheless, this categorisation is a convenient way to examine the different and sometimes overlapping ways in which tourism is planned, and the research and planning methods, problems and models associated with each'. To these four approaches, Hall (1995) added a further approach, that of sustainable tourism planning. The main emphases of these approaches are outlined in Table 1.1.

According to Hall (1995) the dominant approach to tourism planning within the private sector is that of boosterism, while the attention of government to the potential economic benefits of tourism has also provided a major driving force for tourism planning. The result has often been 'top-down planning and promotion that leaves destination communities with little input or control over their own destinies' (Murphy, 1985 : 153). However, attention is gradually becoming focused within academic discussion of tourism planning on the need to integrate social and environmental concerns into the economic thrust of much tourism development (Pearce, 1989; Murphy, 1994; Hall, 1995). Therefore, it should not be surprising that Getz (1987 : 3) defines tourism planning as 'a process, based on research and evaluation, which seeks to optimize the potential contribution of tourism to human welfare and environmental quality'. Similarly, Murphy (1985 : 156) observes that 'planning is concerned with anticipating and regulating change in a system, to promote orderly development so as to increase the social, economic, and environmental benefits of the development process'.

The approaches of Getz (1987) and Murphy (1985), as well as those of Gunn (1994) and Inskeep (1991) are based on prescriptive models of tourism planning as a basis for public participation within a community. Prescriptive (normative) models serve as a guide to an ideal situation. However, while these may be useful rational models against which to compare reality, they do not provide detailed insights into the real world of planning and its associated set of values, power and

Table 1.1 Approaches to tourism planning

Approach	Characteristics
Boosterism	The simplistic attitude that tourism development is inherently good and of automatic benefit to the hosts. Residents of tourist destinations are not involved in the decision making, planning and policy processes surrounding tourism development.
Economic/Industry	Tourism as a means to promote growth and development in specific areas. The planning emphasis is on the economic impacts of tourism and its most efficient use to create income and employment benefits for regions or communities.
Physical/Spatial	Tourism is regarded as having an ecological base with a resultant need for development to be based upon certain spatial patterns, capacities or thresholds that would minimise the negative impacts of tourism on the physical environment.
Community	Emphasis on the social and political context within which tourism occurs. Advocates greater local control over the development process.
Sustainable	An integrative form of tourism planning which seeks to provide lasting and secure livelihoods with minimal resource depletion, environmental degradation, cultural disruption and social instability. The approach tends to integrate features of the economic, physical/spatial and community traditions.

Source: Hall (1995).

interests. As the discussion of the case studies below indicates, such idealised representations of the opportunities for communities to participate in the tourism planning processes appear overly optimistic.

Mega-events

Mega tourist events, otherwise referred to as hallmark or special events, are major fairs, festivals, expositions, cultural and sporting events which are held on either a regular or a one-off basis (Hall, 1992, 1997). Mega-events have assumed a key role in urban and regional tourism development and promotion strategies. Their primary function is to provide the host community with an opportunity to secure high prominence in the tourism marketplace (Ashworth and Goodall, 1988). Mega-events are also extremely significant not just because of their visitor component of the event itself but because of the impact they have on host communities (Ritchie, 1984; Ritchie and Smith, 1991; Roche, 1992, 1994; Hall, 1995, 1997). Mega-events such as the Olympic Games or World Fairs have been associated with large-scale public expenditure, the construction of facilities and infrastructure, and the redevelopment and revitalisation of urban areas which may have substantial impacts on local communities (Hall, 1992). According to Law (1993 : 107), the mega-event

> . . . acts as a catalyst for change by persuading people to work together around a common objective and as fast track for obtaining extra finance and getting building projects off the drawing board. This is not without its problems, since some would argue that it gives priority to development issues over those of welfare. The physical aspect of this strategy is that it has been linked with inner city regeneration and in particular with that of the city centre.

The hosting of mega-events is often deliberately exploited by government and public–private sector partnerships to 'rejuvenate' urban areas through the construction and development of new infrastructure. For example, Hughes (1993 : 157, 159) observed that 'the Olympics may be of particular significance in relation to the "inner city" problems that beset many urban areas of Europe and N[orth] America' and noted that Manchester's bid for the 2000 Summer Olympics were 'seen as a possible contribution to solving some of 'the city's' inner city 'problems'.

The use of tourism as a mechanism to regenerate urban areas through the creation of desirable middle-class leisure-tourism environments appears almost universal in Western society. Roche (1992, 1994) and Hall (1994) have described this as a component of urban re-imaging strategies to provide an urban environment that will attract and retain the interest of professionals and white-collar workers, tourist expenditure, and investors in order to generate employment and redevelopment. According to Roche and Hall, urban imaging processes are characterised by some or all of the following: the development of a critical mass of visitor attractions and facilities, including new buildings/prestige centres; hallmark events; development of urban tourism strategies and policies often associated with new or renewed organisation and development of city marketing; and development of leisure and cultural services and projects to support the marketing and tourism effort (Hall, 1994). The ramifications of such an approach are far-reaching, particularly in the way in which

cities and places are now perceived, by some, as commodities and products to be
sold and promoted (see Chapter 8 of this volume). However, while 'selling places'
through re-imaging and redevelopment strategies may be an effective way by which
cities and regions can compete with each other in attracting capital, investment,
employment and the tourist dollar, substantial questions are now being asked as to
the manner in which the communities which are sold and affected through re-
imaging and the hosting of mega-events are able to participate in the planning
processes which led to the adoption of such strategies (Hall, 1992, 1994, 1997;
Roche, 1992, 1994; Kearns and Philo, 1993; Hughes, 1994). It is to these issues
which we now turn with respect to the development of Darling Harbour in Sydney.

Darling Harbour

Darling Harbour is a major bay off Sydney Harbour which is adjacent to the central
business district of Sydney. Up until the early 1960s Darling Harbour was a key port
area of Sydney, but with the introduction of container shipping the area went into
decline and by the early 1980s it had largely become derelict with impact on its
immediate surrounds. According to the Darling Harbour Authority (DHA)
(1984 : 7):

> With the decline of its major land uses, the functional role of the area within the
> city collapsed. Natural regeneration has not occurred and this is due in large part
> to the sheer scale of physical infrastructures the redundant land uses involved.
> Hence, very major capital inputs would be required to regenerate the area and
> make it available for effective land uses.

Sydney City Council and the New South Wales State Government both started
investigating potential new uses for the area from the early 1970s. Both municipal
and state government identified a mixed entertainment/convention centre/museum
complex as being suitable. Although it was the state government which had both
sustained interest in redevelopment of the area and the financial resources with
which to support such a project. However, critical to the waterfront redevelopment
project was the 1988 Australian Bicentennary which not only served as a catalyst
for government but also provided a justification for substantial public expenditure.
   Initial studies of the Darling Harbour area focused on its potential development
for an International Exposition to coincide with the Bicentennial. However, the
New South Wales and federal governments could not come to an agreement on
financial strategies for such a project which emerged from a secret Federal Treasury
costing (Totaro and O'Brien, 1996) and the project was not pursued but was instead
taken up by the Queensland government. Following the demise of the Sydney Expo
'88 proposal the state premier, Neville Wran, requested the Minister for Planning
and Environment to arrange for the preparation of a Management Plan for the
Darling Harbour area which was then endorsed as a statement of development
intent by the state government in November 1982.
   In 1983 the Premier's Department and the Department of Environment and
Planning undertook a series of Darling Harbour development studies which recommended a specific set of uses including:

- An educational/entertainment park
- A Chinese landscape garden
- A major residential complex of 1200 units
- A waterfront promenade
- A market complex
- A foreshore retail complex and
- A maritime museum (Darling Harbour Authority, 1984).

The basic elements of the premier's Department's recommendations served as the basis for the future redevelopment of the area. That the premier's department was the lead agency is significant in terms of interpreting the political weight and momentum Darling Harbour carried in government circles. In 1984 this momentum led to formal cabinet approval to establish a new statutory authority, the Darling Harbour Authority, to develop the area comprising about 50 ha land and 12 ha water. On 1 May 1984 the premier publicly announced the government's decision for the redevelopment of Darling Harbour as 'the focal point of the bicentenary celebrations for New South Wales' (Unsworth, 1984 : 1485) (see Figure 1.1).

The Authority, under the provisions of the New Darling Harbour Authority Act 1984, was given powers to control all development within the nominated development area, with all public authority lands in area also to be vested in the DHA. One of the most controversial aspects of the Authority's enabling Act was that it gave the Authority absolute planning control exempting it from the Environmental Planning and Assessment Act 1979 as well as other Acts which covered such issues

Figure 1.1 Darling Harbour retail complex with hotel development behind. The Sydney Harbour ferry in the foreground also serves as an Olympic information and exhibition centre

as subdivision approvals, heritage conservation, and heights of buildings. This meant that the Authority was not subject to the City Council, the Department of Environment or Planning or the Land and Environment Court. According to the Authority (1984 : 21) it

> was given an extremely tight timetable in which to complete the bicentennial development strategy. As a consequence there was a real necessity to ensure that the Authority would have the ability to carry out comprehensive development quickly, and to ensure that there existed no avenue for administrative delays.

As the various approval and appeal processes within the existing environmental planning legislation had the distinct capacity to significantly delay the development process, the government decided that such an exemption from the planning Act was justified.

Six years of behind-the-scenes planning for the site were therefore excluded from the legislative requirements for public participation and scrutiny by the exigencies created by the demands of a mega-event. All this took 'place under a government whose own recent legislation explicitly enshrined community participation and provided for the dissemination of information through the publication of environmental impact statements' (Thorne and Munro-Clark, 1989 : 156). As premier Unsworth commented 'It means we are determined to have this done – to see it finished – and we're not going to be frustrated by legal technicalities . . . This is a national project, it's something for Australia, and we cannot have government aldermen or anyone else frustrating our intentions to achieve one of the great features of 1988' (*The Australian*, 2 May 1984, p.13).

The importance and prestige attached to hallmark events by governments often means a commitment to 'fast-track' planning practices which ignore community opposition to the hosting of events (Thorne and Munro-Clarke, 1989). The establishment of special Acts and Regulations to control hallmark events has important political dimensions. Acts and Regulations may serve to reinforce the powerlessness of certain groups and individuals within the planning process. The law often acts to protect the integrity of the event and associated physical development, not the impacts of the event on the host population (Hall, 1992). As Thorne, Munro-Clarke, and Boers (1987) commented in the case of Sydney's Darling Harbour bicentennial project:

> National 'hallmark' events . . . are prone to generate (at least in prospect) a heady atmosphere. In some government quarters in particular, time comes to be experienced as a count-down interval, in which everything must be made ready for the day the show begins, and any call for deliberation amounts to sabotage. In the excitement of putting a good face on things, more sober, long-term commitments are apt to be lost sight of or denied, and normal legal safeguards are set aside, in the spirit of a state-of-emergency.

One of the most controversial aspects of the scheme was the development of a 'people mover' system between Darling Harbour and the central city. The government's selection of a raised monorail system was subject to intense public criticism, however. As with the rest of the project, it was not subject to normal planning legislation.

Furthermore, as Thorne and Munro-Clarke (1989) recognised, one of the most contentious aspects of the whole process was the manner in which information was withheld from public debate. The withholding of information and lack of meaningful consultation with the wider community was symptomatic of the whole Darling Harbour development experience.

At no time in the development proceedings were people given an opportunity to scrutinise proposals in a manner which would enable them to reject them. The demands of having the development ready for the Australian Bicentennial and the political loss for the government to be had by not doing so created a climate in which participation in the planning process ceased to exist. The New South Wales government directly invested at least A$950 million into the project with subsequent private sector investment of A$1431 million (Darling Harbour Authority, 1996). Nevertheless, in the immediate years following its opening by the Queen on 4 May 1988, it was regarded as something of a white elephant with difficulties in attracting conferences to the conference and exhibition centre and sufficient expenditure by visitors to the retail complex.

According to the DHA (1996) the Darling Harbour area generates direct employment of approximately 4000 jobs per annum and has a similar visitor profile to that of Sydney overall, with Sydney residents making up 70% of visitors, outside Sydney 23% and overseas visitors 7%. Table 1.2 provides an official breakdown of visits to Darling Harbour. However, the longer-term viability of Darling Harbour has become interrelated with two associated major projects, the development of a casino as part of the City West project and the Sydney 2000 Olympics.

City West is a Commonwealth-State urban redevelopment project of the Ultimo-Pyrmont area situated adjacent to the Darling Harbour Complex. A casino was initially mooted for Darling Harbour but was dropped following opposition by church and community groups. However, proposals for a Sydney casino were revisited in the early 1990s following the stock exchange crash and economic recession, and the subsequent need of the state government to attract capital and increase their tax base.

The Sydney casino will be built on the site of a former power station at Pyrmont in Sydney's inner Western suburbs. The planned development of a 352-room hotel, 139 serviced apartments, a 2000-seat lyric theatre, a 700-seat showroom and convention facilities for 1000 people, and a light-rail station opened in

Table 1.2 Total visits to Darling Harbour

Year	Visits (million)
1988	13
1989	10.1
1990	13.2
1991	15.25
1992	14.61
1993	14.23
1994	13.78
1995	13.7

Source: Darling Harbour Authority (1996).

March 1998. Until the permanent casino is opened, a temporary casino, which features 150 gaming tables, 500 slot machines and four restaurants, is in operation beside the National Maritime Museum in Darling Harbour (Hall and Hamon, 1996). Undoubtedly, the casino development has proved a boon to Darling Harbour and served to attract hotel development which might not have been forthcoming.

As in the case of the initial Darling Harbour project, it is important to note that the planning process was controlled at the state government rather than the municipal level. Indeed, the Lord Mayor of Sydney, Councillor Frank Sartor, argued that the state government's decision to approve a modified design proposal for the Sydney Harbour Casino from the preferred tenderers, was 'probably the worst planning decision Sydney has seen in decades' (Morris, 1994a : 4). The original design featured a 16-storey, split ziggurat-style structure. Following opposition from the Sydney City Council and architects who claimed that the proposed building exceeded existing height limits and was inappropriate for Pyrmont, the twin towers were recast as a lower, longer and simpler building of approximately 12 storeys in height (Morris, 1994a).

The notion of 'a world-class casino' is clearly in keeping with the re-imaging strategies being employed by the New South Wales state government (Hall and Hamon, 1996). However, the casino is also expected to bring in a substantial income to the state government through gaming taxes and the casino license fee itself. Even prior to the court action being taken by an unsuccessful bidder, the state government had accepted an upfront fee of A\$376 million from the winning consortium. The fee gave the licence holder a 12-year monopoly on the casino market in Sydney and a 99-year lease on the Pyrmont site. According to the then premier of New South Wales, Mr John Fahey, a 'great deal' of the licence fee was to be used to fast-track urban renewal projects in Sydney, including the area around where the casino is to be situated. In addition, Sydney Harbour Casino estimates that the project could generate in excess of A\$1.2 billion over the 12-year exclusivity agreement (Morris, 1994b).

Given the role of Darling Harbour to regenerate the inner city, it may well be asked why further fast-tracking is necessary. However, the successful bid of Sydney to host the 2000 Summer Olympics has provided yet another justification for top-down, fast-track development, with Darling Harbour as one of the premier venues for Olympic events.

Public participation in the case of the Sydney 2000 Summer Olympics bid took the form of consultation with significant individuals and leaders of interest groups including labour, key public sector agencies, and the Director of the New South Wales Office of Aboriginal Affairs. In addition, a telephone poll was conducted to gauge reaction to a potential Sydney bid for the 2000 Summer Olympics. According to the Sydney Olympic Games Review Committee (1990 : 47), 'The poll showed widespread community support for a bid by Sydney . . . with 82% of respondents either strongly or mildly in favour'. The Committee concluded 'As a result of these meetings and consultations, the Committee is confident that a Sydney bid would have bi-partisan political support and the support of leading media executives and news editors, the aboriginal community, the NSW Labor Council and key trade unions, along with critical public sector agencies' (1990 : 47). The Sydney Olympic bid exercise supports the notion that Olympic bids are increasingly becoming tests of public relations strength in which public participation in the decision-making process and community consultation occurs through media opinion polls rather than any independent social analysis or formal, ongoing, process of community participation:

> Moreover, assessment of 'public opinion' in a contrived climate of ignorance is no more than a propaganda exercise. If any weight at all is to be placed upon the corrective value of the judgement of ordinary citizens in such practical issues, it needs to be informed by an adequate knowledge of real contexts and consequences, and some basis for comparing and weighing alternatives (Thorne and Munro-Clark, 1989 : 168).

Indeed, it is ironic that for an Olympic Games proposal which focused on the environment or a 'Green Games' as a central platform of its bid that the mistakes of the 1980s with respect to Darling Harbour would be repeated. In its August 1993, news release as to 'why Sydney would stage a great Olympics in 2000', the Sydney Olympics 2000 Bid Limited (1993 : 2) argued that Sydney was 'Pioneering environmentalism for the Olympics. Throughout Sydney's Olympic plan, from venue and residential construction to event management, the highest environmental principles are applied. Sydney's Olympic Village design, prepared in collaboration with Greenpeace, foreshadows the sustainable city of the 21st century.' However, as with Darling Harbour, the Games bid, particularly with respect to the major Homebush Bay site, was not subject to the conditions of the Environment and Planning Act which meant that not only was public consultation minimal but the project was not even subject to a formal environmental impact statement, even though the Homebush Bay site is a former industrial waste dump (Hall and Hodges, 1996).

The importance of Darling Harbour to the Games is illustrated by the Authority now being responsible to the Minister for the Olympics (Darling Harbour Authority, 1996). Moreover, the Games has provided for a new round of development investment in order to provide for the needs of the Games. In 1994 the DHA launched a review of the Master Plan for the area. According to the DHA (1994 : 15) 'The successful Olympic bid gives Darling Harbour a clear timetable for completion of development. The authority should position itself now to capitalise on any benefits flowing from the Olympics.'

Out of the Games bid and the Master Plan has come a second wave of developments for the area with the image of Darling Harbour being 'relaunched' by the Olympics Minister, Michael Knight, on 1 November 1996. According to the Minister 'It has always been popular with visitors to Sydney however the appeal to locals was limited . . . Darling Harbour is now undergoing something of a revolution with the approval of $1 billion worth of new attractions and facilities' (Australian Associated Press, 1996). Open-air sports facilities for netball, volleyball and tennis were ripped up to make room for an A$18 million IMAX cinema and a A$70 million Segaworld video complex. Further development includes:

- Aquarium expansion (A$9 million)
- Darling Park retail, parkland and entertainment complex (A$500 million)
- Darling Walk entertainment and retail complex (A$30 million)
- Expansion of convention and exhibition space (A$57 million)

- Refurbishment of Harbourside shopping complex ($60 million) and
- The development of a light rail link (Australian Associated Press, 1996; Totaro and O'Brien, 1996).

Undoubtedly, Darling Harbour has served as a focal point for both public and private investment. It has transformed the physical space of the Bay as well as the social space. The motto of Merlin International, the initial developers and managers of Darling Harbour's Festival marketplace, was 'Making Cities Fun'. Yet, as Huxley (1991 : 141) questioned:

> The whole concept of the city as 'fun' is redolent with the post-modernist approach to playful spectacle, display and ironical references to other eras. It is the essence of the 'yuppy' lifestyle and yet our cities contain increasing numbers of unemployed, homeless, disadvantaged people: urban infrastructure is inadequate or non-existent at the fringe and outdated and overloaded at the centre. What sort of 'fun' can Merlin bring to the city?

As Sydney approaches the 2000 Olympics the answer is becoming clearer. The Darling Park development is designed to be 'upmarket' to 'bring in the suits' much loved by marketing specialists (Totaro and O'Brien, 1996). While perhaps even more indicative of the appeal of the development is the DHA's own research which indicates that the majority of visitors come from the affluent North Shore and is much less popular with the lower socio-economic residents of the Eastern suburbs and the Inner West (Totaro, 1996; Totaro and O'Brien, 1996). Finally, we can note that the DHA are still exempt from standard planning procedures. They do consult, but consultation is not participation. Instead, consultation is defined in terms of 'liaison' (Darling Harbour Authority, 1994 : 12) and the community is invited to input into a predetermined agenda. In terms of the 1994 Master Plan, for example, comments were requested on the following:

- What aspects of Darling Harbour you do or don't like and possible improvements
- Whether there are new or different activities or facilities that you would like to see in Darling Harbour or its environs and
- Any other suggestions that would ensure Darling Harbour continues to be a major attraction for Sydneysiders and visitors alike (Darling Harbour Authority, 1994 : 31).

In the case of Darling Harbour the planning agenda has been driven from the top since the late 1970s. The ability to make and influence planning decisions remains firmly within the grasp of government, the Darling Harbour Authority, and select public–private partnerships. The supposed urgency of meeting the timetables for hosting mega-events has provided the justification for the suspension of broader public participation in the planning process and relevant planning legislation. Where consultation has occurred it has been focused on very specific questions, not wider issues of alternative developments and what communities actually want their city and waterfront to look like. In short, the rules of the game have been drawn up in such a way as to exclude many groups from the development process. Rather

Hall, C.M. (1995) *Introduction to Tourism in Australia: Impacts, Planning and Development*, 2nd edn, South Melbourne: Longman Australia.

Hall, C.M. (1997) 'Mega-events and their legacies', in P. Murphy (ed.), *Quality Management in Urban Tourism*, Chichester: John Wiley, 75–87.

Hall, C.M. (1998) *Introduction to Tourism Development, Dimensions and Issues*, 3rd edn, South Melbourne: Addison-Wesley Longman.

Hall, C.M. and Hamon, C. (1996) 'Casinos and urban redevelopment in Australia', *Journal of Travel Research*, 34, 3, 30–36.

Hall, C.M. and Hodges, J. (1996) 'The party's great, but what about the hangover? The housing and social impacts of mega-events with special reference to the 2000 Sydney Olympics', *Festival Management & Event Tourism*, 4, 1–9.

Hall, C.M. and Jenkins, J. (1995) *Tourism and Public Policy*, London: Routledge.

Hall, C.M., Jenkins, J. and Kearsley, G. (1997) 'Introduction: issues in tourism planning and policy in Australia and New Zealand', in C.M Hall, J. Jenkins and G. Kearsley (eds), *Tourism Planning and Policy in Australia and New Zealand*, Sydney: Irwin, 16–36.

Hall, P. (1982) *Urban and Regional Planning*, 2nd edn, Harmondsworth: Penguin.

Harvey, D. (1990) 'Between space and time: reflections on the geographical imagination', *Annals of the Association of American Geographers*, 80, 418–34.

Heeley, J. (1981) 'Planning for tourism in Britain', *Town Planning Review*, 52, 61–79.

Hughes, H.L. (1993) 'Olympic tourism and urban regeneration', *Festival Management and Event Tourism*, 1, 157–62.

Hughes, H.L. (1994) 'Urban tourism and the performing arts: the constraints of current research on the analysis of the role and significance of the performing arts in urban tourism', in P.E. Murphy (ed.), *Quality Management in Urban Tourism: Balancing Business and Environment, Conference Proceedings*, Victoria: University of Victoria, 224–33.

Huxley, M. (1991) 'Making cities fun: Darling Harbour and the immobilisation of the spectacle', in P. Carroll, K. Donohue, M. McGovern and J. McMillen (eds), *Tourism in Australia*, Sydney: Harcourt Brace Jovanovich, 141–52.

Inskeep, E. (1991) *Tourism Planning: An Integrated and Sustainable Development Approach*, New York: Van Nostrand Reinhold.

Jenkins, J. and Hall, C.M. (1997) 'Tourism planning and policy in Australia', in C.M Hall, J. Jenkins and G. Kearsley (eds), *Tourism Planning and Policy in Australia and New Zealand*, Sydney: Irwin, 37–48.

Kearns, G. and Philo, C. (eds) (1993) *Selling Places: The City as Cultural Capital, Past and Present*, Oxford: Pergamon Press.

Law, C.M. (1993) *Urban Tourism: Attracting Visitors to Large Cities*, London: Mansell.

Matthews, H. (1978) *International Tourism: A Political and Social Analysis*, Cambridge: Schenkman Publishing.

Mommaas, H. and van der Poel, H. (1989) 'Changes in economy, politics and lifestyles: an essay on the restructuring of urban leisure', in P. Bramham, I. Henry, H. Mommaas, and H. van der Poel (eds), *Leisure and Urban Processes: Critical Studies of Leisure Policy in Western European Cities*, London: Routledge, 254–76.

Morris, L. (1994a) 'Casino green light makes lord mayor see red', *Sydney Morning Herald*, 10 December, 4.

Morris, L. (1994b) 'Govt won't wait to spend casino fee', *Sydney Morning Herald*, 7 December, 17.

Murphy, P. (1985) *Tourism: a Community Approach*, New York and London: Methuen.

Murphy, P. (1994) 'Tourism and sustainable development', in W. Theobald, (ed.), *Global Tourism: The Next Decade*, Oxford: Butterworth-Heinemann, 274–90.

Pearce, D. (1989) *Tourist Development*, Harlow: Longman.

Ritchie, J.R.B. (1984) 'Assessing the impact of hallmark events: conceptual and research issues', *Journal of Travel Research*, 23 (1), 2–11.

Ritchie, J.R.B. and Smith, B.H. (1991) 'The impact of a mega-event on host region awareness: a longitudinal study', *Journal of Travel Research*, 30 (1), 3–10.

Roche, M. (1992) 'Mega-events and micro-modernization: on the sociology of the new urban tourism', *British Journal of Sociology*, 43, 563–600.

Roche, M. (1994) 'Mega-events and urban policy', *Annals of Tourism Research*, 21, 1–19.

Schattsneider, E. (1960) *Semi-sovereign People: A Realist's View of Democracy in America*, New York: Holt, Rinehart and Winston.

Sydney Olympics 2000 Bid Limited (1993) *News Release: Sydney's plans for an environmental Olympics in 2000*, Sydney.

Sydney Olympic Games Review Committee (1990) *Report to the Premier of New South Wales*, Sydney.

Thorne, R. and Munro-Clark, M. (1989) 'Hallmark events as an excuse for autocracy in urban planning: a case history', in G.J. Syme, B.J. Shaw, D.M. Fenton and W.S. Mueller (eds), *The Planning and Evaluation of Hallmark Events*, Aldershot: Avebury, 154–71.

Thorne, R., Munro-Clark, M. and Boers, J. (1987) 'Hallmark events as an excuse for autocracy in urban planning: a case history', in *The Effects of Hallmark Events on Cities*. Nedlands Centre for Urban Research, University of Western Australia.

Totaro, P. (1996) '$3m plan to broaden Darling Harbour's appeal', *Sydney Morning Herald*, 31 October.

Totaro, P. and O'Brien, G. (1996) 'Sydney's Darling', *Sydney Morning Herald*, 31 October.

Unsworth, B.J. (1984) New Darling Harbour Authority Bill, *NSW Parliamentary Debates, Legislative Council*, 26 November, 1485–1489.

Veal, A.J. (1992) *Research Methods for Leisure and Tourism*, Harlow: Longman.

World Travel & Tourism Council (1996) *Australia Travel & Tourism Millennium Vision*, London.

2 Community-oriented tourism strategy development: Kalisz, Poland

GARY AKEHURST

CHAPTER SUMMARY

An urban development programme has been undertaken recently in the Polish city of Kalisz, which is some 200 km south-west of Warsaw. The project was funded by the Foreign and Commonwealth Office of the United Kingdom government, as part of its Local Authority Technical Links Scheme, the Southampton City Council and the City of Kalisz Council. This case illustrates the all-embracing nature of tourism planning and the range of choices which must be made in consultation with the local and regional communities. Many agencies and organisations are involved in these tourism planning and development activities and coordination of the diverse activities engendered is absolutely essential in order to generate acceptable tourism outcomes which benefit both local inhabitants and visitors.

Introduction

The project outlined in this chapter was funded by the Foreign and Commonwealth Office of the United Kingdom government (as part of its Local Authority Technical Links Scheme), Southampton City Council and Kalisz City Council. The objective was to provide technical assistance to the city of Kalisz in Poland, in the preparation and implementation of a City Development Plan, covering the areas of retailing, tourism, land-use planning and traffic management.

Work on Stage 1 started in September 1993, on an interim report covering the essentials of land-use planning, retail policy, traffic management and tourism development (Walters, Sanger and Whitehead, 1994). This stage was completed in April 1995 following the presentation of an urban development plan to the assembled City Council of Kalisz (Walters *et al.*, 1995). Stage 1 essentially laid the planning ground rules following a period of intensive discussions with interested

Managing Tourism in Cities. Edited by D. Tyler, Y. Guerrier and M. Robertson.
Copyright © 1998 John Wiley & Sons Ltd.

parties, which included elected City representatives, City Council Officers and local tourism organisations. Stage 2, the detailed implementation of the agreed tourism plan, is currently underway. A major brief of the project was to attempt to transfer urban planning and local government knowledge and experience to the Polish people and this transfer was designed to help in the development of the city of Kalisz as a major regional economic centre. Such a brief would be difficult at the best of times but there is a fine line to be drawn between the unbiased transfer of knowledge and experience and a paternalistic 'hand-down' of knowledge from on-high. The latter approach was clearly not acceptable but it is difficult, and indeed, presumptuous to believe that tourism planning concepts and principles developed in Western, developed economies can be transferred in their entirety to a country only recently removed from Communist central control. Transferring knowledge and experience, however well intentioned, can lead to misunderstandings, tension and difficulties, although the project reported here has been described by the British ambassador to Poland as 'one of the best British projects currently being undertaken in Poland'. Obtaining unanimous agreement on what tourism development is needed has not proven to be easy and many elected City Councillors were not (and are still not) convinced that tourism in all its various forms should be developed rather than manufacturing activities, which, to be fair, constitute the main wealth and job generators in the city. This viewpoint is understandable when one looks at unregulated and environmentally destructive tourism development in certain parts of the world.

It is rather rare for the practical issues, detailed planning considerations and implementation problems of a tourism development plan to be placed into the public domain for public consideration and debate. Occasionally we have glimpses of the practical development of tourism plans and their implementation (see, for example, the splendid work of Inskeep, 1991, Inskeep with the World Tourism Organisation, 1994, and Laws, 1995). Many consultancy firms have been engaged to a varying extent in the development of national and regional tourism plans but these rarely get published and the methodological rigour (often suspect at the best of times) is rarely debated and dissected in public. The Kalisz case provides an insight into who decides what, in terms of the nature, scale and speed of tourism development, and how and to what extent the legitimate concerns of the various stakeholders involved (such as residents, visitors, organisational employees and investors) are recognised and responded to (Laws, 1995 : 4).

This Kalisz case is presented as a modest offering to the continuing development of a rigorous and structured understanding of the realities and practicalities of tourism planning and its implementation based on a living, developing city. There is no theoretical development here – this is left to others.

This case outlines first, the development of a tourism plan (as a subset of a city plan encompassing urban land-use planning, retailing, traffic management and tourism), and second, how this plan can be implemented. The tourism plan establishes what needs to be done to achieve the city's objectives, what tourism products should be developed, when, where and how. The plan also establishes who will coordinate, promote, monitor and evaluate the proposed actions. Accordingly, three subplans have been developed – an organisation, marketing and promotion plan, a tourism product plan and a quality plan. This has required the starting up of a tourism section within the Kalisz City Council's Department of Economic Initiatives (to promote standards, formulate policy, monitor implementation and advise City Councillors), a commercial Tourism Investment Promotion and Marketing Agency (as a one-stop shop of practical assistance for investors) and a Tourism Development Agency to develop the infrastructure at a relatively small number of chosen sites.

Background

Poland, as most people are aware, has a deeply tragic and disturbing history of annexation and extermination. Even in post-1945 peacetime the Poles suffered under a Communist regime whose legacy can be seen everywhere in the awful greyness of apartment blocks which disfigure the towns and cities. But all is not gloom, for over the past five years or so, considerable progress has been made towards the stabilisation and reform of an economy that for too long had been subservient to the Communist Soviet Union. Poland was the first former Warsaw Pact country to embark on 'fast-track economic reforms' and early in the new liberalising government's life restrictions on currency movements and foreign trade were removed. Attempts are being made to encourage foreign inward investment and great efforts are being made to expand the tourism industry (Wickers, 1995; *Financial Times*, 1995). The Polish tourism industry is going through a time of rapid transformation with the former state tourist organisation, ORBIS, being split up and its businesses of hotels, tour operation and travel agencies privatised. ORBIS had once been the controlling organisation in Poland – all inward and outward visitor movements were controlled by it.

Generally, tourism data are still rather unreliable and difficult to obtain but an upward trend can readily be seen. Tourist arrivals are (according to the Institute of Tourism in Warsaw, based on World Tourism Organisation data) steadily increasing, rising from 3.8 million in 1991 to 18.8 million in 1994, and estimated at 24.5 million in 1996. Foreign currency tourist receipts have grown from US$1 billion in 1991 to US$6.2 billion in 1994 (Jermanowski, 1994; Hunt, 1992).

The main Polish tourist areas are the Baltic Coast (very popular with domestic tourists), the Western Carpathian and Tatra Mountains, the Mazurian Lake District in north-east Poland and the Sudeten Mountains in the south of the country. Kalisz is not in a popular tourist region although a major centre of religious worship is within travelling distance (Dawson, 1991 : 196–9). Kalisz is located in the valley of the Prosna river on the eastern edge of the Calisian heights, some 200 km south-west of Warsaw (see Figure 2.1). It is Greater Poland's second biggest city and capital of the province since 1975. It covers an area of 55 km^2 and has a population of 107 000. Claudius Ptolemy, the Alexandrian cartographer, mentions the city in the second century. The fastest growth took place in the fifteenth and sixteenth centuries although numerous wars and epidemics in the seventeenth and eighteenth centuries hampered its development. During the First World War around 80% of the old city was destroyed but during the 1920s and 1930s the picturesque old city was completely rebuilt. In September 1939 the city was occupied by the Germans, and there followed a period of relentless repression. Following the war,

Figure 2.1   Location of Kalisz in Poland

manufacturing and food processing industries were developed. Kalisz lies in a rich agricultural region but the main industries within the city limits include textiles, food processing, aircraft components and piano manufacture.

The first-stage interim tourism plan

The Kalisz Project team prepared an interim Urban Development Report which was published and presented in April 1994 (Walters, Sanger and Whitehead, 1994). It is not the purpose of this chapter to describe in detail the contents of this interim report, which was essentially a working document, but it painted a picture of Kalisz as a city of considerable potential which could draw on the resources and skills of a very productive region. Strengths and weaknesses were analysed in terms of urban land use, traffic management, retail and tourism development and the challenges of a lengthy transitional stage towards a market-led city economy were outlined in some detail. This report further presented the city's strategic priorities (as seen by the project team and discussed with city representatives) for the next five years. It was not surprising (because so much consultation and discussion had taken place with stakeholders, mainly in public meetings, one-to-one meetings and organised seminars) that the City Council accepted this interim Stage 1 report almost in its entirety although it was abundantly clear that developments would need to be phased in over many years because of intractable funding difficulties. Although it was relatively easy to identify key tourism issues that the city would need to address over the next five to ten years, the project team went to great lengths to explain that tourism and its attendant activities are not a wealth and jobs panacea but, provided tourism development was carefully thought out, there were rewards to be gained from adopting a well-focused and well-designed tourism plan.

Kalisz has, despite a relatively poor infrastructure, tourist potential because of three specific factors:

- Its claim to be Poland's oldest city
- Its wealth of buildings of architectural interest, set in a pleasant environment
- It is a major cultural centre, historically associated with famous actors, musicians and artists.

The city is, however, poorly placed in relation to express railways, motorways and airports, and the level of support services to sustain tourism is low. Tourism infrastructure and amenities (such as hotels and cafés) are relatively poor and will need extensive development. However, funds for tourism development are limited, and what funds are available means that tourism will need to compete with other, possibly more pressing, priority developments.

The Interim Report recommended that urgent attention should be given to basic infrastructure, such that:

- Tourism must be *packaged*, with the city giving attention to establishing a tourism unit within the City Council's management structure, which is quite separate from the existing Culture Department
- Wherever possible, buildings of historical interest must be opened to the public and noticeboards (in Polish, German and English) erected to allow more consumer interpretation
- Hotel and guest house accommodation at affordable prices must be provided
- A one-stop Tourist Information Bureau should be established at a central location
- Taxis must be regulated and adhere to minimum standards of service.

To the credit of the city and its officers, and with little fuss or lengthy discussion with the project members, several recommendations were taken up – a Tourist Information Bureau with a new computer accommodation service was opened in October 1994 with specifically recruited staff and work began on the construction of a visitor interpretation centre (built as a traditional Polish-style log cabin) at an important site of Roman remains. The provision of affordable low-cost accommodation was, and still remains, a major constraint, but in the next two years at least one new mid-range hotel and a budget hotel will have been constructed within the city centre.

Because of its location towards the western edge of Poland, the majority of tourists that Kalisz can realistically hope to attract are likely to be domestic weekenders and people visiting friends and relatives. Overseas visitors are likely to be those of Polish origin but a small number of independent tourists may visit because of the architectural and historical qualities of the city. Car-borne visits are likely from the Czech Republic and Germany. With careful and sustained promotion, Kalisz may be able to attract business people on visits to other towns and cities in the region (particularly people visiting the important religious centre at Czechtohowa), but this may not be easy in the medium term.

As Kalisz is a city with a fine historical tradition and architectural heritage, it is possible to identify and recommend a range of tourism products which could include:

- Development of existing city events such as the Chopin concerts, music festivals and competitions, jazz and piano festivals, cycling Grand Prix and super-marathons, and new festivals of culture
- Interpretation and tours of medieval and Napoleonic architecture
- Organised excursions, for example to the chateau at Goluchow
- Reconstruction of the Roman past and the development of associated tours
- A country park linking city-centre parkland, the river and the lake at Golochow, and development of cycling and walking trails
- Conferences and
- Religious tourism, given the proximity to Czechtohowa (home to Poland's most sacred religious centre).

Underlying all these possible tourism products there exists the opportunity to promote Kalisz as 'the birthplace of Poland'. This is both exciting and an exacting challenge because, frankly, the people of Kalisz had been held back by the 'dead hand' of Communism with its ill-conceived central planning regime and distrust of personal initiative. Although they may have been constrained by Communism, nevertheless, they are quick to learn the skills of the marketplace. This is not surprising – a hard-working nature coupled with a natural intelligence and hospit-able rapport with visitors and a fine school and university system is an attractive prospect for investors. The project team found, however, that there is a natural distrust of, indeed hostility towards, 'planning' and planning processes, for plan-ning is forever associated with the Communist regime. As a result, the project team quickly learned to talk about 'planning' processes which were wrapped up in the language of marketing and strategic management. This hopefully non-threatening but necessary approach did, over time, persuade people that while free markets can deliver wealth they cannot be relied on to deliver an *equitable* distribution of wealth generated by economic growth. For a more equitable dis-tribution of societal wealth, free markets need elements of planning in order to determine and secure desired goals. Planning thus becomes a facilitating process, *not an end in itself*.

Development of a tourism plan for Kalisz

The Final Report as written by the project team, built on the work undertaken for the Interim Report and has established through consultation and discussion *a tour-ism blueprint for action*:

- *What* needs to be done to achieve the city's objectives
- *What* tourism products should be developed
- *When*, *where* and *how* these tourism products should be developed given the potential international and domestic demand and

- Who will *coordinate*, *promote*, *control*, *monitor* and *evaluate* the proposed tourism development actions.

Development timescales have been linked to these fundamental and basic questions, that is, short term (up to three years), medium term (four to eight years) and long term (over eight years). It was important to keep things clear and focused, not least because meetings and reports had to be translated into the Polish language. At times it was felt that something sometimes gets lost in the translation process (some of the subtleties and underlying meanings, perhaps) and sometimes the project members have found their suggestions and recommendations have been quietly forgotten. Rather than get precious about this, the project team recognised the thought and action processes involved – this is a transfer of knowledge process and the people of Kalisz and their elected representatives need to take ownership of *their* tourism plan, because they will be living with its consequences in years to come (while the project team quietly walk away and move on to other projects elsewhere). One thing became very clear, however, that as a project team ostensibly from a developed economy we were guilty of assuming that developed countries have all the tourism answers and we perhaps also assumed too much of Polish people in this time of transition from Communism to a free-market system. There is a clearly a fine line to be drawn between assistance and patronisation. This line can so easily be crossed.

Within the tourism action plan three essential subplans were prepared:

- An *organisation, marketing and promotion plan* (to encourage investors, develop marketing research, promote the city, provide information services and an efficient accommodation booking service)
- A *tourism product plan* (attractions, amenities and essential infrastructure) and
- A *quality plan* (to ensure environmentally friendly tourism and protection, and high-quality services for tourists).

Such plans and sub-plans required careful consultation with city councillors and representatives and this continues at regular intervals with the people of Kalisz. Consultation included a lengthy process of carefully prepared public meetings led by the city's vice-president, where tourism interests and city people could meet the project team, city officers and city representatives to debate (often in robust style) the reasons for developing tourism, what tourism products should be prepared, where and why. Sensitivity is needed in this process of consultation as well as careful preparation and a willingness to listen, and take on board alternative views. The plans which subsequently emerged in this process of debate need the support of everyone who lives and works in the city, a clear sense of ownership and a willingness to make them work. Outside people or so-called 'experts' cannot impose their thoughts and plans on the city, and rightly, the people of Kalisz would not allow this. Such sensitive considerations also raise issues of whether Western tourism planning concepts, principles and procedures are the most appropriate within a developing economy. There is no easy answer to this, and indeed the only answer must surely be to listen carefully to what objectives are being sought and devise plans that are realistic and sympathetic to both people and environment in the attainment of those objectives.

The objectives identified, agreed and developed for the Kalisz city tourism plan are:

- To promote Kalisz as an attractive destination for tourists
- To develop a sustainable, environmentally sound tourism industry
- To generate income and employment opportunities for the people of Kalisz
- To encourage and facilitate profitable investment in tourism, which leads to the refurbishment and enhancement of the city's infrastructure and
- To enhance the cultural and educational life of the city.

The articulation of these tourism objectives shows that tourism needs to be developed and promoted to establish a very clear and distinctive image for Kalisz, which exploits to the full the tourism potential of the city and its surrounding region, and which clearly differentiates Kalisz from other Polish cities.

In the short term the project team recommended (and the City Council agreed) that the development of tourism products should be small-scale, thus requiring only modest levels of investment, such as:

- Letting of private residents' rooms to visitors
- Special-interest trips in relatively small groups of around 12 to 15 people, including architectural and heritage appreciation, trekking, cycling and water sports
- Bus and minibus tours with local guides
- Chauffeured car tours with local guides and
- Private sector investment in bed and breakfast accommodation and camping facilities.

In the short term, tourism action is clearly focused on organisation, promotion and small-scale product development requiring only modest levels of investment. This recognises the sharp realities of investment in Poland and the current (and foreseeable) lack of investment funds.

In the medium term (that is, between four to eight years) the project team recommended that tourism product developments should continue with the modest investments but investment in accommodation (particularly hotels and guest houses) should be a top priority. Medium-term recommendations are subject to further consultation in due course. Inward investment is beginning – a German company has started work on the building of a mid-range hotel in the city but long-term developments will depend on economic stability (of the state and region) and the success, measured in payback terms, of previous tourism ventures.

The organisation, marketing and promotion plan

The project team found early on that there was an urgent need to define very clearly the functions and responsibilities of all parties in the public and private sectors involved in tourism within the city and region. There was a needless confusion as to who would do what and when, and above all, who would coordinate often disparate activities that were likely to be undertaken in parallel rather than in any strict sequential time path. The project team recommended that the functions of tourism marketing and promotion and investment promotion be devolved to a new body – a tourism investment promotion and marketing agency, that would be accountable to a new department of tourism within the City Council. Following detailed analysis and lengthy audit, it was decided that what was required was:

- The effective organisation of tourism within the City Council
- Attention to the requirements of investors
- Manpower planning and training
- Effective marketing and promotion of tourism within and outside Kalisz.

Suggested guidelines were carefully developed by the project team to establish the short-, medium- and long-term actions required, with a definite articulation of priorities.

The City Council will, in the opinion of the project team, need to ensure over time that tourism policy formulation and implementation is democratically debated and controlled with reference to city, government and regional objectives. This will not be easy and neither will it be easy to encourage and assist potential investors, or ensure that standards of services to tourists are promoted and maintained, including the classification and registration of accommodation. Furthermore, information and research services, such as data collection and analysis, must be provided for decision makers in the City Council and its agencies and departments, while manpower for the tourism industry is planned for and trained to high standards.

A clear organisational structure is obviously required in this developing city which provides reliable and efficient services to tourists, tourism operators, potential investors and City Council agencies. Each organisation must be clearly defined, with *clear lines of accountability* and *well-defined areas of responsibility*. Anything less than this is a recipe for intractable problems. Coordination of these diverse functions, by a new department of tourism accountable to elected representatives of the city, was felt to be absolutely essential. However, the City Council decided that in the medium term it would be too costly to establish a new Council department of tourism, so a tourism officer was appointed and located within the Department of Economic Initiatives. This officer was charged with undertaking the preparatory work for a draft tourism plan prior to coming to the UK for specific training in tourism plan development, tourism assets audits and tourist attractions evaluation at Portsmouth University, Southampton Institute of Higher Education and the City of Southampton Economic Development Division. Subsequently, in April 1996, the tourism officer came to the UK with the Head of the City of Kalisz Economic Initiatives Department for a one-week stay. Regrettably, the young man appointed to this post of tourism officer proved to be rather unsuitable for the job in both temperament and experience. Lack of experience could have been overcome had the person shown a willingness to listen, had he consulted widely and asked for help when unsure of what to do next.

Following the establishment of a definite organisational structure, and following the UK visit of the tourism officer and the Head of the City of Kalisz Economic Initiatives Department, a draft tourism plan was prepared by the City Department of Economic Initiatives and submitted for debate within the City Council. This plan was discussed first, in a specially constituted Kalisz Tourism Forum, consisting of elected representatives and members of tourism organisations, and chaired by the City vice-president. This Tourism Forum has an agreed written constitution and working arrangements and has proved so far to be the most durable of the many actions taken. The Tourism Forum is working well. It has given the various stakeholders in tourism development a real voice in shaping that development. The establishment of a tourism investment promotion and marketing agency has so far not materialised. This is not surprising at this time in post-Communist Poland, where there is a relatively cautious attitude to risk and a lack of investment funds, but the main reason for the delay may lie in the relative lack of Polish individuals willing and financially able to take the risk in developing such an agency.

In theory this draft tourism plan, as prepared by the City Council, should have outlined proposed developments in the short, medium and long term and should be reviewed annually, with a major review every three to four years, to examine the attainment of objectives and the organisation of tourism in terms of efficiency, effectiveness and other performance indicators. In reality, and at the time of writing this chapter, things are in a state of flux – the tourism officer produced a first draft plan which was frankly less than adequate and with little regard for the recommendations made by the project team. Perhaps something had been missed in the translation from Polish to English or perhaps the project team had not communicated their thoughts sufficiently and in depth, or perhaps there was a certain stubbornness (on all sides). Whatever, the reason, a tourism plan structure was faxed to Kalisz Council with a recommendation to use it in preparing a new draft tourism plan (see Appendix for the structure to be used in a revised tourism plan). Consequently the city of Kalisz has recruited the services of a Polish tourism specialist from Poznan to drive forward the tourism plan on a day-to-day basis and the tourism officer has been dismissed.

Three new organisations were proposed and, subject to City Council approval, will be established in the medium term (within three years) in order to develop tourism in Kalisz. First, a *City Council department of tourism* which advises City Councillors, formulates policy, monitors and evaluates implementation, promotes standards and promotes the city. Much of this coordination work will be undertaken in partnership with other Council departments, the Wojewodstwo (Regional Government) and the private sector. Second, a commercial *Tourism Investment Promotion and Marketing Agency* (Kalisz Marketing), reporting to the proposed department of tourism, which will act as a 'one-stop shop' for investors by providing practical assistance to investors, including identification of suitable opportunities; vigorously promote the city to potential investors and tourists; maintain, in collaboration with the City Council department of tourism, and departments of economic initiatives and planning, a comprehensive list of possible investment sites; advise potential investors on planning, investment and tax laws (including laws concerning possible repatriation of profits to foreign countries and foreign corporations owning land and property) and possible fiscal incentives; evaluate the merits of proposed projects and assist (if necessary) in obtaining finance and act as an intermediary between developers, City, regional and central government and funding sources to secure project implementation. Lastly (but not least) it will prepare, publish and distribute an investors guide which gives clear, concise information about the

5. Origin of visitors
6. Age of visitors
7. Average spend of visitors per day and by spend category and
8. Percentage of repeat visitors.

The tourism plan will need to forecast tourist arrivals, mode of travel, and other market research data. Plus, there will need to be a regular accommodation survey collecting data such as number of bedrooms available, average length of stay in accommodation, average room and bed occupancy, average achieved room rates, numbers of staff and possible recruitment difficulties.

Other marketing actions will include:

1. A programme of press visits, identifying and inviting key journalists
2. Promotion to the travel trade, including preparation of a multilingual travel guide
3. Preparation of a target list of Polish towns and regions and foreign country towns, to circulate promotional material
4. Preparation of a student travel initiative, including poster campaign in Polish university cities
5. Ensuring promotional literature is regularly sent to Polish embassies abroad and tourist information centres in Warsaw.

This is not a comprehensive list but is indicative of promotional activities which must, in the view of the project team, be carried out if the city of Kalisz is to fulfil its tourism potential in the short to medium term.

In the short term (up to three years or so) the city must clearly concentrate resources on markets which offer the greatest potential returns. Kalisz Marketing will need to actively promote the growth of the city's tourism industry, with marketing research and promotional material which is reliable, consistent and attractive but cost-effective. Public relations in the form of newspaper and magazine articles is a cheap and effective way of building awareness in potential and existing markets. Over time, Kalisz Marketing will need to actively promote 'flagship' tourism developments which set the tone, scale and sense of direction. In addition, it will need to go on to establish good working relationships with tour operators, coach operators and other tourism businesses in order to establish profitable products and services.

In the medium term, consumer and investor awareness will have been increased by the activities of the Department of Economic Initiatives or the new Department of Tourism and Kalisz Marketing. Marketing strategies will need modifying where necessary in the light of experience and following prolonged and systematic collection of market data.

In the long term, the markets for tourism in Kalisz could well have matured beyond the 'tour operator phase' into ones where direct selling to independent tourists becomes important. Long-term actions include the continued promotion of the city by Kalisz Marketing, identifying further priorities and market gaps and close attention being given to the development and promotion of domestic tourism, as disposable incomes begin to increase significantly. The marketing and promotion functions of Kalisz Marketing will be reviewed in the light of experience.

A tourism products plan

A tourism products plan needs to consider with extreme care the accommodation, products, attractions and facilities which will be needed. Short-term actions are highlighted in Table 2.1 (Accommodation, Attractions and Facilities) and Table 2.2 (Tourist Information Services). Medium-term actions are shown in Table 2.3. The medium term is defined as being from four to eight years.

Following successful implementation of essentially small-scale tourism developments in the short term (including refurbishment of existing hotel and other accommodation stock) a more extensive development of tourism products may be possible. This presupposes a relatively stable economy together with an inward flow of investment funds into Poland. In the long term (that is, over eight years) product developments will depend on a number of factors including the pace of development in preceding years, investment funding and growth in the economy.

A tourism quality plan

The city of Kalisz must develop tourism which is sympathetic to the environment and which enhances the life of the people of the city, nothing less will be acceptable. All involved (City Council, project team, people of the city and tourism organisations) are agreed on this fundamental point. A tourism quality plan is therefore being developed by the City Council guided by the project team which:

- Establishes clear and unambiguous guidelines which actively encourage environmentally friendly tourism, protects the countryside and enhances the life of the city
- Ensures quality services to tourists, such that the city promises only that which can successfully be delivered and no more.

The City Council will need to establish very clear physical planning and environmental control guidelines. Consideration of these issues is really outside the scope of this chapter but to be able to control and monitor tourism development, and coordinate tourism development with other types of construction, coordinated planning must take place at national, regional and city levels. Building construction needs coordination with the detailed topography of an area in order to minimise environmental impacts. Those matters which need to be considered in a tourism quality plan are listed in Table 2.4.

Conclusions

This chapter describes a possibly distinctive approach to the development of tourism within a city. It is readily acknowledged that there are different ways of promoting the development of urban tourism. The methodology developed by the project team recognises that there are several discreet stages in the development process, founded on audit, analysis, dialogue, commitment, stakeholder and visitor

Table 2.1 Tourism products plan – accommodation, attractions and facilities

Accommodation	*Tourism products, attractions and facilities*
• Reviewing existing hotel and guesthouse accommodation stock and encouraging private businesses to refurbish to acceptable standards (as defined by marketing research)	• Kalisz Marketing to set up a comprehensive inventory of existing and potential attractions
• Kalisz Marketing to review and update existing site portfolio and circulate details to commercial attachés, investment agencies and major hotel groups	• The Department of Tourism to appraise state of daytime and evening entertainments, festivals and concerts
• City Council to consider a Hotel Development Incentives Scheme in order to increase stock of acceptable accommodation	• The Department of Tourism in partnership with Kalisz Marketing to generate a priority system for improvement of individual sites at different levels of expenditure. Implementation will depend on resource availability but priority should be given to improvements likely to generate income
• The Department of Economic Initiatives or the new Department of Tourism and Kalisz Marketing to encourage the provision of private rooms for visitors by preparing a comprehensive list of private city residents willing to let rooms	• Private businesses with Kalisz Marketing to develop key trekking, walking, cycling and horse-riding routes and centres
• The Department of Tourism, in consultation with the City Council, to agree standards, classification and registration scheme with code of conduct for the operation of accommodation	• Kalisz Marketing to identify centres for special-interest holidays (archaeology, architecture, etc.) particularly archaeological and heritage trips focusing on Roman remains (target market – older persons over 40 primarily from Western Europe)
• The Department of Tourism to agree a standard sign for registered accommodation and encourage its display in a prominent place	• Kalisz Marketing to encourage private chauffeured car tours with guides, beginning with one-day tours with official licensed cars, drivers and guides
• Private businesses with Kalisz Marketing assistance encouraged to develop bed and breakfast accommodation with donor aid	• Identify and develop with private firms a limited number of camping and caravanning centres
• Establish an efficient self-funding accommodation booking system based on the new Tourist Information Centre, established in October 1994	• The private sector encouraged to develop minibus tours with guides, and with the active support of Kalisz Marketing and donor aid
	• Kalisz Marketing to assist private businesses to establish restaurants and cafés, particularly in the city centre
	• The Department of Tourism to establish a guides, taxis and chauffeured car driver registration and licensing scheme
	• Kalisz Marketing to review ways of extending the tourism season
	• To examine the feasibility of establishing small handicraft and souvenir production centres, which can be visited

Table 2.2 Tourism products plan – tourist information services

Tourists of whatever nationality need good information services – where to stay, at what price, where to eat and what to see. A number of actions are being carried out, which include:

- A review of existing tourist publications and their distribution arrangements

- A review of existing hotel bedroom literature, and agreement on production of new publicity material and distribution

- Assurance that the new Tourist Information Centre (now located in premises near the City Hall) has agreed annual funding, management, responsibilities, accountabilities and operational plans

- Production of simple tourist guides in Polish and foreign languages (German and English)

- Preparation and publication of a simple foreign-language 'What's on' guide, which is designed to be self-funding

- Agreement on the number and siting of information boards

- Agreement on standard design and contents of information boards, adding foreign-language captions where necessary

- Review of signs at individual attractions, replacing or supplementing where necessary

- To ensure adequate directional signs throughout the city

- To ensure that there are knowledgeable and helpful wardens at attractions

- Preparation of an independent restaurant guide

- Preparation of a simple shops guide, particularly crafts, souvenirs and antiques

- To encourage shops to display attractive tourist products

- To ensure that all restaurant menus are translated into at least English

Table 2.3 Tourism products – medium term

- Continue to identify and develop with private firms a limited number of camping and caravanning centres

- Kalisz Marketing to assist in the development of cultural centres with music and folklore festivals

- The private sector encouraged to develop and present conferences, seminars and business meetings

- Private companies encouraged to develop upmarket coach tours, using Kalisz as the main centre

- Kalisz Marketing with the tourism department to encourage the development of additional hotels of various standards (luxury, middle range and budget) on the periphery of the old city centre

- Limited development by the private sector, with Kalisz Marketing encouragement, of self-catering accommodation just outside the city

- Private sector development of sports facilities (including golf) at the lake at Golochow with perhaps multi-activity centres based around low infrastructure requirements

Table 2.4 Tourism quality plan – issues

- Desirable development densities in designated zones, given availability of building land, the supply of services such as water and power and the level of existing infrastructure

- Avoidance of ribbon development and control of creeping development

- Using the natural topography with its opportunities and constraints

- For quality tourist developments, a maximum building density for hotels and apartments (including ancillary facilities, car parking and landscaping) of 100 tourist beds per hectare of land should be adhered to, together with a maximum height for buildings depending on topography

- All development should be based on local vernacular (styles, materials, colours and features) and designed to create as little change to the natural environment as possible. Maximum benefit is gained by exploiting local views, sunsets and natural topography in building design

- Building height should not exceed that of surrounding buildings and be in sympathy with the overall town

- Tight planning control is necessary to prevent indiscriminate industrial development spoiling tourism attractions

- Clustering of small tourist developments is more sympathetic to the environment and local economy

- The city should offer mixed developments, geared towards providing interest and services for both tourists and residents.

This is clearly not an exhaustive list but is indicative of those matters which deserve special consideration.

Source for Tables 2.1–2.4 from Walters, J. et al, (1995). Reproduced with permission.

feedback, overall strategy, plans for action, target setting, and regular monitoring and evaluation of results. Above all, the local community through elected representatives must agree and take ownership of their own plan for development.

This development process requires a very clear plan as to what needs to be done, when, where and how, and who will coordinate, promote, monitor and evaluate actions. A tourism development plan needs three essential subplans, using three broad planning timescales of short, medium and long term – first, an organisation, marketing and promotion plan (paying particular attention to investment encouragement and support, and market research); second, a tourism product plan (amenities, attractions and infrastructure); and third, a tourism quality plan (environmentally friendly tourism and quality services for tourists).

So far, the most successful development in Kalisz has been the establishment of a Tourism Forum, which has led to intensive and extensive discussion about what kind of tourism development is needed in this part of Poland. It is wagered that this project is different because those who have prepared an urban development plan are now charged with the responsibility of implementing their tourism development proposals. This gives an opportunity for tourism planning consultants and tourism educators to put cherished theories into practice in a creative but simple way. The project team believe that this approach can be successfully applied elsewhere, in both developed and developing economies, and are now working with other clients to put this methodology into practice.

Appendix: Kalisz tourism plan – Recommended structure

Foreword by City President

(Commending plan to the people of Kalisz)

Executive summary

(Main recommendations in bullet points or listed paragraphs)

Terms of reference

(Carefully formulated to achieve desired results and outputs)

Overall tourism development objectives and policies

(What needs to be done; natural, cultural, economic and tourism resources con-
served for continuous use in the future – i.e. sustainable development plus income
generation, employment enhancement, integration into overall city development
plans and policies, etc.)

Existing tourism markets and forecasts

• Numbers of current visitor arrivals, visitors profiles (length of stay, transport
  mode, etc.), patterns of movements
• Accommodation currently used by each market segment with trends if possible
• *Projected* visitor arrivals – short, medium and long term.

Current tourism policies, planning and organisational structure

(Currently, who does what and how; limitations to current organisational structures
and processes – setting the scene for the development actions)

Audit or inventory of existing and planned tourism resources

• Summary of existing and planned tourism sites, attractions, facilities, accommodation, infrastructure, etc. *with most details in appendices*
• *Map or plan* showing location of principal tourism attractions, hotels, etc.

Recommended development actions

(With clear timescales, cost estimates and identification of *who* is responsible and accountable for *what*)

Divided into sections – product developments, organisational/institutional proposals, manpower, quality and environmental guidelines, investor promotion and support, etc. (Clearly shown as short term: 1–2 years; medium term: 2–5 years; long term: +5 years)

- Possible alternative development scenarios
- Organisational structures (from review of current structures with recommendations for changes – city council, public and private sectors – roles of various organisations and agencies including Voievodship, PTTK and regional development agencies)
- Manpower planning, education and training (projected manpower requirements and development of competencies and skills)
- Marketing strategies, promotion programmes and market research
- Development of accommodation required (B & B, hotels, camp sites, etc. with projected accommodation needs in short, medium and long term broken down by market segment)
- Development of a fully integrated accommodation reservation system linked to other regional and national systems
- Development of clearly defined tourism products with clearly identified market segments
- Quality, physical and environmental guidelines (ways to control tourism developments, lessen impacts, conserve natural environment, etc.)
- *Plan for actions in seeking financial capital for defined developments* (tourist attractions, facilities, infrastructure and services); the mechanisms for attracting capital investment especially development of an investor's guide to Kalisz.

Monitoring, control and evaluation of progress

- Very clear lines of responsibility and accountability, including Tourism Forum arrangements
- Clear and quantified performance targets with control functions to correct variances
- Feedback from stakeholders and visitors.

Appendices

- Checklist for evaluation of tourist attractions and services
- Inventory of current and planned tourist attractions, facilities, etc.
- Detailed projections of visitor arrivals, manpower etc. (if prepared)
- List of all agencies and organisations involved in tourism.

Acknowledgements

Thanks to the officers and members of Kalisz City Council, who have made this project possible, and in particular, the contribution of Wojciech Bachor, President of Kalisz City Council, Zigismund Kasmierczak, former Economic Development Officer, City of Kalisz, Iwana Duda, Head of the Economic Initiatives Department, City of Kalisz, Marius Tomasiewski and Pavel Wozny our translators and James Beadle, Local Government International Bureau, London. To project colleagues – Jeff Walters (Economic Development Manager, City of Southampton Council), Alan Whitehead (now MP for Southampton Test constituency) and Andy Sanger (transportation department, City of Southampton Council) – thanks for your good-humoured company and we can now, after much practice, catch the right train to Kalisz from Warsaw railway station.

References

Financial Times (1995) 'Poland's progress', 5 June.
Dawson, A.H. (1991) in D.R. Hall (ed.), *Tourism and Economic Development in Eastern Europe and Soviet Union*, London: Belhaven.
Hunt, J. (1992) *Poland*, EIU International Tourism Reports 199, No. 2, London: Economist Intelligence Unit.
Inskeep, E. (1991) *Tourism Planning: an integrated and sustainable development approach*, New York: Van Nostrand Reinhold.
Jermanowski, C. (1994) *Tourism Development Objectives*, Warsaw: State Sports and Tourism Administration.
Laws, E. (1995) *Tourist Destination Management*, London: Routledge.
Walters, J., Sanger, A. and Whitehead, A. (1994) *A Development Plan for Kalisz*, Interim Report, Southampton City Council, Overseas Development Administration, Kalisz City Council and Public Policy Research Centre, Southampton, April.
Walters, J., Sanger, A., Akehurst, G. and Whitehead, A. (1995) *A Development Plan for Kalisz*, Final Report, Southampton City Council, Overseas Development Administration, Kalisz City Council and Public Policy Research Centre, Southampton, March.
Wickers, D. (1995) 'In pole position', *The Sunday Times*, 23 July, 5–6.
World Tourism Organisation (1994) *National and Regional Tourism Planning. Methodologies and case studies*, London: Routledge.

3 Getting tourism on the agenda: policy development in the London Borough of Southwark

DUNCAN TYLER

CHAPTER SUMMARY

Tourism has only recently become an item on the economic agenda of many inner-city local authorities. There are many reasons for this including the need to replace lost traditional industries, economic development pressure from central government, the effects of new forms of urban governance, and pragmatism replacing political ideology at national and local levels. The case study considers how these pressures lead one inner London local authority to reconsider the role that tourism could play within its regeneration strategy.

Introduction

Tourism in London has received much attention recently from academics (Evans and McNulty, 1995; Bull and Church, 1996; Bull, 1997), government (Department of National Heritage, 1995; London Tourist Board, 1993) and the public (a series of public meetings 'The London Debates' organised by *The Evening Standard* newspaper attracted several thousand people to discussions which included, indirectly, tourism and leisure uses within London). This recent interest has largely come about because of the rise in tourism's importance to the London economy as the service sector became dominant in the 1980s at the expense of the manufacturing sector.

London has always been a focus for travellers to and within the UK. Historically, a city of merchants, financiers and courtiers, London has always attracted those who wish to gaze on the fine buildings and palaces, but mass tourism for leisure purposes, even on a domestic scale, is a post-Second World War phenomenon. Bull and Church (1996) note a slow increase in overseas tourist numbers to the capital through the 1950s until a startling growth in the 1960s saw a sixfold increase from

Managing Tourism in Cities. Edited by D. Tyler, Y. Guerrier and M. Robertson.
Copyright © 1998 John Wiley & Sons Ltd.

about 1 million to 6 million overseas visitors by 1970. Growth since has been steady
rather than spectacular with 12.2 million overseas visitors to the capital in 1995
(LTB, 1996).

Such growth, however, hides three main problems for London's tourism development (Bull, 1997). The first is a shortfall in quality, budget accommodation
especially in the central areas where planning restrictions make conversion of
offices and large houses difficult. Second, as Figure 3.1 shows, London experiences
a concentration of tourist activity and provision in its three most central boroughs
(the City of Westminster, the Royal Borough of Kensington and Chelsea and the
London Borough of Camden). These boroughs provide 70% of London's bed
spaces and the majority of the world-class attractions (e.g. Houses of Parliament,
Westminster Abbey, Madame Tussaud's, Oxford Street, Leicester Square, Covent
Garden and all the major museums). This concentration of resources brings with it
the associated negative impacts of congestion, noise and inconvenience to those
who live and work in these densely populated boroughs.

The third issue arises from this: how can London decentralise its tourism industry
to relieve the pressure on the central boroughs? The LTB has had a policy of
decentralising hotel and attraction provisions to neighbouring boroughs since 1987.
Little happened, however, until the early 1990s when other boroughs such as Is-
lington, Tower Hamlets (including the London Docklands) and Greenwich actively
began to court tourism through marketing and product development initiatives.

The London Borough of Southwark (LBS), which is immediately south of the
River Thames, opposite the City of London, St Paul's Cathedral and The Tower of
London, was slower to adopt positive tourism development policies than many
other inner London boroughs, despite having a number of established attractions.

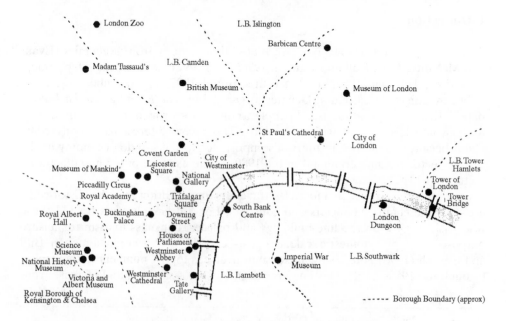

Figure 3.1 Clusters of major London tourist sights (adapted from McKinsey & Co., 1994)

Since 1993, however, policy initiatives have sought to establish a major cultural quarter for London on the south bank of the Thames. This includes, through hundreds of millions of pounds of investment in infrastructure, attractions and services, two new tourism clusters within the LBS, known as Bankside and the Pool of London (Figure 3.2). A third adjoining cluster known as the South Bank is in the neighbouring London Borough of Lambeth.

This chapter will discuss how changes in urban policy have helped shape the tourism planning agenda in the LBS since the 1970s, and how along with changes in the nature of the local policy-making environment this led to the LBS slowly developing and implementing positive tourism policies which, since 1993, has seen the borough play a positive role in helping to attract over £300 million of tourist-related investment.

Tourism and London's economic restructuring

Planning for tourism in London has been contentious since early 1970, when the former Greater London Council (GLC), along with the City of Westminster and the Royal Borough of Kensington and Chelsea, argued that tourism had negative impacts on housing stocks, land and transport resources, while the LTB argued for positive tourism planning policies (GLC, 1971; Bull and Church, 1996). The GLC, central London boroughs and the Tourist Board continued to struggle to find a compromise between growth of tourist numbers and control of negative impacts. On top of these arguments it was felt that tourism provided poor-quality, seasonal, low-paid jobs which were no substitute for jobs in the manufacturing sector (Eversley, 1975, as cited in Bull and Church, 1996).

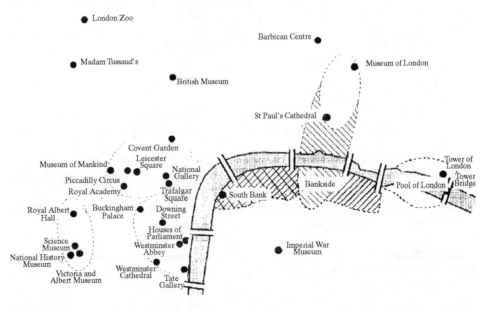

Figure 3.2 New tourist clusters south of the River Thames (adapted from McKinsey & Co., 1994)

However, from the late 1970s and through to the early 1990s London lost its manufacturing base. Between 1981 and 1996 male employment in the manufacturing sector fell from 21.3% of London's employment to 11.7%, while the service sector rose from 66.7% to 77.1% of male employment, with financial services and distribution/hotels/catering/repairs being the main growth areas (London Research Centre *et al.*, 1996).

The GLC was abolished in 1986, and the London Tourist Board (LTB) took over the strategic tourism planning role for London, but itself lacked the resources and power to implement the strategies it developed. Many of the London boroughs, including Southwark, remained very sceptical of the worth of tourism jobs, and remained loyal to the re-establishment of a manufacturing base for the inner-city economy. However, a deep recession in 1982–4, compounded by another between 1989 and 1995, meant little hope of the return of the manufacturing base. The final closure of the London docks and loss of riverside manufacturing activities were a major blow to the riparian London boroughs such as Southwark. The Big Bang (deregulation of the City finance markets) in the mid-1980s saw London's economy become dominated by the service sector and with the majority of economic activity firmly located within central London.

Changes in urban governance

In response to these structural changes in the economy it became vital to regenerate whole swathes of inner cities throughout the UK, and inner London in particular. The national government began to adopt a deregulatory yet centrally controlled approach to urban regeneration. National urban policy (that directed at regenerating the inner cities) took on typically free-market characteristics. Harding and Garside (1995) considered that although urban policy was an important arm of government policy it was never well articulated. They noted over thirty programmes in this field showing six typical characteristics:

- Private sector action was essential
- The role of government was to make urban areas attractive to business
- Programmes prioritised employment and economic regeneration through capital expenditure
- A proliferation of schemes, each with its own administration and resources
- Initiatives were often short-lived reactions to major shocks such as riots, and perceived potential, rather than needs
- The local authorities' role in the new implementation agencies was subordinate to government regional offices and the private sector.

Until 1989 the local authorities had no statutory economic development role, and new government initiatives such as Urban Development Corporations (UDCs) left the local authorities in 'ambiguous situations' (Harding and Garside, 1995 : 168). Some of their authority, such as awarding planning permission in Urban Development Areas, was removed and resources channelled directly to the UDCs from government departments bypassing the local authorities. Occasionally, where resources were channelled through them they were often not in control of the programmes.

Some local authorities outrightly refused to cooperate with the emerging mixed governance of the inner city: tensions rose between the local authorities wishing to develop people through training and central government whose regeneration strategy was dominated by land development and capital investment. But the move towards a weakened local state and a mixed urban governance of private/public sector partnerships was inevitable, as the resource demands were too high for one sector alone to bear. The result was initially the creation of new urban agencies (e.g. UDCs), and later multi-sector partnerships.

Local authorities in the late 1980s and early 1990s were, therefore, no longer at the centre of urban regeneration. They no longer had the resources to actively regenerate large areas of cities in the manner they may have wished.

The local authorities struggled to find a role for themselves in urban regeneration at this time. They had to wait until the mid-1990s for a newly defined role. Their task was that of helping to create the right climate for regeneration rather than to undertake that regeneration themselves:

> Based on the current economic climate, the extent to which local authorities are creating the right environment in which to plan for renewal is a critical issue. (Agarwal, 1997 : 14).

The way that this climate and environment was created was through the new era of mixed urban governance and partnership arrangements.

Governance through partnership began to develop in 1992 when the government instigated a competitive process for bidding for urban regeneration monies. City Challenge was a five-year programme offering mixed public/private sector scheme regeneration grants for run-down inner-city areas. Some early schemes (e.g. Deptford City Challenge, adjacent to Greenwich) had a tourism element to them. This was a clear move away from the single-agency approach of the UDCs.

Later, in 1993, the Single Regeneration Budget (SRB) unified over 20 different central government regeneration schemes to form a £1.44 billion regeneration package. Monies were to be bid for competitively by partnerships of the local authorities, private sector and not-for-profit or community groups. Ward (1997 : 78) notes that the central government saw this as a departure from the centralist/private sector urban development corporations of the 1980s by claiming that the SRB approach was designed to 'give local people more influence over spending priorities' and sought to evoke a sense of civic pride through the development of environmental improvement, housing, employment and training schemes.

Other regeneration projects also followed similar partnership formats including the City Pride schemes, which sought to provide manifestos for the regeneration of Britain's major cities. London Pride saw tourism as one of four economic growth sectors along with financial services, the media, and a vestigial yet re-emerging manufacturing sector (Newman, 1995).

Williams (1995 : 100) considered that one result of the years of erosion of local authority powers and resources was the 'loss of competencies from the local authorities' and as such new partnership arrangements were inevitable, with local

authorities becoming enablers and managers rather than 'doers'. Stewart
(1994 : 144) sees this as a shift in urban governance from urban managerialism of
the old-style local authorities to urban entrepreneurialism, to which local authorities took time to adapt having to develop new skills such as 'the brokerage of
support, the negotiation of mutual positions, the packaging of collective resources,
and the orchestration of stakeholders'.

Harding and Garside note that the slow thawing of local–central relations started
to begin with the third consecutive Conservative Party's election victory in 1987.
Noting the reduction in their powers and the continuance of the re-engineering, the
Labour-controlled local authorities slowly, over the next five years, began to adopt
a new pragmatic approach to urban governance, taking advantage of the new
partnership arrangements to reclaim some influence over the development within
their constituencies.

Partners and enablers

As stated above, the emergence of multi-sector urban governance brought about,
by necessity, the need to form partnerships in order to identify practical ways
forward for economic regeneration projects. This is seen by Bailey (1994) as re-
aligning the balance of powers within and between local authority constituencies
away from central government-imposed UDCs to locally generated partnerships.
The new partnerships were to allow for improved agenda setting, leveraging of
regeneration monies from the private sector, place marketing, infrastructure improvements and confidence building.

However, providing enabling legislation and actually making partnership
schemes happen are two different things. Clarke (1996) notes that the complexity of
the urban problems (polarisation of society, problems of decline, resource demands
of regeneration, social exclusion and deprivation) demand a variety of agencies to
be involved. He further notes that the Society of Metropolitan Chief Executives
(the highest-ranking officers in local authorities) did not think that regeneration
was 'capable of being tackled by national politicians and their officers on their own'
(p.13) and that 'partnerships, collaboration and personal networks and the like are
the emerging pattern of local – and national – governance' (p.14) which require
local authorities to develop new skills of:

• Enabling rather than controlling
• Eliciting debate rather than dominating it
• Achieving consensus rather than dictating
• Mediating between stakeholders rather than to forcing through their own
  agenda.

The willingness to develop these skills indicates a softening of attitude towards
the new order by local government, or as Valler (1996 : 840) states, local authorities
now begin to 'facilitate market functions in stimulating enterprise and identifying
investment opportunities' where bargaining and negotiation are the skills required
to make the partnerships work. He sees this reorientation as requiring, first,

in-depth research by local authorities into their local economies and second, internal reorganisation to enable external relationships to develop.

Local authorities thus became strategic enablers, working with others to achieve their aims and the aims of government. Sir George Young, Minister for Housing, Inner Cities and Construction, addressed the Association of Metropolitan Authorities in 1993 saying:

> I regard local authorities as uniquely placed to lead and encourage regeneration . . . I believe that the changing role of authorities does open up opportunities for them to take a more strategic view of the needs and priorities of their area . . . the enabling role means taking responsibility for looking to the future, working with others to map out a strategy for an area's development (from Valler, 1996 : 852).

Local authorities, therefore, have now adopted a more strategic role, working with others to achieve broad economic and social aims. However, there is no single ideal partnership arrangement, although others (Sellgren, 1990; Huxham, 1996) have outlined some common characteristics of collaborative arrangements between sectors.

What is clear, however, is that local authorities are the only body at the local level that have an economic and social remit. In the new order of local governance it is to be their job to be able to show the necessary leadership to be able to present regeneration or development schemes to potential partners in such a way that it is worth-while for them to join in and bring valuable resources with them.

An added complication for the development of urban tourism, however, is the well-known fact that tourists do not recognise administrative boundaries, and so local authorities have to work with each other to be able to develop coherent programmes. This is a particular problem in a city such as London where administrative jurisdiction is divided between 33 boroughs, and where the central and emerging tourist quarters cross boundaries between local authorities that do not necessarily share the same political ideologies (see Chapter 5 in this volume for more on jurisdictional impacts on urban tourism).

The need for leadership

Given the emerging fragmented, but dynamic, nature of Britain's local governance in the 1990s there is a clear need for quality leadership from within the local authorities. Gone are the days when local leaders (officers and politicians) could merely preside over an administrative structure to massage their egos and prove their powerbase. The nature of competitive resource allocation, the needs of the slimmed-down, dynamic, enabling authority and the scale of urban regeneration problems require a well-informed flexible approach.

Leadership in local authorities in Britain is usually bound up with the major political parties who dominate both national and local government. The council leader, although a non-statutory post, is key. The leader is elected by the controlling party and it is he or she who shapes the thinking of the local authority during his term of office. He and the rest of the councillors have to work with and through the council's officers in order to develop and implement policy. The senior advisor to the local councillors is the Chief Executive Officer, who works with the heads of departments to ensure that councillors are acting both legally and in a coherent manner (Elcock, 1995).

Leadership in London has been a major political issue since the abolition of the Londonwide authority (Greater London Council) with various calls for a reformed version of the GLC or a New York-style elected mayor. At present, however, the political leaders of London are the 33 council leaders along with the government's Minister for London. The council leaders are, therefore, both powerful and potentially influential, depending on their style of leadership and their ambitions for both themselves and their boroughs.

Elcock (1995) sees the political leaders often achieving 'dominance through the force of their own characters' (p.560) with the 'role of the political leaders . . . important not only in relation to the internal policy making and administration of their authorities but also in relation to the wider community' (p.561). Hence, the leaders' views on the council's reaction to the new patterns of governance and regeneration issues are key to shaping the council's response.

Stoker and Mossberger (1995) suggest four types of response to all the changes in the local authority roles described above:

- Early adherents: display leadership and adherence in implementing new local authority structures
- Pragmatic compliers: followers that wish to be seen playing the game, but often lack innovation
- Critical compliers: delay entry into the new system but can be innovative, they try to reshape or interpret policies to fit local needs
- Late adopters: little enthusiasm; compliance with new methods limited.

The nature of the response is often related to the economic conditions and political orientation of the local authority. Typically, the early adherents are government-friendly; pragmatic adherers have little reason to worry about these changes as their local economy is stable, but are willing to comply; critical compliers need to react because of local economic difficulties, but undertake reforms by necessity rather than ideological adherence; and late adopters are usually rural areas where little regeneration pressures exist.

Innovative leadership, therefore, is required in both the early adherers and the critical compliers. In the former leadership is driven by political ideology while in the latter it is driven more by necessity and social need, while maintaining a central role for the local authority itself rather than handing the majority of tasks over to the private sector in typical boosterist fashion.

The London Borough of Southwark

The case study that follows shows how the London Borough of Southwark has reacted to these changes in the urban economy and local governance. It traces the pragmatic development of policy that has:

- Taken advantage of the thawing relations between central and local government
- Actively participated in multi-agency urban governance and
- Been guided by the development of clear, decisive local leadership.

This has led to a traditional manufacturing borough adopting a regeneration strategy which has tourism and visitor management at its centre.

The London Borough of Southwark has not always embraced the tourism industry as it does today. At present major attractions, accommodation and infrastructure projects are underway within the north of the borough. These include the Tate Gallery of Modern Art Extension and the Globe Theatre (Figure 3.3), Wine World Experience, London Bridge Experience and other attractions. Several mid-range hotels are now being built while the multi-million-pound Jubilee Line extension links Southwark, for the first time, directly to the West End of London via the underground railway system.

These developments have been hard fought for by the voluntary, public and private sectors, not always, it has to be said, in harmony. But how did the London Borough of Southwark shift its position from a council whose former Planning Officer allegedly told Sam Wanamaker, when seeking planning permission to reconstruct the Globe Theatre, that 'Frankly, I think Shakespeare is over-rated', to a council that put up £2 million to help pay for the feasibility study for the Tate Gallery of Modern Art Extension in a successful attempt to woo the developers away from competitor sites?

For the answer to this conundrum we must begin by looking at the recent history of economic decline and the failure of past economic development strategies to deal

Figure 3.3 The Bankside cluster: the Globe Theatre on the left with Bankside Power Station at the beginning of its refit to become the Tate Gallery of Modern Art Extension

with the underlying problems. We shall then trace how the themes discussed in the first half of this chapter helped the Council to change its policies towards tourism.

Policy background – London Borough of Southwark in the 1970s and 1980s

The Labour-led London Borough of Southwark in the late 1970s and 1980s was a radical left-wing organisation. Its style was confrontational and protective. The London Docklands Development Corporation (LDDC), one of the Thatcher government's first UDCs, was established in the old Docklands of London, including the Surrey Docks and wharves upstream as far as London Bridge. This organisation based its regeneration policies on land development, bringing about massive change to the north of the borough where hundreds of acres of open dock, wharves and warehouses were filled in or demolished. Traditional lumber, aggregates, distribution and boat-building activities were replaced with new housing and commercial office developments.

The UDC, however, was autonomous of LBS. Greenland Dock became a battleground; community-led development (supported by the Council) took on and lost to the *laissez-faire* development philosophies promoted by the LDDC. Such a battle made relations between the two organisations difficult for the whole of the 1980s. During this time the LDDC were beginning to encourage the visitor market to north Southwark with developments such as speciality retail mall of Hay's Galleria, converted from the old Hay's Dock (Figure 3.4).

The 1982 local elections saw the local councillors elected on an anti-development manifesto. The North Southwark Community Development Group, a very influential and radical lobby, was particularly strident in its views. It did not wish to see Southwark become dominated by office development and visitor attractions which would, it believed, make the area dead outside working hours, and local shops and amenities replaced by services only for those working in and visiting the area. In fact the group wished to see major potential tourism assets such as Bankside Power Station demolished to make way for local housing.

The Council also sought to establish housing on the land in north Southwark. It successfully gained resources to help build a housing estate as a planning gain in 1986 in return for granting permission for the Midland Bank to site its main clearing house on a site abutting that sought by Sam Wanamaker for the Globe Theatre. At the same time the Council refused to move a sweeper's yard from the proposed site of the Globe to allow the purchase and development of the site.

The attitude of the early/mid-1980s was, therefore, very much anti-development, justified as the protection of local residents from the vagaries of speculative development and nuisance. At this time the North Southwark Local Plan (the statutory town planning document) became the first, and only, local plan to be rejected by the Secretary of State for the Environment because of its anti-development overtones.

By 1988 the atmosphere towards development and tourism began to thaw. The process began two years earlier when the local Chamber of Commerce, at the behest of some of its members, set up a Tourism Committee to explore the possibilities

Figure 3.4 Hay's Galleria: one of the first leisure/tourism developments formally planned on the south side of the River Thames

of promoting the tourism industry and resources of the borough. The Chamber commissioned Lawson Price consultants to make an assessment of economic and employment benefits that tourism could bring to the borough. Their report concluded that no matter what the Council's attitude to tourism was, the industry in the borough was developing of its own accord with Tower Bridge attracting 284 000 visitors, the Imperial War Museum 695 000 and the London Dungeon 380 000. Mindful of the Council's concerns about nuisance it assessed that 'these numbers have a long way to go before they become a diseconomy to the local area' (Lawson Price, 1986).

By 1987 the Chamber of Commerce sought to establish a tourism association with a wide membership, based around the slogan 'Historic Southwark Alive Today' (Southwark Chamber of Commerce Tourism Committee, 1987). The Chamber of Commerce committee began networking with the local attractions, historical and amenity societies, the LDDC and local Council. It sought funds to open a tourist information centre and produce a newsletter, its ambition being to employ a project officer to promote tourism's cause.

Their networking looked to have paid dividends after two years' work when in early 1988 the Chairman, Canon Peter Challen, reported that:

> We have reached a critical point. We have gathered evidence and can make a case for potential development of tourism in Southwark (Southwark Chamber of Commerce Tourism Committee, 1988).

Indeed, the Council's powerful Policy Committee had:

> agreed proposals to work out a tourism strategy. An Officers Working Party meets on 27th January, will make an initial report in February and a full report in June (Southwark Chamber of Commerce Tourism Committee, 1988).

In April 1988 the committee split with the Chamber of Commerce to form the Southwark Heritage Association (SHA), a networking and campaigning organisation that would lobby all necessary parties to secure resources for promoting tourism development in Southwark. One of its first actions was to arrange a 'Swap Shop' where all the attractions and catering managers in the borough could meet and find out what was actually 'going on.'

SHA secured funding from the Council by the back door, using a new government urban policy mechanism, the City Action Team, which sought to improve the economies of the inner cities of the UK. The City Action Team 75% funded SHA in 1988/89 with the council providing, by default through the new mechanism, 25%.

The Council Officers Working Party report on tourism was published as a committee paper in November 1988. This took a wide-ranging view of tourism and concluded that tourism could 'perform a valuable public relations function for the Council'. It also recognised that tourism may help Southwark become a better place to live and work. However, it highlighted the conditions of employment within the industry:

> People working in the hotel and tourism industry often suffer from low pay, poor conditions, casualisation and low unionisation (London Borough of Southwark, 1988).

The report, like the Lawson Price document two years earlier, recognised that market-led tourism development was underway in Southwark as a result of the LDDC's development policies, and that planning for tourism could help to mitigate any negative effects of unbridled development. The report became a landmark hailing the Council's official, albeit still grudging, recognition of the role of tourism. It concluded:

> Tourism is not a panacea for Southwark's economic and unemployment problems. It could, however, be a key strand in a development strategy for the borough. Market-led developments are now so well established and Southwark so natural a venue that tourism will expand irrespective of the Council's wishes.

> The Council should, therefore, take the opportunity to influence and manage
> tourism in ways it finds acceptable for the residents of the borough. (London
> Borough of Southwark, 1988)

These sentiments were echoed by the local trade unions (Southwark Trade
Union Support Unit, 1990) which reviewed the pressures on local councils to
develop tourism – the Conservative government planning guidance, Labour party
reports, voluntary sector activity and examples of success from other Labour
boroughs. Echoing the Council's concern with the conditions of employment it
urged the Council to seek unionised jobs with large employers such as theatres,
the public sector, large hotel groups and other forms of unionised employment.
The unions themselves saw this qualified endorsement of tourism as a major step
forward and urged the Council to identify tourism development zones in its
formal plans. However, all these good words actually led to little action on the
Council's behalf, and until 1991 SHA were always leading and the Council playing a passive role.

Policy change in the 1990s: the emergence of a new leader

Major changes happened in the early 1990s. A small, largely inconspicuous, Council
committee called Land, Investment and Economic Development Sub-Committee
(not without some irony known as LIED) was chaired by Jeremy Fraser, soon to be
leader of the full Development Committee and in 1992 Leader of the Council. He
recognised the importance of the borough's tourism potential to its general economic regeneration – not just to the north of the borough but also to the more
impoverished mid-borough areas. LIED began to promote interest in the 'Cultural
Industries', a euphemism for tourism, for the 'T' word was still viewed with some
suspicion within the Council.

Fraser then became Chairman of the Development Committee. At this time,
economic fortune shone on the Council. Unlike many councils, Southwark had
not disposed of much of its capital assets such as land and buildings, and a
change in government policy giving the local authorities a capital holiday on
certain asset sales allowed Southwark to become a reasonably cash-rich borough. Fraser, as chairman of the Development Committee, oversaw much of
this disposal and use of the assets. With his positive attitude to tourism, key
projects such as the Thameside walkway, streetscape improvements, and new
leisure facilities were implemented. A new Tourist Information Centre, public
art and environmental improvements were also realised. Tourism had found a
champion within the Council, not for tourism's own sake but as a means to
economic regeneration.

A new vision of integrated economic regeneration

In 1992 Fraser became the Leader of the Council. He brought with him a new mind-
set not just to tourism but also to the regeneration of the whole borough.

Throughout the 1970s and 1980s the Council had focused its regeneration strategy on the middle of the borough, which was dominated by massive council housing estates and high rates of unemployment. Solutions were typically sought to encourage manufacturing jobs to this area, and to adopt social policies to address issues of crime, poor housing quality and other social ills.

Recognising that such policies had achieved very little, Fraser switched the focus of development to linking the middle of the borough to the north, creating in the north the jobs to be taken up by those living in the middle. At the same time he instituted major environmental improvements to housing stock in the middle of the borough to try to stabilise communities characterised by estates with 20–30% resident turnover per year. Linked to increased job opportunities in the north of the borough it was hoped to help cure these social problems.

This new strategy was implemented through three mechanisms:

- Viewing Southwark as part of central London rather than inner or outer London and, therefore, made links with the City of London, the City of Westminster and the London Pride organisation
- Positively using the new forms of multi-sector urban governance to tap into sources of regeneration funds
- Reorganising the Council administrative structure to realise a more proactive, enabling style of organisation. To do this many of the established officers were relieved of duties and new positive-thinking officers given key positions as Chief Executive, Head of Regeneration and Head of Leisure Services, among others.

All these mechanisms worked together and with a certain synergy . The shift in mind-set that saw Southwark as part of central London was an important confidence-boosting exercise and foundation for tapping into key central government regeneration resources. The leadership skills needed to make a typical inner-city borough see itself as a central player in London's conversion to a service-driven economy should not be underestimated.

Noting that tourism and the service industries were the way forward for the economic wellbeing of the borough, Fraser, on being elected Leader of the Council, immediately apologised to Wanamaker for the Council's past attitudes towards the Globe Theatre. Planning permission swiftly followed. This act was a key symbol of the new proactive approach to tourism and economic regeneration.

Fraser, together with local Liberal Member of Parliament, Simon Hughes, joined forces to secure the Jubilee Line extension through Southwark, securing a key station close to Bankside Power Station and the Globe, and another at London Bridge – the site of Southwark's other attractions cluster, the Pool of London.

The third major show of proactive leadership was to invest £2 million of the Council's money in a feasibility study to help convince the Tate Gallery's trustees that Bankside Power Station was the right choice for its new extension. The report concluded that the site would help generate 430–1000 jobs for the residents of Southwark and £16–35 million turnover for the trustees (McKinsey and Co., 1994).

Using the new forms of urban governance

Building on such success, the Councillors and officers were now confident to join in with the government's new urban initiatives, rather than turn their back on them as they did in the 1980s. The Single Regeneration Budget part funded three major multi-sector partnerships projects within Southwark:

- The Cross River Partnership (LBS together with the Borough of Lambeth, the City of Westminster and the City of London and other key public sector organisations) seeks to develop Bankside and the South Bank (slightly upstream of Bankside) as a major new destination helping to relieve tourist congestion within the centre of London by developing a 'cultural quarter for London', improving the infrastructure and landscape of the area, creating 10 000 full-time equivalent jobs, 1000 hotel bedspaces, 4000 new restaurant covers and training places for 6000 people to fill local skills gaps (Cross River Partnership, 1994). The partnership has attracted £19 million of public money and seeks to generate £31 million from the private sector.
- Further downstream the Council takes part in another SRB project known as the Pool of London Partnership. The partners include the Borough of Tower Hamlets, the City of London, SHA, and the Royal Historic Palaces and commercial tourism operators to improve the visitor environment in a £52 million scheme between London Bridge and Tower Bridge.
- In the middle of the borough the Five Estates Partnership was the biggest SRB project in the UK, attracting £60 million of public funds, plus private sector investment, to redesign 1960s estates and improve the quality of life for tens of thousands of families, who it is hoped will be enabled to take up the jobs generated in the north of the borough.

In addition to these SRB partnership projects the Council also joined in other more *ad hoc*, pure tourism partnerships, including TourEast, a public/private partnership to promote tourism in the LDDC area (this would be unheard of in the 1980s) and the South East London Visitor Initiative (SELVI), a LTB-sponsored partnership to help south-east London boroughs market themselves to those arriving by car from the Channel Tunnel. Taking advantage of such new forms of multi-agency governance has been possible because of a new mind-set, brought about by pragmatic political philosophies that did not see an area's economic problems as intrinsic to that area. It allowed politicians to seek solutions by looking outwards, working with others to benefit from synergy, and to work across administrative boundaries in order to bring benefits to one's own constituency (see also Chapter 4 in this volume).

The enabling team

However, this would not have happened if the leadership had not convinced what was once a radical, inward-looking officer group of the new strategy. This was achieved by reorganising departments in order to get them working together and by working with chief officers who were willing to share a vision. Steven Wray, Head of Leisure Service, brought with him experience in tourism matters gained from Edinburgh Council. A new Chief Executive was appointed, internally, a man who had drive and vision (Bob Coomber) and a new Head of Regeneration (Fred Manson, again an internal appointment) and a planner with responsibility for tourism issues (Terry Wilden, also internal) who possessed the skill and flexibility to embrace the new economic regeneration policies promoted by Fraser. These individuals have led the integration of tourism into the general economic planning undertaken by the Council.

The new tourism strategy

This transformation led to the Council appointing a tourism officer in 1995. Formerly with SELVI, she (Gwen Owen) along with Terry Wilden have helped to redefine the role of the Council in terms of tourism development, visitor management and promotion (London Borough of Southwark 1995a,b). The Council's tourism strategy seeks to move on from the 1988 Officers Working Party report. Significantly, the changes are what Bob Coomber calls a change of approach from considering tourism in terms of 'the conditions of employment, to the conditions for employment' (personal interview, May 1997).

As the Council were defining their new role within tourism, SHA were also redefining theirs. For years the leaders within Southwark in the field of tourism, SHA welcomed the Council's strategy and saw the Council as the new leaders. This allowed SHA to concentrate on becoming a mass-membership amenity society that would act as a catalyst encouraging further partnerships to promote the cause of Southwark's rich heritage through events and lobbying. The latter was recognised as a key role by Fraser, who described SHA as a 'welcome thorn in the side of the Council' (personal interview, Fraser, 1997) keeping it on its toes and acting as a guardian of Southwark's rich past.

The Council's strategy has five main aims, leading to five main areas of action for the Council (Figure 3.5). Central to this strategy is education and training. Training has been given a top priority, as creating jobs that are not taken up by local people is of little benefit to a borough that at the last census point in 1991 (the time that LIED began addressing tourism issues) had a male unemployment rate of 21.3% compared with 13.5% for the whole of London and 11.2% nationally (London Borough of Southwark, 1992) and which by 1994 had risen to over 26% in some wards adjacent to the River Thames (Cross River Partnership, 1994). Training initiatives have formed major parts of all three SRB projects and have been negotiated with the Tate Gallery (Bankside Arts Training Trust) to allow local residents to be trained for the new jobs before the Gallery Extension opens.

Visitor management will ensure that mitigating measures are taken before the mass of the new attractions open around the year 2000, while infrastructure and environment projects make Bankside and the Pool of London both accessible and inviting. Hotel and catering development, such as Terence Conran's gastrodome at Butler's Wharf next to Tower Bridge, and the trendy Oxo Tower Restaurant run by

STRATEGIC AIMS:
Define areas within Southwark
to become **destinations**
and make the areas
understandable and memorable

Attract more visitors

Retain visitors and **increase** their spending

Ensure **local people** have the **skills** to take
advantage of **jobs** generated by tourism

KEY AREAS OF COUNCIL ACTIVITY:
Infrastructure, access and environment projects

Visitor Management

Education and Training

Marketing

Monitoring and Evaluation

Figure 3.5 Outline of London Borough of Southwark's Tourism Strategy. From presentation made by Gwen Owen, London Borough of Southwark Tourism Officer, to Southwark Heritage Association, February 1997

the upmarket department store Harvey Nicholls, and Gabriel's Wharf (Figure 3.6) help to retain visitors and drive up visitor spend.

This positive strategy symbolises how far Southwark Council have moved towards tourism over the past decade, and the last five years in particular. Current priorities are to ensure that progress is to be maintained in ensuring that local residents are able to take up the jobs created by the new tourism developments. These developments are still being encouraged with the possible relocation of the English National Opera to the banks of the Thames by Tower Bridge, a new centre of excellence for London's food industry in the old Borough Market and, importantly, encouraging shops, restaurants, cafés and hotels to ensure longer visitor stay and higher spend.

Without doubt the Council have moved a long way from their position in the 1970s and 1980s. Although the job is not finished the momentum now seems unstoppable, and Southwark Council, along with its partners, would seem to be creating London's new cultural quarter through what Bob Coomber calls 'Sense with Vision'.

Figure 3.6 Gabriel's Wharf: a community-led development of speciality shops and restaurants. One of the earliest and most popular 'service areas' along the south side of the River Thames

Conclusion

Since 1991 the London Borough of Southwark has systematically changed its approach to tourism development. Previously it had been very inward-looking, harking back to the days of manufacturing employment, and worried about the pressure that development would bring to the residents of the borough. In 1991 a newly emerging leadership with a willingness to widen the vision and appreciation of the nature of economic decline and regeneration led to tourism being accepted as part of the post-Fordist service economy of London, which Southwark could not ignore. Southwark has without doubt been what Stoker and Mossberger (1995) call 'critical compliers' but they have used the new mechanisms provided by central government, and the new forms of urban governance, to their and tourism's advantage.

The key feature, therefore, which makes this case example a useful addition to the urban tourism literature is the way in which the Council have used the new urban processes to their advantage. It is these characteristics that make this a true *urban* tourism case study.

Acknowledgements

I must express my gratitude for the time given by, and frank discussions with, Jeremy Fraser (Leader of the Council), Bob Coomber (Chief Executive), Steven Wray (Head of Leisure Services), Terry Wilden (planner with responsibility for tourism development) and Gwen Owen (Tourism Officer) – all from the London Borough of Southwark. My thanks are also extended to the help given by Canon Peter Challen, Chairman of the Southwark Heritage Association, both for his time and the access he has given me to the SHA archives.

References

Agarwal, S. (1997) 'The public sector: planning for renewal?, in G. Shaw and A. Williams, (eds), *The Rise and Fall of British Coastal Resorts: Cultural and Economic Perspectives*, London: Mansell.

Bailey, N (1994) 'Towards a research agenda for public–private partnerships in the 1990s', *Local Economy*, 8(4), 292–307.

Bull, P (1997) 'Tourism in London: policy changes and planning problems', *Regional Studies*, 31(1), 82–85.

Bull, P. and Church, A. (1996) 'The London tourism complex', in C. Law (ed.) *Tourism in Major Cities*, London: International Thomson Business Press.

Clarke, M. (1996) 'Urban policy and governance', *Local Government Policy Making*, 23(1), 13–18.

Cross River Partnership (1994) *Single Regeneration Budget Bid Document*, September, London Borough of Southwark.

Department of National Heritage (1995) *Tourism Competing With the Best*, London: DNH.

Elcock, H. (1995) 'Leading people: some issues of local government leadership in Britain and America', *Local Government Studies*, 21(4), 546–67.

Evans, G. and McNulty, A. (1995) 'Planning for tourism in London: world city, whose city? A critique of Local Development Plans and Tourism Policy in London', paper presented to The Urban Environment: Tourism Conference. South Bank University, London, September 1995.

Eversley, D. (1977) 'The ganglion of tourism', *The London Journal*, 3(2), 186–211.

Greater London Council (1971) *Tourism and Hotels in London*, London: GLC.

Harding, A. and Garside, P. (1995) 'Urban and economic development', in J. Stewart and G. Stoker (eds), *Local Government in the 1990s*, Basingstoke: Macmillan.

Huxham, C. (ed.) (1996) *Creating Collaborative Advantage*, London: Sage.

Lawson Price (1986) *A Report on the Economic and Employment Benefits to be Gained by the Borough from Tourist Related Development*, a report for the Southwark Chamber of Commerce.

London Borough of Southwark (1988) *Towards a Strategy for Tourism:* Report of the Inter-departmental Working Party.

London Borough of Southwark (1992) *Summary of Census Data.*

London Borough of Southwark (1995a) *Tourism Strategy for Southwark.* A Report to the Regeneration and Environment Committee, 17 January.

London Borough of Southwark (1995b) *Tourism Strategy for Southwark – Update.* Report to the Regeneration and Economic Development Sub-Committee, 12 September.

London Research Centre, Government Office for London and Office for National Statistics (1996) *Focus on London 97*, London: The Stationery Office.

London Tourist Board (1993) *Tourism Strategy for London: Action Plan 1994–97*, London: LTB.

London Tourist Board/English Tourist Board (1996) Regional Fact Sheet for London, ETB.

McKinsey & Co. (1994) *Assessing the Economic Impact of the Tate Gallery of Modern Art at Bankside (Version 2)*, Report for the London Borough of Southwark and The Tate Gallery.

Newman, P. (1995) 'London pride', *Local Economy*, 10(2), 117–23.

Sellgren, J. (1990) 'Local economic development partnerships – an assessment of local authority economic development initiatives', *Local Government Studies*, July/August, 57–78.

Southwark Chamber of Commerce Tourism Committee (1987) *Minutes of Meeting held 25 November 1987*.

Southwark Chamber of Commerce Tourism Committee (1988) *Minutes of meeting held 10 January 1988*.

Southwark Trade Union Support Unit (1990) *Tourism in Southwark*.

Stewart, J. (1994) 'Between Whitehall and town hall – the realignment of urban regeneration policy in England', *Policy and Politics*, 22(2), 133–45.

Stoker, G. and Mossberger, K. (1995) 'The post-Fordist local state: the dynamics of its development', in J. Stewart and G. Stoker (eds), *Local Government in the 1990s*, Basingstoke: Macmillan.

Valler, D. (1996) ' "Strategic" enabling? Cardiff City Council and local economic strategy', *Environment and Planning A*, 28, 835–55.

Ward, K.G. (1997) 'The single regeneration budget and the issue of local flexibility', *Regional Studies*, 31(1), 78–81.

Williams, G. (1995) 'Local governance and urban prospects: the potential of City Pride', *Local Economy*, 10(2), 100–7.

Personal interviews with:

Challen, P., Chairman, Southwark Heritage Association

Coomber, R., Chief Executive Officer, London Borough of Southwark

Fraser, J., Leader of Council, London Borough of Southwark

Wilden, T., Planning Officer, Regeneration Department, London Borough of Southwark

Wray, S., Head of Leisure Services Division, London Borough of Southwark.

4 The tourism explosion: policy decisions facing Singapore

HABIBULLAH KHAN

CHAPTER SUMMARY

Tourism in Singapore has shown remarkable success. Despite a recent slowdown in arrivals and receipts, it is still one of the fastest-growing industries in Singapore. The government has always played an important role in tourism development by reacting quickly to the changing needs of the industry. The slowdown in tourism growth observed in the 1980s and 1990s can at least partly be explained by the Life Cycle Hypothesis, which describes the evolution of tourism through the stages of introduction, growth, maturity, and decline. Although it is also argued that the recent slowdown in arrivals and receipts has mainly been caused by external factors rather than any past policy mistakes, studies have shown that pre-1984 there were structural problems which the Singapore government were required to address. In 1996 the government unveiled a comprehensive tourism plan for the sustained development of the tourism sector. It is recognised that small city states, such as Singapore, may reach their carrying-capacity limits more readily than capital cities in larger countries. Recognising this, the Singapore strategy seeks to improve the domestic product and expand the domestic industry's influence by developing throughout the ASEAN region, seeking healthy competition and cooperation as a route to sustainable growth. This chapter bases its analysis of this policy on an extensive investigation of visitor and economic trends and considerations on carrying-capacity issues.

Introduction

In 1965, when Singapore (originally called 'Singapura', the Lion City in ancient Sanskrit) became politically independent, only 98 500 visitors visited the new Republic. In 1995, the country's tourism authority recorded 7.14 million arrivals, showing that the number of visitors had increased seventy-twofold over the past three decades. The earnings from tourism experienced an even a larger increase (nearly one hundred and thirty-threefold) during the same period, rising from S\$88 million in 1965 to S\$11.7 billion in 1995. These statistics reveal remarkable achievements for such a small island-state which currently measures only about 648 km² including its 57 offshore islets and is inhabited by less than 3 million people. Based on arrivals and receipts, Singapore is now classified by the World Tourism Organisation (WTO) as one of the 'Top 20' tourist destinations in the world. For example, in 1994, Singapore occupied nineteenth and eleventh positions in the world in terms of tourist arrivals and receipts respectively (WTO, 1996). Singapore now experiences the same level of visits (measured in terms of tourist density, such as daily visitors per 1000 residents and per km²) as other popular tourist destinations in Western Europe and the Carribean Islands.

The massive explosion of tourism in Singapore was caused mainly by its spectacular economic success. The size of the economy in 1995, as measured by real GDP, was more than fifteen times that in 1965. On average, the economy has grown 9.5% annually during the past three decades and has consistently maintained an upward trend with only two exceptions (i.e. a slow real growth of only 4% in 1975 and a minus 1.6% growth in 1985).The sustained economic growth and gradual appreciation of the Singapore dollar have resulted in Singapore having the highest per capita income among developing countries.

Modern Singapore is an economic powerhouse with the second highest standard of living in Asia (after Japan), and according to recent estimates (World Bank, 1996), its per capita GNP has already exceeded those of Australia, Canada, and the UK. Although Singapore has very few natural attractions and recreational resorts (see Figure 4.1), it has an international reputation for safety and cleanliness. Although most of the land-intensive activities (such as agriculture) in Singapore have been replaced by skill-intensive industrial activities over the years, the city-state has successfully maintained a number of public parks and open spaces decorated with ornamental plants and magnificent greenery (Singapore is often regarded as the 'garden city' of Asia). Other factors which have promoted tourism in Singapore include its excellent infrastructure (Singapore has among the world's best airports and busiest seaports), its strategic location, and political stability. Located at the confluence of three major Asian cultures (Chinese, Malay, and Indian), Singapore is a gourmet's delight, and with an open economy, has become a shopper's paradise. Thus, it is regarded by many as the 'Jewel of the East', attracting tourists from all over the world.

Tourism development in most cities has been spearheaded by the private sector. Governments have usually played 'supportive' roles by providing essential services (such as helping to ensure the safety of foreign tourists). The growth of 'mass tourism' in many cases has created undesirable social and environmental consequences and there is a growing demand for greater government initiatives such as systematic tourism planning.

This chapter seeks to identify the role played by the government in the development of tourism in Singapore. Has there been any systematic tourism planning? What are the main problems and issues the tourism industry is facing today? What is the 'optimal' target for tourism growth in Singapore? What are the future plans for tourism development in the city-state?

Figure 4.1 Main Tourist attractions in Singapore. Reproduced from *The Official Map of Singapore* by permission

The tourism industry: an overview

Tourism in Singapore is a fast-growing industry. The number of visitor arrivals increased at an annual average rate of 15% during the past three decades and reached a record high of more than 7 million in 1995. Double-digit annual growth rates were recorded in most years in the 1960s and 1970s but the rise in visitor arrivals became relatively slower in the 1980s and 1990s. The visit rate suffered a major setback in 1982 when the number of tourist arrivals rose by only 4.5% (Table 4.1), compared to increases of over 10% in the previous years. The following year, the number of tourist arrivals was down by 3.5%, the first time that numbers fell for 20 years. This was caused mainly by a drastic decline in the number of visitors coming from Indonesia as a result of the imposition of US$150 exit tax on residents by the Indonesian government. Tourist arrivals registered a marginal increase of 4.8% in 1984 and 1.3% in 1985. The growth of tourist arrivals was quite steady for the next few years but it suffered another setback in 1991 (when it rose by a meagre 1.7%) due to the Gulf War.

Although it is difficult to make year-on-year comparisons of tourism receipts due to data gaps, the available evidence shows that Singapore's tourism revenue grew from about 5% of the country's GDP in 1970 to more than 12% of GDP in 1980. The contribution of tourism earnings to the GDP usually becomes magnified when the multiplier effects are taken into consideration and several studies (e.g. Khan, Chou and Wong, 1990; Toh and Low, 1994; Khan, Phang and Toh, 1995) have already been undertaken to identify the knock-on effects of tourism expenditure on the various sectors of the Singapore economy. While these studies suggest

Table 4.1 Visitor arrivals and receipts in Singapore, 1980–95

Year	Arrivals (000s)	% change in arrivals	Receipts (S$ billion)	% change in receipts
1980	2562.1	—	3.07	—
1981	2828.9	10.4	3.79	23.5
1982	2956.7	4.5	4.03	6.6
1983	2853.6	–3.5	4.21	4.5
1984	2991.4	4.8	3.97	–5.7
1985	3031.0	1.3	3.65	–8.1
1986	3191.1	5.3	3.85	5.5
1987	3678.8	15.3	4.40	14.3
1988	4186.1	13.8	5.30	20.5
1989	4830.0	15.4	6.40	20.8
1990	5322.9	10.2	8.60	34.4
1991	5414.7	1.7	7.80	–9.3
1992	5989.9	10.6	8.50	9.0
1993	6425.8	7.3	10.10	18.8
1994	6899.0	7.4	10.90	7.9
1995	7137.3	3.5	11.70	7.3

Note: Arrivals in Singapore do not include Malaysian day-trippers coming by land.

Sources: Singapore Tourist Promotion Board (STPB), *Singapore Annual Report on Tourism Statistics 1996* (Singapore: STPB, 1996); Singapore Tourist Promotion Board (STPB), *Annual Report 1995/96,* and previous issues.

that the tourism multipliers in Singapore are highly significant, they also reveal that the 'net foreign exchange' earned by tourism is substantially lowered by high 'import leakage' caused mainly by the factors related to the small size of the economy. The figures on tourism earnings (Table 4.1) are computed on a 'gross' basis, and show uneven growth over the years. In line with tourist arrivals, tourism receipts increased at a faster rate in the 1960s and 1970s, but the growth rate decelerated in the 1980s and 1990s. The growth was particularly weak during 1982–6 and in 1991 due to the factors responsible for the slow growth of arrivals in these years. On average, growth of receipts was much stronger than that of arrivals.

Although tourists in Singapore come predominantly from Asia (roughly 70%), marked shifts in visitor origins can be noticed from the recent data (Table 4.2). An increasing number of tourists are coming from the neighbouring ASEAN countries, which in 1995 accounted for more than 30% of total visitors. The Japanese constitute the second largest group among foreign visitors to Singapore, but a slight downward trend since 1990 is noticeable, probably attributable to the prevailing recession in Japan.

Declining trends can also be observed in the percentages of tourists coming from some other developed countries such as Australia and the UK. In contrast, the proportions of visitors coming from the newly industrialised countries (NIEs) such as Taiwan and the Republic of Korea have been rising consistently in recent years due to their strong economic growth. Another surprising change that has occurred is the emergence of China as an important tourist market, accounting for nearly 3% of total visitors to Singapore in 1995. This is more than the proportion of tourists coming from India, another traditional source of visitors to Singapore.

Tourist expenditure data (Table 4.3) shows rather a disturbing trend. It is evident that since 1990, the average level of tourist spending has declined quite significantly. It is clear that although total tourist receipts in recent years (particularly since 1992) have increased, the rise came from sheer numerical growth in tourist arrivals, which

Table 4.2 Top eleven visitor-generating markets for Singapore, 1990–95 (percentage distribution)

Markets*	1990	1991	1992	1993	1994	1995
ASEAN	27.11	31.03	30.23	30.34	31.24	30.68
Japan	18.25	16.09	16.71	15.58	16.08	16.52
Taiwan	4.22	5.30	6.45	6.65	7.40	7.89
Korea (Republic)	2.05	2.46	2.61	3.09	4.20	4.92
Australia	8.58	6.80	6.43	5.68	5.04	4.86
USA	4.91	4.69	4.80	4.78	4.98	4.84
UK	5.57	5.07	5.06	4.84	4.38	4.04
Hong Kong	3.65	3.93	3.88	3.93	3.93	3.92
China†	—	—	1.55	3.51	2.39	2.83
Germany‡	2.65	2.63	2.68	2.93	2.84	2.67
India	4.07	3.87	3.26	2.80	2.52	2.64

* The countries are ranked in order of their performance in 1995.
† China entered the chart only after 1992.
‡ Data prior to 1991 refer to West Germany only.

Sources: Singapore Tourist Promotion Board (STPB), *Singapore Annual Report on Tourism Statistics* (Singapore: STPB,1996).

Table 4.3   Average expenditure (Singapore dollars) per tourist in Singapore by country of residence

Countries*	1990	1991	1992	1993	1994	1995
All countries	1229	1065	758	829	729	746
South Africa	na	na	983	1404	1039	1188
India	1273	1066	785	1049	832	939
ASEAN	1386	1054	774	965	800	891
Switzerland	951	1012	628	671	567	772
New Zealand	1078	818	648	821	582	744
Japan	1357	1256	752	838	813	732
Italy	1391	1195	908	719	680	716
USA	1120	971	684	714	734	701
Australia	1055	964	786	770	646	698
UK	824	678	584	625	610	665
France	1170	1105	754	815	580	664
Hong Kong	1037	968	597	627	584	594
German	807	849	631	605	590	592
Taiwan	1402	891	691	664	622	523
Netherlands	893	669	565	560	669	514
Canada	1051	975	554	532	549	509
China	na	na	440	640	510	475
Korea (Republic)	1196	1124	628	655	513	416
Scandinavia	1086	1164	na	na	na	na
Others	1272	1358	na	na	na	na

* The countries are listed in order of their performance in 1995.
na: Not applicable

Sources: Singapore Tourist Promotion Board (STPB), *Survey of Overseas Visitors to Singapore 1996* (Singapore: STPB, 1996).

outweighed the precipitous drop in average spending, especially among ASEAN and Japanese visitors. The fall in average spending has mainly been caused by the appreciation of the Singapore dollar against other currencies, which tends to make the whole range of tourist products relatively more expensive for the overseas visitors.

It is too early to say whether the Goods and Services Tax (GST), implemented from 1 April 1994, has adversely affected tourism spending. Several measures have, however, been taken to minimise the impact of GST on tourism. For example, tourists are reimbursed the GST paid on all merchandise taken from Singapore if the total amount of purchases equals or exceeds S$500. Furthermore, to keep the hotel industry in Singapore internationally competitive, the cess tax (equivalent of VAT) paid by the hotels has already been reduced by 3%. While average tourist expenditure is falling, the emergence of new markets such as South Africa and China has raised hopes among local tourism officials about the possibility of reversing the trend, if the growth potential of these new sources of tourist dollars can be fully realised.

Table 4.4 shows visitor arrivals to Singapore by purpose of visits. Although Singapore is quite deficient in natural attractions and recreational facilities, pure holidaymakers (i.e. pleasure/vacation travellers) constitute the bulk of tourists coming to Singapore and the proportion of such visitors has increased significantly since

Table 4.4 Visitor arrivals to Singapore by purpose of visits, 1985–95 (percentage distribution)

Purpose	1985	1990	1995
Pleasure/vacation	37.6	55.2	50.2
Business	23.6	9.6	15.5
In transit	17.2	4.2	10.3
Business/pleasure	7.6	7.2	6.1
Visit friends/relatives	5.3	4.1	3.7
Convention/exhibition	na	1.9	2.0
Stopover	4.4	10.5	6.2
Honeymoon	na	1.5	1.3
Shopping	0.9	2.9	1.6
Medical/dental treatment	1.5	1.2	1.1
Sports and recreation	na	na	0.1
Others/not stated	1.9	1.6	1.1
Education and travel	na	na	0.7
Incentive travel	na	na	0.1

Sources: Singapore Tourist Promotion Board (STPB), *Survey of Overseas Visitors to Singapore 1996* (Singapore: STPB, 1996).

1985. The number of business travellers fell quite sharply after 1985 but increased again after 1990 and in 1995, nearly 16% of travellers came for business reasons alone.

Although only a small percentage of tourists visit Singapore for the sole purpose of shopping, it still represents the main category of tourist expenditure, accounting for more than half of total spending by the tourists (Table 4.5). It is clear that Singapore still remains a 'shopper's paradise' in spite of the growing strength of the Singapore dollar.

The proportion of convention travellers is small but growing. Singapore in recent years has developed world-class convention facilities and it is already ranked as the 'first convention destination in Asia'. The city-state is trying to attract more delegates as their average spending is found to be more than three times that of the 'average' tourist. The tourism expenditure survey also shows that the Republic is

Table 4.5 Expenditure pattern of travellers to Singapore, 1985–95 (percentage distribution)

Expenditure category	1985	1990	1995
Accommodation	19.3	22.3	21.1
Food and beverage	13.8	13.3	10.7
Shopping	59.7	55.8	55.6
Sightseeing	0.6	1.5	2.0
Local transport	3.9	3.5	4.6
Entertainment and recreation	1.2	1.7	1.1
Medical/dental treatment	na	0.4	4.7
Miscellaneous	1.5	0.5	0.2
Total	100	100	100

Sources: Singapore Tourist Promotion Board (STPB), *Survey of Overseas Visitors to Singapore 1996*, and previous issues.

increasingly becoming a 'regional' centre for health care services with 1.1% of total visitors arriving for medical treatment alone in 1995. Their medical bills accounted for 4.7% of total tourist expenditure in that year.

The average length of stay for a tourist in Singapore is fairly low by Asian standards, presently hovering around 3.5 days and has always been less than 4 days (Table 4.6). This compares to 5.2 days for the Republic of Korea, 4.8 for Malaysia, 11.5 for the Philippines, 7.5 for Taiwan, 7.0 for Thailand, and 3.9 for Hong Kong (Pacific Area Travel Association, 1996). Although the shortness of stays can be explained by the smallness of the country, local tourism experts have lamented the loss of natural attractions (due to rapid industrialisation), the absence of good cultural attractions, and the lack of a vibrant nightlife because of strict puritanical standards.

In line with the growing number of arrivals, Singapore's hotel industry has expanded rapidly, almost doubling in size over the past ten years. The industry experienced an oversupply of hotel rooms in the 1980s. Widespread optimism resulting from robust growth in the 1960s and 1970s led to the overdevelopment of new hotels and the excessive expansion of the existing ones. The average occupancy rate in 1980 was more than 86% but it fell to 64.7% by 1986 (Table 4.6). Due to this overexpansion, average hotel rates declined from being the highest in Asia in the early 1980s to among the lowest in 1985–6. This situation, however, did not last long as the market reacted quickly, resulting in a slowdown in hotel construction. The process of revival started in 1987 and the hotel occupancy rate is currently back to about its 1980 level. Room rates have now even exceeded their previous peak. It should, however, be noted that the fundamentals of the hotel industry still remain somewhat weak. For example, the profitability of the industry has declined in recent years due to the change in visitor markets from 'high-yielding' Western visitors to 'value-for-money' visitors from Asia, and increased operational costs. Hotel managers are particularly concerned over rising costs and deteriorating service standards resulting from the serious labour shortage.

Table 4.6 Average length of stay, hotel occupancy, and hotel tariff in Singapore, 1980–95

Year	Average length of stay (days)	Occupancy (%)	Tariff* (1982 = 100)
1980	3.7	86.1	76.9
1985	3.5	65.9	79.6
1986	3.5	64.7	65.2
1987	3.4	68.7	60.5
1988	3.4	79.3	64.2
1989	3.3	86.4	87.9
1990	3.3	84.0	125.6
1991	3.9	76.7	124.3
1992	3.7	79.8	121.8
1993	3.6	83.4	115.2
1994	3.5	86.6	116.3
1995	3.4	84.1	120.6

* Double occupancy.

Sources: Department of Statistics (DOS), *Singapore, 1965–1995 Statistical Highlights: A Review of 30 Years' Development* (Singapore: DOS, 1996).

Role of government in tourism development

Singapore's economic philosophy is often explained by using the 'Governed Market' theory (Wade, 1990). This says that the superior economic performance of the East Asian economies is due mainly to the adoption of a specific set of economic policies which enabled the government to 'guide' or 'govern' the process of resource allocation to produce a different production and investment profile than would result under a free-market system. The theory also claims that the corporatist and authoritarian political arrangements of East Asia have provided the basis for market guidance. Being strongly 'efficiency-conscious' and 'achievement-oriented', the government of Singapore has, since independence, regulated the private sector activities with various policy instruments in order to attain its long-term development objectives. Such an interventionist policy was clearly indicated by the then deputy prime minister of Singapore, Dr Goh Keng Swee, in the following statement:

> The *laissez-faire* policies of the colonial era had led Singapore to a dead end, with little economic growth, massive unemployment, wretched housing and inadequate education. We had to try a more activist and interventionist approach. The roles of the government are not only to perform the traditional roles of a government – defence, law and order, and to provide infrastructure for private enterprises – but also to participate actively in economic activities as well as to lay down clear guidelines to private sector as to what they could and should do (Devan Nair, 1976 : 74).

The Singapore government had no ideological commitment to any particular economic system – free enterprise, socialism or whatsoever. Its only concern was the betterment of living for Singaporeans and in order to achieve this objective, it implemented a host of 'pragmatic' policies which involved extensive government intervention in many areas of Singaporean life, including population control, housing, education, medical and health services, compulsory savings, industrial relations, pollution control, etc. Economic pragmatism also motivated the government to adopt an open-door policy not only to foreign investment and technology but also to foreign managers, engineers and technicians. Singapore never suffered from a xenophobic post-colonial hangover. Moreover, there was a realisation that, given its small size, it could not possibly develop a critical pool of high-level manpower required to run the economy.

In tandem with its open-door economic policy, Singapore adopted a liberal 'tourism policy' right from the beginning. Tourists from all over the world were welcome into the Republic and there were hardly any visa or foreign currency restrictions. Strict laws were enforced to ensure safety for the visitors. To keep the environment clean, tough pollution-control measures were introduced. To increase the growth of air travel, liberal aviation policies were implemented with little or no restrictions on the landing rights of scheduled airlines and on the operation of charter flights. The Singapore Tourist Promotion Board (STPB) was created in 1964 as the national tourism organisation entrusted with the responsibility of developing the country's tourist industry. Besides its main functions of marketing and planning tourism, it acts as an agent for the government on a wide range of tourism-related matters. It also acts as a lead agency when in partnership with the Civil Aviation Authority of Singapore, Economic Development Board, Urban Redevelopment Authority and the Ministry of Information and Arts. In 1972 the Sentosa Development Corporation (SDC) was established as a statutory body to develop 'Sentosa' island (formerly known as Pulau Blakang Mati) into a tourist resort. Currently, it is the 'top' tourist attraction in Singapore with many recreational facilities (Figure 4.2). In 1995/6, a total of 3.9 million people visited the island, of whom 2.5 million (64%) were overseas visitors (Sentosa Development Corporation, 1996).

Has there been any 'shift' in government policy towards tourism? Tourism experts such as Wong (1997) identified four phases of government support:

- No support before 1955
- Conflicting interests from 1956 to 1962
- Strong support from 1963 to 1983 and
- More concerted support and strategies from 1983 to present.

Richter (1993), in her review of tourism policies in South-east Asia, claims that Singapore has always adopted a 'centralised' approach, characterised by a high degree of government intervention and a regulatory climate towards tourism planning and development.

Given that Singapore adopted a 'statist' model of political economy, which embodies strong state action for achieving high economic growth, it is somewhat difficult to determine precisely the level of government support for the development of the tourist industry at different points in time. Even if government support is found to be lacking at one time or another, it can be justified from the point of view that such an action was necessary for growth enhancement, which remains the single-minded priority of the government.

Tourism and recreational activities are basically labour-intensive (as well as land-intensive) in character and spending too many state resources in such activities at the cost of other higher value-added activities such as manufacturing, particularly in the context of a city-state economy where both land and labour resources are very scarce, though not stifling economic growth, may slow down the pace of economic progress. Another popular perception is that the benefits of the tourist industry largely go to the foreigners and the government should, therefore, not overinvest in such industries. The perception could be right if the focus of the tourism policy is to develop certain recreational resorts which exclusively serve the interest of the foreign visitors. If investment is made, however, in the development of resorts which serve the recreational needs of both foreigners and locals, the perception is obviously erroneous. It is germane to mention at this point that the demand for recreational activities by the residents would usually increase as a country makes economic progress and as the demand for basic goods and services is gradually being met. So in a governed-market economy, government investment in tourism may be expected to increase when the growing industry is required to become efficient and to achieve objectives that benefit domestic as well as overseas visitors.

It can be clearly observed that there has been a marked shift in the government's attitude towards tourism development since 1983. The government has always been

75

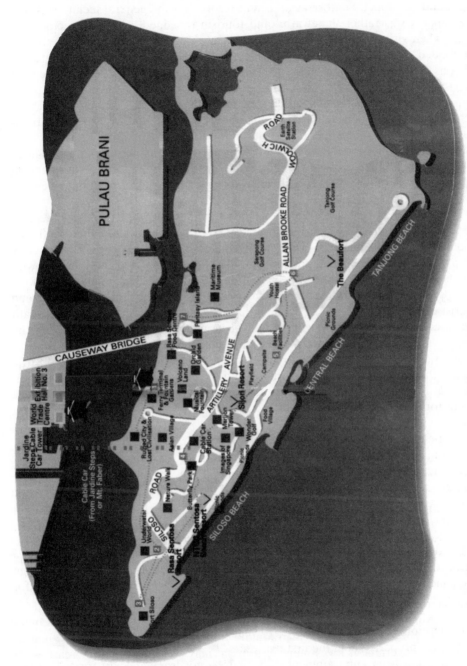

Figure 4.2 Recreational facilities in Sentosa island. Reproduced from *The Official Map of Singapore* by permission

supporting tourism by providing tourism-related infrastructure – it is a major share-holder in Singapore Airlines (SIA), built Changi Airport at a cost of S$1.3 billion in 1981, and developed Sentosa as an island resort. But the general feeling was that the support was rather 'lukewarm' and tourism remained a low-key sector until 1983, when visitor arrivals declined, for the first time, by 3.5%. The government responded quickly and appointed a high-powered task force to investigate the reasons for such a decline and to formulate guidelines for the development of tourism. The team of experts produced a meticulous report and found that the tourist industry faced serious structural (rather than cyclical) problems which in-cluded travel restrictions imposed by some ASEAN neighbours (particularly Indo-nesia), Singapore's uncompetitive position as a tourist destination, and the loss of attractions (Ministry of Trade and Industry, 1984). It was noted that a sustained high growth of tourist arrivals was required to justify the huge public investments in infrastructure projects. This report represents the first major official document on Singapore's tourist industry.

The STPB was reorganised and expanded in 1984 in order to reflect the new needs of the industry. A Tourism Product Development Plan (Ministry of Trade and Industry and Singapore Tourist Promotion Board, 1986) was subsequently prepared by the STPB in conjunction with the Ministry of Trade and Industry, with inputs from various other ministries and statutory bodies. The main objective of the proposed S$1 billion plan was to raise the rate of visitor arrivals, length of stay, and tourist expenditure. It was felt strongly that Singapore needed to pause for breath because, in its race for achieving higher economic growth, it was destroying the country's heritage. Accordingly, the plan recommended the restoration and re-vitalisation of some of the older areas of Singapore (such as Chinatown and Little India), the greening of the whole island, and the cleaning of the Singapore River. The various conservation and restoration projects aimed to give Singapore five major touristic themes:

- Exotic east
- Colonial heritage
- Tropical island resort
- Clean and green garden city and
- Centre for international sporting events.

Each theme was expected to generate half-day or day-long visit by the tourists.

Besides giving tourism a billion-dollar boost, the government also offered a package of attractive tax incentives to encourage both domestic as well as foreign investments in tourism-related projects. These incentives, which were designed for investments in excess of S$20 million, included:

- Exemption of tax on profits for 5–10 years
- A lower property tax in the first five years
- Exemption from entertainment duty (a 15% government levy) for 5–10 years depending on the size of investment
- Accelerated depreciation allowances and
- Investment allowances.

Singapore has always offered generous tax and investment incentives to investors and it receives the bulk of foreign investments coming to Asia. However, the stock of foreign direct investment (FDI) in the hotel and tourism sector is rather minimal and the most common form of foreign investment in this sector is the management contract followed by franchise agreements (Khan, 1991).

The STPB in 1993 prepared a Strategic Plan for Growth, 1993–95 (Singapore Tourist Promotion Board, 1993), which was a logical extension of the earlier plan. It emphasised the need for diversifying the tourism product by various means (such as expanding the cruise market and improving convention facilities). Realising that it would be extremely difficult, if not impossible, to increase the average length of stay for a tourist in such a small city-state environment, the new plan sought only to maintain the prevailing length of stay rather than raise it. It also recognised the constraints imposed by various external factors (e.g. competition and restrictive trade policies of some neighbouring countries), and many internal factors (e.g. rising business costs and increasing labour shortages).

The Economic Planning Committee of the Ministry of Trade and Industry produced a major planning document in 1991 (Ministry of Trade and Industry, 1991), called 'The Strategic Economic Plan (SEP)'. It is an extension of the Committee's earlier works on the causes of 1985 economic recession (Ministry of Trade and Industry, 1986) and it sought to chart the long-term economic policies for Singapore to realise the ultimate objective of attaining the status of a first-league developed country within the next 30 to 40 years (i.e. the GNP per capita of the United States by 2030 or the Netherlands by 2020).

The main thrust of the SEP's industrial strategy was to select some industrial 'clusters' (i.e. groups of industries based on horizontal and vertical linkages) and then channel all the available resources to make them world-class. Tourism was one of the fourteen industrial clusters selected for development and the principal objective, as announced in SEP, was 'to establish Singapore as a premier visitor destination with universal appeal and a leading international hub for aviation, convention/exhibition and travel/tourism-related services' (The Ministry of Trade and Industry, 1991 : 144). The detailed composition of the tourism industry was developed (Figure 4.3) and several policies, such as exporting travel-related services, increasing the intensity of land use for hotel development, and improving the efficiency of workers (employed in the travel industry) through automation and training were suggested for the attainment of the main objective.

Despite detailed industrial analysis and the successful implementation of several tourism plans since 1984, the industry is currently facing the problem of falling growth in tourist arrivals and receipts. The average length of stay for a tourist has also shown no improvement over the years, though a wider variety of attractions have been provided under the plans. One cannot argue that the lack of systematic planning in the earlier years of tourism development is responsible for a slower growth in later years simply because the government has always adopted a pro-growth strategy in order to achieve sustainable development for tourism, as discussed above.

Why could not the high growth rates of tourist arrivals be sustained? Has there been any deliberate attempt by the government to impose some restrictions on the entry of visitors for the sake of environmental (or social) preservation? Not at all.

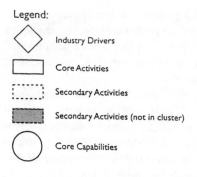

Legend:

◇ Industry Drivers

▭ Core Activities

┈ Secondary Activities

▨ Secondary Activities (not in cluster)

○ Core Capabilities

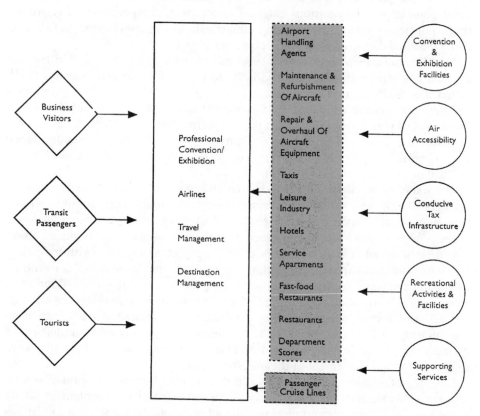

Figure 4.3 Tourism cluster proposed in the Strategic Economic Plan (SEP)

In fact, immigration procedures have been streamlined over the years to promote both in- and outbound travel. With the exception of a very few countries, travellers do not require a visa to enter the Republic. Although there are very few studies on the social and environmental impacts of tourism in Singapore, the general perception is that the social and environmental costs of tourism were rather minimal in the city-state (Khan, Chou and Wong, 1990). The tough stance taken by the government against all types of crime (e.g. mandatory caning for acts of vandalism, molestation, and even for overstaying) and pollution (e.g. stiff penalties for littering, failing to flush the toilet after use, selling chewing gum, etc.) has largely helped to control the adverse effects of tourism. It is highly unlikely that these measures, which are primarily designed to ensure the safety of citizens (as well as overseas visitors), would dissuade tourists from coming to the Republic. The falling growth of tourist arrivals in recent years could be a natural phenomenon as Singapore's tourist industry has already matured, and seems to be nearing its carrying capacity.

The small island-state cannot certainly hold an unlimited number of tourists due to limited carrying capacities and it would be extremely useful if tourism planners could set some kind of an 'upper limit' on tourist arrivals. This would help to maintain a quality product and give a frame of reference within which to interpret growth figures. The determination of an 'optimal' growth target for visitor arrivals involves several considerations, and any such measured optimum is likely to be very tentative in nature, as discussed in the following section.

An optimal target for growth

Tourism experts often use 'stage theoretic' approaches to study the evolution of a tourist destination and the changing marketing strategies over time (e.g. Butler, 1980; Cooper, and Jackson, 1989; Cooper, 1990). It is usually believed that from the time a new tourist resort (or area) is opened for recreational activities until the time that it loses the majority of its market appeal, it passes through four stages of development, namely; introduction, growth, maturity, and decline. At the 'introduction' stage, the rate of visitation is quite small due mainly to the lack of visitor awareness on the quality of recreational facilities available at the new site. The visitation rate increases rapidly at the 'growth' stage when the facilities are further expanded and the resort becomes widely known among potential visitors. The popularity of the resort will eventually peak and as the resort becomes 'mature', the growth of visitor arrivals is likely to level off or start falling. Finally, the tourist area becomes overcrowded (and loses its popularity to other new recreational sites) and the visitation rate sharply declines. Applying the theory to a tourist destination such as Singapore (rather than a tourist attraction such as Sentosa island), one can easily observe that the city-state Republic entered the maturity stage in the early 1980s when relatively slow growth in tourist arrivals was experienced.

In order to prevent the country's tourism industry from a 'decline', the planning and marketing strategies should be reoriented towards a sustainable growth of tourist arrivals. While the rejuvenation of existing tourist attractions (and the opening of some new ones) and more effective promotional measures have already been undertaken for this purpose, it is also necessary to set an 'optimal' target for tourism growth, say, up to the year 2000. This involves several considerations.

First, it is necessary to establish Singapore's capacity to accommodate its visitors. This will enable us to arrive at some kind of upper limit for accommodation. Based on various projections (e.g. STPB, 1996), it is unlikely that the number of rooms available in Singapore would exceed 40 000 by the year 2000. Assuming that all these rooms have double beds, the total bed capacity will be 80 000. Since the average length of stay of visitors to Singapore is around 3.5 days, the maximum number of visitors that Singapore can accommodate is 8.34 million (we assume 100% occupancy rate for estimating this upper limit). Based on past trends, we may assume that roughly 25% of all visitors do not stay in hotels. Incorporating this into our estimation, the maximum number of visitors that Singapore can host by the year 2000 is 10.43 million. Interestingly, a regression-based forecasting model has also predicted that the tourist arrivals in Singapore will surpass 10 million by the year 2000 (Ng Tze Chieh, 1997).

Second, too many visitors may strain local resources. Although it is virtually impossible to determine an exact acceptable threshold, a comparison of density-related indices across countries might provide some answers. An examination of data presented in Table 4.7, shows that in 1990, Singapore had 16 visitors daily per 1000 residents, and 69 visitors daily per square kilometre of land (day trippers from Malaysia arriving by land are not included in this estimation).

Thus, it appears that Singapore is more densely visited than popular European destinations such as France, Spain, and Italy. The tourist densities in Hong Kong, another popular destination in the Orient, are also lower than those of Singapore. The eight high-density Caribbean Islands average approximately 180 visitors daily per 1000 residents and 58 visitors per square kilometre (in the case of the area-based density index, Singapore exceeds the average for the Caribbean Islands). Considering that by the year 2000 Singapore could accommodate 10.43 million tourists, the tourist densities will be roughly 37 visitors daily per 1000 residents and 175 visitors daily per square kilometre.

Finally, while the tourist densities in Singapore in the year 2000 are sustainable by Caribbean standards, the socio-economic effects of excessive tourist arrivals must be considered. Although the adverse social effects of tourism have largely

Table 4.7 Tourist densities for a few selected countries, 1990

Countries	Total visitors (000's)	Daily visitors per 1000 residents	Daily visitors per km^2
Caribbean*			
St Martin	976	283	193
British Virgin Islands	547	132	141
Bahamas	3220	286	23
Bermuda	414	221	4
Caymans	614	147	41
US Virgin Island	1555	119	37
Aruba	414	147	15
Anguilla	70	101	8
Others†			
France	51 462	16	2
Spain	34 300	5	0.4
Italy	26 679	4	0.8
Singapore	**4842**	**16**	**69**
Hong Kong	5933	9	51

* All figures are valid for 1989–90 and are extracted from McElroy *et al.* (1993).
† The tourist density indices for 1990 were compiled by the author by taking the relevant information from World Tourism Organisation (WTO), *Yearbook of Tourism Statistics 1992*, and United Nations (UN), *Demographic Yearbook 1991*.

been checked by appropriate government policies, the uncontrolled growth of tourism may result in overcrowding, congestion, and inflated prices. Also, tourism is primarily a labour-intensive industry, thus imposing a serious constraint on the Republic's scarce labour resources. The import of foreign workers to reduce the labour shortage in itself creates a host of socio-political problems. The economic impact, measured by the input–output multipliers, shows that tourism played a positive role in the economic development of Singapore. It should, however, be mentioned that such impact studies do not truly reflect the real economic significance of tourism, which can only be measured by using cost–benefit techniques. Both public and private sectors have invested billions of dollars in developing tourism-related projects (e.g. building of hotels, airports, recreational resorts, etc) and any economic impact study should incorporate these expenses (i.e. pure economic costs of tourism development) into its calculation. The economic benefits of tourism, based on the results of visitor expenditure surveys, tend to ignore this fact.

Considering the above factors, it is believed that although by the year 2000 Singapore could accommodate more than 10 million visitors, a target of 9 million would be more manageable, resulting in an average 6% annual increase in tourist arrivals over the next few years. By carefully restraining hotel construction and expansion, both occupancy and room rates can be improved, resulting in an increase in the overall profitability of the hotel industry. The number of tourists will keep on rising as Singapore revitalises its tourist attractions but the emphasis should be on increasing the quality instead of the quantity of visitors. It should continuously strive to attract a sustainable number of high-spending tourists who stay longer and who can make a maximum contribution to the local economy at minimum social cost.

Planning for the future

The STPB in conjunction with other public and private sector agencies recently launched a tourism plan called 'Tourism 21' (STPB, 1996), with the long-term vision of making Singapore the world's 'Tourism Capital' in the twenty-first century. Singapore has already made significant contributions to the development of global tourism and in future it wants to flourish not only as a tourist destination but also as a tourism business centre and as a tourism hub. To turn the vision of a Tourism Capital into reality, a new broad strategy called 'Tourism Unlimited' (which is a part of 'Singapore Unlimited' strategy) has been announced, which again has two dimensions. The first, 'Bringing the World to Singapore', is about enhancing Singapore's own attractiveness as a 'must see' destination, attracting people from all over the world to visit Singapore and encouraging companies to use Singapore as a test-bed for new ideas and products. The second, 'Bringing Singapore to the World' involves Singapore's active participation in the development of tourism in the region through 'Co-opetition', a term coined recently to combine both cooperation and competition that will bring about greater long-term benefits to Singapore and its partners than competition alone. In short, the 'Tourism Unlimited' strategy is built upon the premise that the perceived problems of Singapore's smallness can be overcome by pulling together the complementary strengths of regional countries through effective partnerships. For example, Singapore can create new tourism space outside its border by investing jointly with Malaysia in developing certain tourist attractions in Johor and then promoting these attractions as a 'package'.

For ease of implementation, the broad strategy of 'Tourism Unlimited' has again been divided into six components or strategic thrusts (Figure 4.4), which are as follows:

- Redefining tourism
- Reformulating the product
- Developing tourism as an industry
- Configuring new tourism space
- Partnering for success and
- Championing tourism.

To achieve the vision of a Tourism Capital, it is necessary to redefine tourism in a wider perspective. Singapore is already well known as a top tourist destination in Asia, but in order to realise the full potential of tourism as an industry, it should now concentrate on the business aspects of tourism. By promoting tourism-related investments and ideas within the Republic and across the region, Singapore can play a new role as a Tourism Business Centre. With its strategic location and excellent infrastructure, Singapore is well suited to be a Tourism Hub, not only for the tourists using Singapore as a base for travelling into the region but also for entrepreneurs venturing into tourism-related businesses in the region. As the global community increases its awareness of the great economic potentials of the Asia-Pacific region, the adoption of a broader perspective in promoting the tourism industry will certainly help to create new opportunities for Singapore and its partners.

In order to perpetuate Singapore's reputation as a prime tourist destination, it is necessary to continuously upgrade existing tourism products and offer new ones so that the tourists keep coming back to the Republic, stay longer, and spend more. While upgrading the tourist products, attempts should be made to keep their prices as low as possible so that the budget travellers coming from the neighbouring countries can easily afford them. In adding new attractions, the recreational needs of both foreigners and locals should be considered equally. With these objectives in mind, Tourism 21 aims to reformulate the tourism product so as to make Singapore 'a world-class memorable destination'. It adopts a thematic approach to develop a unifying character of existing tourist products which will be strongly reflected in terms of activity clusters, services, and facilities. Altogether, eleven 'thematic zones' (Entertainment District, Theatre Walk, Museum and Heritage Trail, The Night Zone, Island Escapade, Rustic Charm, Mall of Singapore, Nature Trail, Singapore Heartland, Ethnic Singapore, and International Vacation Gateway) have been targeted for development under this plan and it is intended that visitors will spend at least half a day in each of these zones. The development of such thematic zones is also expected to enhance the quality of life in Singapore by beautifying the surrounding areas and creating a wide variety of recreational opportunities for its citizens.

Although tourism has played an important role in the Singapore economy, it received an explicit recognition as an 'industry' only in 1991 when the government

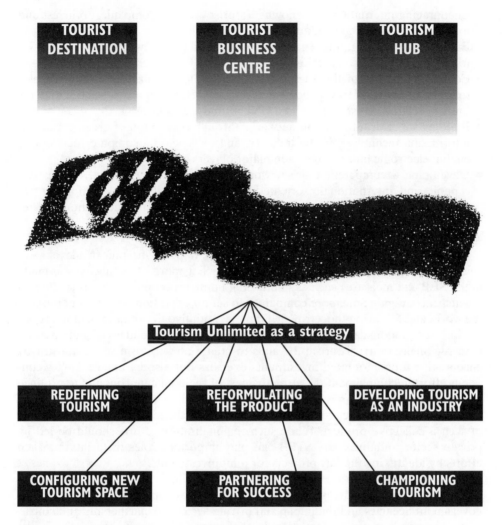

Figure 4.4 Tourism 21: The strategies for making Singapore 'The Tourism Capital'.
Reproduced by permission from Singapore Tourism Promotion Board 1996

announced its long-term 'Strategic Economic Plan'. Unlike most other industries, tourism is characterised by the diversity of sectors it embraces, such as hotels, travel agencies, restaurants, shops, airlines, etc., and this composite industry can only be developed by adopting a 'cluster development' approach.

The industrial strategy proposed in the SEP is built upon this premise and it received further refinements in the recently announced 'Tourism 21'. A number of measures are suggested in this new tourism plan for the future development of the tourist industry, and these include:

- Encouraging the upgrading efforts by local companies so that they are always at the forefront of business know-how
- Product development and regional expansion

- Encouraging internationally renowned tourism-related companies to invest and to set up their regional headquarters in Singapore
- Enhancing the operating environment by building new tourism-related infrastructure (such as a mega-exhibition hall, and Cruise terminal)
- Continuous review of the administrative procedures impacting on the industry (e.g. the licensing of travel agents and tour guides, tax incentives and grants for tourism-related investments, and a GST refund mechanism)
- Building superior information networks through promotion of greater usage of information technology in the industry; and to develop a computer network to enable electronic link-ups between major players in the industry
- Developing a competent tourism workforce by nurturing a pool of creative, capable and internationally oriented managers; developing a comprehensive skills and attitudinal training programme; and encouraging automation and re-engineering of work processes which can improve efficiency.

Given its size constraint, Singapore can only hope to become a 'developed' country through globalisation. A call for making Singapore a 'global city' was made in the SEP and measures such as liberalising immigration policy to attract foreign talents, encouraging Singapore companies to set up operations in different parts of the world and following the 'Growth Triangle' initiative to promote regional cooperation were announced in the plan. Being motivated by the ideas of globalisation (and regionalisation), 'Tourism 21' aims to create new tourism space not just by encouraging tourism-related investments overseas but also by undertaking a conscious effort to complement the attractiveness of regional countries and to produce a stronger 'collective product' to the benefit of all parties involved. Blending Singapore's city sophistication with Indonesia's rustic beach charms is one example of such a collective product. While such regionalisation efforts should be led by private sector initiatives, the STPB can play important roles in facilitating such efforts by identifying the key projects for joint investments.

Given the multi-component nature of the tourism industry, the successful implementation of various strategies depends largely on the cooperation between various government agencies and the public and private sectors. A partnership and collaborative approach is critical in achieving alignment and synergy, especially for the development of the tourism industry, which is characterised by the diversity of interests reflecting different aspects of hospitality.

'Tourism 21' plans to organise seminars, workshops, and conferences regularly so that tourism enthusiasts from both public and private sectors can deliberate on key policy issues and chart new directions for the future development of the industry. It also suggests the formation of a Destination Marketing Council (DMC), involving members of the public and private sectors, to serve as an integrated marketing platform to create a better and lasting image of Singapore among the potential visitors. Besides performing these tasks, the STPB will also undertake the role of an overall 'champion' for the tourist industry. It will be a one-stop agency, offering all relevant information on the various segments of the tourist industry, and incentives for tourism-related business developments. To reflect the broadening of its role beyond tourism promotion, the STPB will be renamed the 'Singapore Tourism Board'.

'Tourism 21' thus draws a comprehensive plan for the future development of tourism in Singapore.The different tasks set out in the plan will be carried out in phases ranging from one to ten years. As far as visitor arrivals and tourism receipts are concerned, the plan aims to achieve the targets of 10 million visitors and S$16 billion receipts by the year 2000. Although the growth rates of both arrivals and receipts have fallen in recent years, these targets might be achieved if Singapore's tourist markets (including the newly emerging ones) in the region continue to thrive and Singapore remains attractive to them. It is also essential that Singapore continues to maintain friendly relations with all the countries, including its neighbours. Needless to say, tourism grows out of friendships and it sows the seeds of cooperation between people, so vital for realising the Singapore dream of 'Tourism Capital'.

Conclusion

Tourism in Singapore is a success story. Although the industry is currently facing some problems such as a slow growth in tourist arrivals, falling expenditure per tourist and serious manpower shortage in hotels, restaurants, and retail outlets, it is still one of the fastest-growing industries in the Republic. The government has helped the growth of tourism in many ways. It has built the necessary infrastructure so that the industry can thrive. Its open-door policy towards foreign investments has made it possible for multinational hotel and restaurant chains to extend their businesses to Singapore primarily through management contracts and franchise agreements. Its liberal immigration policy has allowed millions of visitors from all over the world to enter the Republic without any visa restrictions and its tough stance against all anti-social activities has made it possible for the tourists to stay in Singapore safely and comfortably. Its 'open skies' policy has made the tiny island-state accessible to virtually all countries of the world, which greatly facilitated the growth of air traffic between Singapore and other destinations, resulting in a tourism explosion.

A closer examination would, however, reveal changing roles of the government over the years. This essentially reflects the 'reactive' nature of government policy which implies that government intervention depends largely on market signals. The basic philosophy is based on pragmatism – the government will intervene as and when necessary to correct market failures. This explains why tourism in Singapore did not receive much attention from the government before 1983. The industry was experiencing double-digit growth and it did not require direct government assistance. The government developed a billion-dollar rescue package immediately after 1983, when the industry experienced negative growth in tourist arrivals for the first time in Singapore's history. More systematic efforts have been made since then to ensure sustained growth of tourist arrivals and receipts.

The long-term vision of making Singapore the 'Tourism Capital' can be achieved if the strategy of 'Tourism Unlimited' is well implemented. The main motivation behind this strategy is to increase Singapore's tourism space through regional cooperation. What are the prospects of such cooperation, for example, in ASEAN countries? From among these countries, Singapore (and to some extent Malaysia) is perhaps the only one capable of making substantial investments in hotels and resort developments in other ASEAN countries. In fact, Singapore investors have already shown significant interests in Vietnam's hotel and tourism-related projects. The scope for Foreign Direct Investment (FDI) from ASEAN sources, however, remains extremely limited, although there is good potential for developing some tourist resorts jointly (e.g. Singapore with Malaysia and Indonesia can jointly develop the Johor, Batam, and Bintan areas; Thailand with Vietnam can develop the Mekong River area).

The potential areas for future cooperation include mainly the activities related to promotion, marketing, tourism planning and research, development of transport and communication networks, technological upgrading, environmental protection, and manpower training. The joint efforts in these areas will benefit everyone by creating economies of scale, e.g. they can save on advertising expenses by selling ASEAN countries as a single destination rather than promoting them individually through campaigns such as 'Visit Malaysia Year' or 'Visit Indonesia Year'. Singapore, as the most advanced country in the region, should perhaps provide technical assistance (e.g. consultancy services, manpower training, etc.) to other ASEAN partners not only to promote tourism but also to upgrade the quality of tourism-related services.

Singapore can also collaborate with Japan (or some Japanese organisations such as The International Tourism Development Institute in Tokyo, which has been trying to promote tourism in South-east Asia) by providing such assistance. It should also be remembered that conflicts may arise between member states on certain tourism-related issues, but these should not undermine the spirit of ASEAN cooperation. Malaysia, for example, is currently considering imposing a levy on tour buses from Singapore which do not stay overnight (i.e. Malaysia wants tourists who will stay in their hotels, not day-trippers). While the imposition of such a levy may increase Malaysia's tax revenue, it may stand in the way of future cooperation between the two countries. It is believed that the countries in the region should be prepared to sacrifice short-term gains for the sake of the long-term benefits to be derived from cooperation.

The future of ASEAN cooperation in the areas of tourism development, however, remains bright. There are several reasons for such optimism. First, these economies are likely to continue their robust economic growth for the next decade and the intra-ASEAN business and trade will receive a large boost in the year 2000 when the proposed ASEAN Free Trade Area (AFTA) becomes a reality. As the ASEAN nationals become more and more affluent and the volume of business transactions grow within the region, intra-ASEAN business travel will see a large increase.

Second, most ASEAN governments are now taking an active interest in the promotion of tourism and such governmental efforts are likely to intensify as they engage in increasing competition to attract more and more tourists. To ensure that competition between them remains healthy (i.e. to promote competition), they should try to identify complementary areas for tourism promotion. For example, while Singapore is now turning its attention to the emerging MICE (meetings, incentives, conferences, and exhibitions) market by developing its convention facilities, others should try to create new niches by developing a wide variety of recreational activities (e.g. sea sports, marinas, hill resorts, mountaineering, rural tourism, culture tourism, etc.).

Finally, the ASEAN region is likely to be a single 'borderless' holiday destination as the road, rail, and cruise links between them and across continents develop significantly over the years. Malaysia, for example, is presently studying a proposed railway line that would run across Asia and link up with the trans-European line. The cruise industry in the region is still at its infancy, though Singapore, Malaysia, and Indonesia are presently drawing up ambitious plans to develop it in line with the successful experience of the Caribbean and the Mediterranean (Ong Poh Chin, 1996). It should also be noted here that the ASEAN countries have significantly improved their air accessibilities over the years. Singapore and Malaysia, for example, have recently signed 'open-skies' agreements with the United States, and other ASEAN members are likely to follow suit.

As cooperation in the region continues to grow, Singapore is likely to achieve its long-term tourism goals. It should not, however, be obsessed with the target of 10 million tourists by the year 2000 as this number may not fulfil all the criteria of optimality. The central focus of the tourism policy in future should be shifted to the generation of more tourism-related businesses (which are relatively higher value-added in nature) rather than increasing the number of tourists. It must be emphasised that the tourism industry, if expanded in this direction, can be an important vehicle for economic growth. Also, the development of the tourism industry, through its various 'beautification' programmes and the creation of a wide range of recreational opportunities for Singaporeans, will certainly help to enhance the 'quality of life' within the city-state, which could not be attained by economic growth alone.

References

Butler, R.W. (1980) 'The concept of the tourist area cycle of evolution: implications for management of resources', *Canadian Geographer*, 24, 5–12.

Cooper, C.P. (1990) 'Resorts in decline: The management response', *Tourism Management*, 11, 63–7.

Cooper, C.P. and Jackson, S (1989) 'Destination life cycle: the Isle of Man case study', *Annals of Tourism Research*, 16, 377–98.

Department of Statistics (DOS) (1996) *Singapore, 1965–1995 Statistical Highlights: A Review of 30 Years' Development*, Singapore: DOS.

Devan Nair, C.V. (ed.), (1976) *Socialism That Works, The Singapore Way*, Singapore: Federal Publications.

Khan, H. (1991) 'Foreign investment in the tourism sector in selected Asian developing countries', *Escap Tourism Review*, 8, 161–88.

Khan, H., Chou, F.S. and Wong, K.C. (1990) 'The social impact of tourism on Singapore', *The Service Industries Journal*, 10(3), 541–8.

Khan, H., Chou,F.S. and Wong, K.C. (1991) 'Tourism multiplier effects on Singapore', *Annals of Tourism Research*, 17(3), 408–18.

Khan, H., Phang, S.Y. and Toh, R.S. (1995) 'Singapore's hospitality industry: the multiplier effect', *The Cornell Hotel and Restaurant Administration Quarterly*, 36(1), 64–69.

McElroy, J.L. *et al.* (1993) 'Applying the tourist destination life-cycle model to small Caribbean and Pacific Islands', in J.R. Brent Ritchie and D.E. Hawkins (eds), *World Travel and Tourism Review*, Wallingford: CAB International.

Ministry of Trade and Industry (1984) *Report of the Tourism Task Force*, Singapore: MTI.

Ministry of Trade and Industry (1986) *The Singapore Economy: New Directions*, Singapore: MTI.

Ministry of Trade and Industry (1991) *The Strategic Economic Plan: Towards a Developed Nation*, Singapore: MTI.

Ministry of Trade and Industry and Singapore Tourist Promotion Board (1986) *Tourist Product Development Plan*, Singapore: MTI and STPB.

Ng Tze Chieh (1997) *Tourism Management in Singapore: Policies, Issues, and Options*, Honours thesis, Singapore: Department of Economics and Statistics, National University of Singapore.

Ong Poh Chin (1996) *Tourism in Southeast Asia: Trends, Issues, and Prospects*, Honours Thesis, Singapore: Department of Economics and Statistics, National University of Singapore.

Pacific Area Travel Association (1996) *Annual Statistical Report 1994*, San Francisco: PATA.

Richter, L.K. (1993) 'Tourism policy-making in Southeast Asia', in M Hitchcock, V.T. King, and M.J.G. Parnwell (eds), *Tourism in South East Asia*, London: Routledge.

Sentosa Development Corporation (1996) *Annual Report*, Singapore: SDC.

Singapore Tourist Promotion Board (1993) *Strategic Plan for Growth 1993–95*, Singapore: STPB.

Singapore Tourist Promotion Board (1996) *Singapore Annual Report on Tourism Statistics 1996*, Singapore: STPB.

Singapore Tourist Promotion Board (1996) *Tourism 21: Vision of a Tourism Capital*, Singapore: STPB.

Toh, M.H. and Low, L. (1994) *Input–Output Tables 1988: Models and Applications*, Singapore: Department of Statistics.

Wade, R. (1990) *Governing the Market: Economic Theory and the Role of Government on East Asian Industrialization*, Princeton: Princeton University Press.

Wilkinson, P.F. (1989) 'Strategies for tourism in island microstates', *Annals of Tourism Research*, 16, 153–77.

Wong, P.P. (1997) 'Singapore: tourism development of an island city-state', in D.G. Lockhart and D. Drakakis-Smith (eds), *Island Tourism: Trends and Prospects*, London and New York: Pinter.

World Bank (1996) *World Development Report*, London: Oxford University Press.

World Tourism Organisation (1996) *Yearbook of Tourism Statistics 1996*, Madrid: WTO.

Section II
Managing visitors and resources in the city

Introduction

Visitor management in cities has become a major concern over the past 5–10 years. The growth of city breaks has led to more tourists visiting urban areas as an alternative to the beach. Short stay and quick throughput characterise these visits. The impact of the visitors on the physical fabric of the city, the loss of city functions from the centre and social impacts of tourism on residents all cause concern to the tourism and city manager. This section presents three case studies that consider the different aspects of visitor management, taking cities that are at different stages in their tourism development cycle.

In the first chapter of this section, Tunbridge considers the issues involved in visitor management in Ottawa. Not an historic city as such, but it has developed its tourist product around a certain interpretation of its history and its wider regional, mostly natural, resources. The drive to develop tourism in a modern city has come from the Federal Government's need to create a worthy federal capital city. Using the tourist historic city framework, Tunbridge considers the problems of developing a tourism product within an area of dual jurisdiction. Having to develop a product, almost from scratch, has led in this political set-up, to a dissonance between the various levels of government and the Anglo/Franco/Aborigine communities.

How should the past be presented? Whose past is being represented? Whose interpretation is correct? Such questions can cause ambiguous messages to be sent to the tourist and to residents, especially as the regional and local begin to dominate the national issues of development, thus changing the icons and meaning of the tourism product. What Tunbridge is driving at is that to manage the tourist you must first manage yourself, your product and your presentation and that this in turn is affected by the political and social environment of the city.

In Chapter 6, Shackley considers the tourism management issues involved in the Syrian cities of Damascus and Aleppo. These World Heritage cities are beginning to experience pressure brought about by an increase in popularity, partly caused by changing entry policies of the government and partly through the advent of more tourist packages. The problems arise due to sudden floods of visitors to Heritage Sites and a lack of on-site management techniques to cope with this. These issues are compounded by the financial and political arrangements concerning the funding of attractions and sites, and the movement of the middle class away from historic centres. Shackley identifies the need for an integrated urban planning scheme that conserves and enhances the tourism product, makes it more accessible to and improves understanding by the tourist and improves infrastructural development to benefit the wider city. Visitor management is clearly not just an issue for the crowded Heritage Site but also for the emerging destinations.

As Khan found in Chapter 4, it is very difficult, and probably commercially and politically unacceptable, to stop visitors entering the city, even when capacity limits are being reached. Issues of overcrowding have to be dealt with in different ways, using marketing, technology and presentational techniques to even out the flow of tourists both to and within the city.

In the final chapter of this section van der Borg discusses the latest theories and techniques of visitor management being developed in Venice. Part of an on-going research and management project, he sets out by describing the type of tourist that visits Venice and the impact that each of these have on the city. He describes how marketing, pre-arrival sales of ticket packages and use of alternative tourist routes within the city are being developed to address the pressure brought on the city by its own popularity, and suggests that such management techniques may be a model for other heritage cities.

These cases show that visitor management is not just a technique that is resorted to when carrying capacities are being reached. Visitor management, like development issues, is affected by the way that the city is developed, presented, managed and funded. The issues are just as broad, and often as intractable, as those of policy development discussed in Secton I.

5 Tourism management in Ottawa, Canada: nurturing in a fragile environment

JOHN TUNBRIDGE

CHAPTER SUMMARY

The development and management of the tourism industry in Ottawa clearly demonstrates that urban tourism is not just concerned with the impact of large visitor numbers but can raise questions of a city's historic and contemporary identity. Taking the tourist–historic city model as a framework for analysis, this chapter explores the need of some cities to nurture tourism products into being, seeing historic areas grow, merge and develop alongside other city functions. It explores how this has been achieved through product development, visitor management and political imperatives. In doing this, tensions rise as to whose history is portrayed, especially in cosmopolitan cities, where some historic actions bear multiple interpretations and where more recent immigration can bring other heritage dissonances into play. The chapter also explores how political changes can or may affect future product development, but how, overall, the tourist industry's imperative to be commercially viable may overcome such strategic issues, at least in the short term.

Introduction: the context of management

The management of tourism in cities is usually associated with strategies to accommodate heavy visitor loads on such European cultural–historic meccas as York, Rothenburg or the archetypal Venice (see Chapter 7 of this volume). In reality, however, there is a spectrum of supply and demand scenarios which calls for a range of approaches in tourism management and marketing (Ashworth and Tunbridge, 1990). Among these there is the scenario of an initially weak tourism resource requiring nurturing management and stimulational marketing to generate a demand. This is widespread, especially in New World urban environments which

Managing Tourism in Cities. Edited by D. Tyler, Y. Guerrier and M. Robertson.
Copyright © 1998 John Wiley & Sons Ltd.

lack obvious natural or cultural interest to tourists but for which the passage of an important milestone in their history, national or local, often stimulates awareness of a potential tourism resource. Given the primacy of historic urban tourism in the post-industrial economy, it is small wonder that so many such hitherto 'uninteresting' places have been scrambling aboard this perceived 'gravy train' with unseemly haste (Ashworth and Tunbridge, 1990).

Such is the tourism setting of Ottawa, in a broad sense, but with the proviso that its status as Canada's capital gave it a critical head-start. Because of this, Ottawa stands as a remarkable illustration of what can be done by systematic nurturing of an equivocal tourism resource – of how, with the single-minded application of resources over time, one can indeed make a silk purse out of a (comparative) sow's ear.

This chapter is concerned with the comprehension of this nurturing process and the contemporary and potential tourism management concerns associated with it. It is necessary to appreciate that what the world and this chapter know as 'Ottawa' is shorthand for the National Capital Region (Figure 5.1), extending over a sizeable portion of Eastern Ontario and Western Quebec and broadly equatable with a series of municipalities within the metropolitan area of Ottawa-Hull (population 1 million in 1996).

Tourism management in Ottawa is a multilateral process with an unequivocally expansionist goal pursued by stimulational marketing strategies, in which control of tourist pressure is but a small and specialised concern. After decades of urban enhancement, the approach to the national Centennial (1967) and the ensuing thirty years have witnessed the progressive expansion of the tourism resource in the interdependent terms of substance, season and space.

In substance: the national institutions in a (quasi) natural setting have created a 'capital tourism' which has been given time depth by the creation of the tourist–historic city (discussed below). The primacy of the capital attraction continues, notwithstanding public expenditure cutbacks and diversification of the regional economy, but initiatives such as sports franchises and a casino have broadened the tourism base. The seasonal expansion is critical: the local climate is often referred to as 'winter and July', an unkind allusion to inclemency which routinely includes four months of snow cover, temperatures dropping to –25°C (exceptionally –30°) and winter wind-chill factors which Europeans west of Moscow could not imagine. Yet Ottawa has contrived to establish the second largest winter festival in North America (after Quebec City) amid a seasonally varied calendar of events. The space expansion beyond the city proper derives chiefly from the political imperative of the National Capital Region and allows a diversity of natural and cultural resources to be co-marketed. It does, however, raise the issue of divided jurisdictions with potentially centrifugal tourism agendas in which (in Quebec) even the national capital legitimacy may be called into question.

An understanding of Ottawa's tourism management requires a prior examination of its resource base, the means whereby this has been nurtured and the significance of the tourist–historic city concept to the overall enterprise. This theoretical framework is central to comprehension of the more recent and critical phases of the nurturing process and must be introduced at the outset.

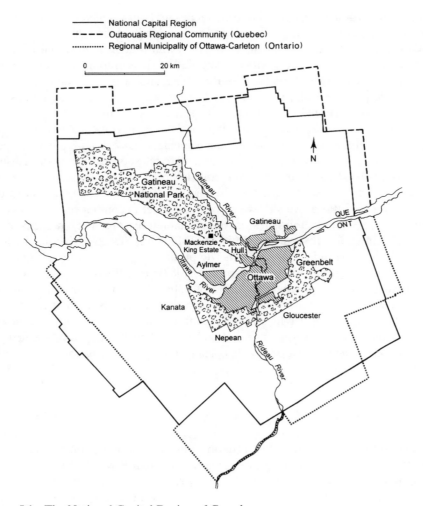

Figure 5.1 The National Capital Region of Canada

The tourist–historic city

The nurturing of Ottawa as a tourism centre has been comprehended by Ashworth and Tunbridge (1990) within the context of the tourist–historic city. The role of the federal government in generating a historic perception, which we shall examine, is in fact a relatively early example of the creation of a perceived historic resource in cities which had previously lacked such a self-perception, in 'New World' environments and more widely. The 1970s in particular witnessed a major articulation of urban historic perceptions simultaneously with, and supportive of, tourism aspirations. Thus the tourist–historic city model was proposed (initially by Ashworth and de Haan, 1985) not as a specialised but as a general framework within which to comprehend urban tourism issues. Not only is tourism often cited as the world's largest industry, but within it cultural tourism – primarily with an urban historic focus – now has pride of place.

While cities in general can now be so characterised (whatever else they may do), in a narrow sense, distinct areas within them can be identified, first, as the basis of the historic resource and, second, as the focus of overall tourist interest and provision. Accordingly, the tourist–historic city is composed of two components which overlap rather than coincide. Over time the historic city expands as newer and more diverse resources are perceived and marked (be they structures, sites or associations with historical or even fictional individuals, features or events); the tourist city likewise expands, as tourist numbers, awareness and specialised interests proliferate. The two components continue to overlap rather than coincide, however, since at a given point in time tourist perceptions and opportunities tend to fall short of current local historic recognition, while tourist service needs and interests extend the tourist city into central, or other, business districts and elsewhere outside the recognised historic city.

In the case of Ottawa, we shall observe this model becoming relevant with the expansion of the focus of tourism from the parliamentary precinct, via the National Capital Commission's resurrected 'Mile of History' on Sussex Drive, to the long-neglected original core in Lower Town. The prodigious growth of the leisure economy here, as the 'place to be' (Tunbridge, 1987), is a vivid manifestation of a widespread phenomenon whereby formerly undervalued inner urban areas (and commonly waterfronts) have been reclaimed as historic tourism resources.

We return to the tourist–historic city concept later in the chapter, following consideration of Ottawa's tourism resource base and nurturing process, which provided the particular foundation for its conspicuous relevance to the city's tourism profile.

The tourism resource base

European settlement originated two centuries ago to exploit the timber resource of the Ottawa Valley, using water power from the Ottawa River. Early settlers came from Quebec but also from the south, largely reflecting the American Revolution which directed many United Empire Loyalists to what became eastern Ontario, then unpromising bush and swampland which would otherwise have been left to its Indian occupants for much longer. Indeed the biggest impetus to the development of Ottawa proper was the building of the Rideau Canal to provide a transportation route from Lake Ontario to the St Lawrence which was strategically safe from the dangerous new republic. The community then known as Bytown (after the canal builder Colonel John By) originated with the construction workers who settled around the locks where the canal met the Ottawa River (Taylor, 1986).

All was not fever-ridden swamp, however: the Ottawa River itself, a glacially deranged sequence of lakes and rapids, was evidently recognised as a scenic as well as economic resource from the military watercolours preserved from that time; especially set against the scarp of the Gatineau Hills which commences the Canadian Shield country extending to the Arctic. While Bytown initially developed as a working-class lumber town, it did so in a location not lacking in potential future recreational resources, to which the canal itself was an important enhancement. Its climate is unforgiving, however, for the summers can be as tropical as the winters arctic. Furthermore its location is relatively peripheral: its choice as capital of

Canada, ostensibly by Queen Victoria, was partly motivated by its remove from the US border. Even today it is a 'spoke' to the 'hubs' of Toronto and Montreal and for most visitors it is the end of the line, there being no major settlement in the harsher (if scenic) Shield country to the north.

Culturally, Ottawa lies on the language frontier between English and French Canada, which is symbolised (though imprecisely delineated) by the Ontario/ Quebec border along the Ottawa River. While this creates a certain cultural tourism resource it has class nuances, francophones being disproportionately working class, and complicates communication, Ottawa being very much the capital of bilingualism (but not unfortunately of individual bilingual competence).

In recent years it has also been the touchstone of political tension, as have the native Indian and, to a lesser extent, the more recent ethnic elements (see below). Ottawa's most obvious cultural tourism resource is, of course, its national capital status and consequent possession of the parliamentary assemblage, 'Westminster of the Wilderness' (see Taylor, 1986 : 119). Even so, Ottawa's intrinsic appeal would be limited in that it is a small metropolis and amenity cluster by comparison with Montreal, the longstanding cultural centre of international stature, and Toronto, now the economic capital and chief anglophone Canadian metropolis.

In an unmanaged state Ottawa's tourism resource would be modest: a physical environment recreationally attractive, but unexceptional in Canada; a historic ambience with distinctive elements, but weak by international standards; and an overall cultural environment which was in the 1960s the butt of jests for Montrealers and Torontonians and a non-place to most from farther afield. Thirty years on this no longer reflects the reality of the tourism resource, for decades of active nurturing and a very specific tourism focus since the 1960s have ultimately borne fruit.

Nurturing a tourism resource

The choice of Ottawa as capital, first of united Ontario and Quebec and in 1867 of the Canadian Confederation, initiated a century-long change in its character from a blue-collar lumber town to a white-collar government centre. Today vestiges of the former identity remain (valued for their heritage if scorned for their residual function!) but the metamorphosis is essentially complete, to the point of further change discussed below.

The management of this transition was structured in the twentieth century, in pursuit of beautification, by a series of federal government agencies culminating in the post-war National Capital Commission (Taylor, 1986). From the outset the process was qualified by the fact that Ottawa possesses no national capital territory, unlike Washington or Canberra: federal agencies exist in uneasy equilibrium with two provincial governments which have ultimate jurisdiction over their land. The NCC's mandate to create an extensive National Capital Region (Figure 5.1) was accordingly in potential conflict with Ontario and Quebec. It has essentially achieved this goal, by virtue of its rights as a property owner, by the acquisition of strategic corridors, through the perception that its improvements have benefited the locality at national expense, and by the federal government's bargaining ability derived from designated powers and ultimate control of the purse-strings.

In association with a regional master plan by the European planner Jacques Greber, the mid-century federal governments under Mackenzie King redesigned the main arteries of central Ottawa to reflect the dignity of a capital, in distinctively Canadian 'Chateauesque' style harmonising with Parliament (Figure 5.2). Improvement was continued on the regional stage by the NCC, which purchased a green belt around Ottawa and created Gatineau Park, a quasi-wilderness green wedge along the Gatineau escarpment, meanwhile developing scenic low-speed 'parkways' along the canal and Ottawa River (Figure 5.1). While these initiatives were not primarily conceived for tourism, so pervasive yet intangible has tourism subsequently become (Ashworth and Tunbridge, 1990) that we can now interpret them as the systematic nurturing of a tourism resource aimed primarily at the nation as a market. This reality has been subsequently recognised by the NCC as it has clearly emerged as the principal agent of tourism management in the Ottawa area.

With the approach of the national Centennial in 1967, the NCC broadened its mandate for primarily aesthetic improvement to include the restoration of what it now perceived as historic buildings. Specifically, it expropriated Sussex Drive in Lower Town West, the heart of the old Bytown, which had slipped into a 'zone of discard' with the creation of the capital focus across the Rideau Canal, but which remained visually sensitive because it connected Parliament with the Prime Minister's and Governor-General's residences (Figure 5.3) (Ashworth and Tunbridge, 1990). This catalysed the reclamation of Lower Town West as a historic district, which thirty years on constitutes the centre of nightlife, restaurant and boutique activity, and the chief tourism magnet aside from the parliamentary precinct.

This reclamation involved many private agents and the City of Ottawa, which notably restored the Byward Market building and ultimately protected the area as a heritage conservation district, under provincial legislation. The NCC's heritage-

Figure 5.2   Parliament and the Chateau Laurier hotel, Ottawa, from Canadian Museum of Civilization, Hull, Quebec

97

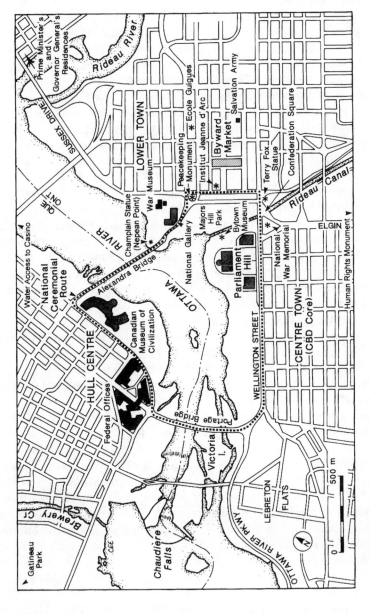

Figure 5.3 Central Ottawa and Hull

related role subsequently expanded to include such aspects as the restoration of riverfront industrial buildings, and above all the orchestration of architecture, monuments and public art around the circuit which has recently become the national ceremonial route (Confederation Boulevard) (Figure 5.3).

While the NCC has played the lead role in the creation of the tourism resource, it has become equally central to the management and marketing of tourism. This is most apparent in its contribution to creating the calendar of festivals and events, currently twenty-six throughout the year. In the case of Winterlude (February) it was directly responsible for creating a linear skating rink along the Rideau Canal and establishing the festival, which draws visitors from overseas as well as the United States. The Canadian Tulip Festival in May is focused upon bulbs along the parkways, while Canada Day (1 July) features multitudinous events culminating in firework displays. These directly involve the NCC's past or present agency (as do the summer 'sound and light' performances outside Parliament) while the numerous music, ethnic and other speciality festivals involve at least the use of its properties.

These initiatives entail not merely the stimulation of tourism throughout the year, to the obvious benefit of the city's economy, but also the specific mastery of the winter problem. The Christmas Lights and particularly Winterlude events and ice sculptures represent a triumph of creative enterprise in using rather than succumbing to the winter environment, an apparently insuperable obstacle in the 1960s. In 1995 the NCC opened a multimedia Capital Infocentre opposite the parliament buildings which employs a comprehensive range of visitor orientation tools: interactive computer systems along with more conventional film, telephone, literature and human guidance. The Infocentre is notable for its national signification of the capital's sites, museums and events, as well as for its holistic promotion of whatever the region has to offer from any source or perspective.

The NCC's initiatives have triggered extensive responses from other organisations; in fact the paucity of public funding in the 1990s has made a virtue of necessity in the forging of cooperative event sponsorship between public, private and voluntary sectors (as for the Tulip Festival). The public sector includes other autonomous branches of the federal government, for example Human Resources contributing make-work funding. Furthermore, the cities of Ottawa and Hull, outlying municipalities and collective regional government bodies on both sides of the Ottawa River have been stimulated into greater tourism efforts by their ability to ride the NCC's coat-tails. But the scope of tourism, describing an activity engaged in by individuals at a moment in time irrespective of the prime reason for their presence (Ashworth and Tunbridge, 1990), automatically embraces business and convention visitors, so that general promotional organisations such as the Ottawa Carleton Economic Development Corporation are involved. The inner-city Convention Centre, in climate-controlled facilities attached to a leading hotel and shopping centre, in itself promotes year-round tourism.

In direct response to public nurturing, private businesses themselves have become the most numerous shapers of the tourism product and, via city tourism councils, contributors to its management and marketing; the enormous increase in restaurants and pubs since the 1960s has in itself created a major year-round tourism resource. Among the most important generators of tourism are season-specific sports franchises, which have partly been attracted themselves, like so much else, by the benificent spiral of tourism-supporting amenities which essentially began with the NCC's resource and management initiatives.

It is important to note that the nurturing of tourism in Ottawa has been greatly facilitated by qualities which tend to be taken for granted by residents of Canadian cities, namely their cleanliness and perceived safety by comparison with those of their US neighbours, who constitute much the largest market for Canadian tourism. In the segmentation of messages which characterises contemporary tourism marketing these qualities are continuously beamed at the US market, while features such as access to open space and outdoor recreation have more meaning to overseas visitors, increasingly Asians, and the historical identity is disproportionately of national (and British imperial/Commonwealth) interest. The hiring of 'street ambassadors', sponsored jointly by business, social and public agencies, was a multifaceted tourism innovation in 1997 which attempts to reinforce the safety image (chiefly by controlling 'panhandling') while dispensing help and information to tourists via various languages and perspectives. The profile of Ottawa's tourism industry has reached the point where it aspires to enter the 'big league' by the appropriation of a 'hallmark' or 'mega' event (see Chapters 12 and 13). To this end it sought an Expo 2002 which (had it been granted) would have raised interesting questions in the light of the political uncertainties of the region, to which we allude below.

The tourist–historic city as management framework

In introducing this concept we have already noted its classic applicability to the creation of a historic resource in Lower Town and the establishment of this area as 'the place to be', for the commercial leisure pursuits of tourists and residents alike. Relevance to recent tourist–historic expansion and to its management concerns us here.

As the model predicts, Ottawa's tourist–historic city has continued to expand as larger areas have been appropriated as historic and have in varying degrees been augmented and publicised to tourists. In the late 1980s its core in the parliamentary precinct and Lower Town was extended by the National Gallery and the Canadian Museum of Civilization (Figure 5.3), spectacular new facilities which variously augment the historic resource, the latter creating a waterfront amenity in common with many tourist–historic cities (Figure 5.4) and extending a potential tourist–historic growth corridor into the older parts of Hull. Meanwhile the historic recognition of some inner suburbs and ethnic districts has increased.

Recession in the 1990s has slowed tourist–historic growth and generated business vacancies, but it is interesting to note that by 1997 the tourist centrality of the Byward Market area was so deeply entrenched that it continued to augment its critical mass of restaurants and pubs in apparent contradiction of economic conditions. Niche and theme businesses (Angelo, 1996) continued to appear in an implicit, if largely oblivious, tribute to the 30-year nurturing of this heart of the tourist–historic city.

As in most other cities (particularly in North America: De Bres, 1994), components of the tourist city, including both service facilities and non-historic attractions,

Figure 5.4   Canadian Museum of Civilization, Hull, showing Ottawa River waterfront and Gatineau Hills (from Parliament, Ottawa: John Tunbridge, 1997)

have continued to appear in discontinuous outlying locations as well as in the inner city. Commonly these augment the historic city also, an example being the Aviation Museum which is necessarily suburban. This returns us to the reality of regional management of tourism in general and the tourist–historic city more specifically, in this case primarily the National Capital Region which extends some 30 miles from Parliament Hill. Within this area, the NCC's management concerns focus upon the green belt in Ontario and the Gatineau Park in Quebec, including cultural as well as quasi-natural heritage maintenance and interpretation. The country estate of former prime minister Mackenzie King is the historic centrepiece of the Gatineau Park and is potentially a bone of contention (see below).

Beyond the NCC's properties, management is the concern of municipalities and of the provinces, which (like other North American provinces and states) have through their tourism ministries established regional marketing jurisdictions which develop circuits of tourist interest, according to their own spatial agendas. The Heritage Canada Foundation, akin to the British National Trusts, illustrates a non-governmental contribution to tourist–historic management with respect to Lanark County, west of Ottawa, one of several Heritage Regions it has sponsored as 'ecomuseums', with public and private collaboration, across Canada (Mountain, 1994).

As is so often the case, however, regional tourism management overall is diffuse and uncoordinated, involving a profusion of public and private decision makers, most of whom (like the federal agency expanding Ottawa's airport and the provincial agency building an expressway to the south) are responding to tourism demands as part of wider mandates.

Before turning to the actual and potential issues of tourism management in the Ottawa region, it is pertinent to consider the significance of management issues applicable to the tourist–historic city in general. The increasingly familiar management issue, indeed the implicit motivation for this volume, is that of excessive tourist pressure upon cities – particularly upon those star attractions within cities emphasised by the selectivity of the tourism commodification process and by tourists' restricted time, money, information and perception (Ashworth and Tunbridge, 1990; Waitt and McGuirk, 1996).

There is an obvious incentive to maximise the urban historic resource, so as to optimise its economic potential and to spread the tourist load upon it where necessary. Moreover, Tunbridge and Ashworth (1996) point out the universally dissonant process whereby an urban historic or 'heritage' resource is recognised, raising questions the most divisive of which is 'whose?', particularly in the light of growing perceived cultural and racial diversity in cities of the Western world. This creates a parallel need for the tourist–historic city to maximise its resource base among the contributions of all sections of its population, thus promoting socially inclusive recognition and participation in the expanded and diversified tourism which can thereby be generated. There is a counter-argument to downplay partisan heritage expressions in favour of the minimum that a society holds in common, but this implies sacrifice of the tourism economy to political priorities of conflict avoidance or alternative community creation.

Expansionary tourist–historic management designed simultaneously to relieve pressure, develop niche markets and promote social equity is well illustrated by Charleston in the US South: tourist flows in the historic core are controlled by a mixture of disincentives (parking) and incentives ('historic' public transport) orchestrated from a peripheral visitor centre, from which tourists are encouraged to explore more recently restored or fabricated outlying attractions and niche itineraries, black heritage being a recent focus of tourism growth. South African tourist–historic cities such as Cape Town and Pietermaritzburg illustrate a different emphasis upon expansionary management in that tourism has yet to reach problem levels and is an urgent economic need, yet the inclusive recasting of the historic resource is a delicate political priority even more than the economic opportunity which the contemporary growth in African township tourism represents (Ashworth and Tunbridge, 1990; Tunbridge and Ashworth, 1996; Worden, 1997; and Dodson and Kilian, Chapter 8 in this volume).

The applicability of such tourist–historic management insights to Ottawa is strongly implicit, in what has already been identified as an expansionary tourism context based upon a nurtured and substantially historic identity, in the presence of an increasingly diverse population. We now consider the reality of tourism management in contemporary Ottawa, with reference to these insights as appropriate.

Contemporary tourism management issues in Ottawa

The creation of the 'silk purse' identity which Ottawa now so largely exudes has been shown to result from multiple actors with, however, one federal government agency as the prime mover. Deliberate creation and then expansion of tourism, in an essentially unquestioned 'the-more-the-merrier' mind-set, has been the long-standing order of the day. Ottawa is a noteworthy illustration of resource maximisation in the tourist–historic city, and the recent concern with social diversity in this respect has been especially prominent here. Canada is pre-eminent as a country of global immigration; it espoused a policy of multiculturalism in the early 1970s which became legally entrenched in its 1982 Constitution. It would be unwise to assume that all is entirely well with this policy: its logic can be assailed and the electorate has signalled some dissatisfaction with an ideology which appears to demand respect for all values other than those of majorities (Tunbridge and Ashworth, 1996; Tunbridge, 1998). Nonetheless, Ottawa as the national capital had an unequivocal mandate to set a national example by extending beyond its Anglo-French roots to accentuate the contributions of all cultural elements to its evolving heritage. Tourist marking and interpretation by the NCC, the Canadian Museum of Civilization, Parks Canada (in the Rideau Canal structures) and all other federal (and other) government agencies have become heavily laced with multicultural sensitivity and indeed reinterpretation. Their representation of the British imperial heritage nationally and locally, especially the United Empire Loyalists (CMC) and the construction of the canal, now tends to accentuate its multicultural/social quality; in sharp contrast to older local voluntary-sector museum collections (as in the canalside Bytown Museum) which tend to display familiar Victoriana very similar to their peers throughout the old British dominions (Tunbridge and Ashworth, 1996). Government-sector (and high-level voluntary-sector) recasting of heritage in multicultural, and otherwise socially multilateral, terms fits and reflects the contemporary academic infatuation with postmodernism and is characteristically lauded by academia in consequence.

However, tourism management and marketing recast in these terms is inevitably subject to their unresolved tensions. The growth of francophone nationalism in Quebec over the past thirty years is the most obvious of these and casts a shadow over all Canadian national representation in Ottawa, notwithstanding the bicultural basis of much of its iconography; we return to the Quebec issue below. Multilateral reorientation itself exacerbates Quebecois nationalism, at root a protective obsession with francophone *survivance*; but it begins to display wider centrifugal tendencies as the diversity of the population increases and sectional rights are emphasised more than collective responsibilities. The most tourist-visible symptoms result from militant elements of the First Nations, the aboriginal peoples, protesting neglect or defective portrayal of their heritage. Their occupation of Victoria Island in the Ottawa River has won their right to an aboriginal social–cultural centre in a place symbolic to Indians; it will be open to all but likely to compromise industrial heritage and recreational use (though not aboriginal tourism, noted below). However, the removal of the 'subservient' Indian scout from beneath Champlain's statue overlooking the river (Figure 5.3) is a demand on which the NCC is stalling (1998). Well it might: the cityscape of Ottawa would be diminished, and the floodgates of sectional interest would then be open to republicans, radical feminists and whomsoever else to dismantle the iconography of the city, nurtured at such cost in time and taxation.

While the diverse imagery of ethnic districts has enhanced the city's tourism appeal (if less so than in Toronto and Montreal), dissonances surface from time to time between various ethnic groups with respect to their heritage representations; in a capital city these can involve the diplomatic representatives of their countries of origin. Recent examples are the monument to the Vietnamese refugees of 1975 in 'Chinatown' which upset some post-cold war Vietnamese interests, and a statue of Simon Bolívar which seemed to please only some Latin Americans. Sectional discord could also touch upon the festivals which are so central to Ottawa tourism, for while many are profitable exploitations of ethnic diversity, some have the potential to attract antagonism; a case in point is the homosexual Pride festival.

The defining characteristic of Ottawa tourism management is that it is first and foremost nationally oriented, by virtue of the NCC's mandate and the large proportion of other tourism enterprise riding on its coat-tails. In practice, however, Ottawa's location and the recent weakness of the national economy prioritise foreign exchange earnings, and tourism marketing targets the United States centrally, Europe substantially and East Asia increasingly. This raises subtle issues of intelligibility, if not of dissonance, in its tourism product. For most foreign visitors, the abundance of French in bilingual marking is a confusing distraction, albeit offset by multimedia access to more tourist-relevant languages. However, the content of messages is of greater significance. The CMC's account of Canadian history might be baffling to an overseas visitor looking for Canada's British imperial roots, since its depiction of the British (as against Loyalist) role emphasises the military presence and in parts implies military occupation of a diverse and restive populace. In townscape iconography those roots are more obvious by virtue of longstanding accretion, as in the War Memorial. However, contemporary public monuments, particularly given their cost and limited capacity for written explanation, mostly avoid reference to sectionalisms and commemorate those (few) national attributes which all Canadians might be persuaded that they share: the Human Rights and Peacekeeping Monuments and the commemoration of disabled athletic achievement are noteworthy cases (Figure 5.3). Such monuments might seem puzzling if not trivial to foreigners unacquainted with Canada's perhaps quixotic nation-building agenda. The Capital Infocentre, discussed earlier, also prioritises the national educational objective.

A positive aspect of city-image and tourist–historic management which moderates the confusion of messages is the geographical separation of the national from more local or sectional emphases. This is accomplished by the NCC's designation and control of 'capital' space within and along Confederation Boulevard, in which the collective Canadian identity is being cultivated in streetscape and iconography. Outside this zone more specific messages and heritages may be projected, with the inevitable risks of dissonances between the various shards of a society fractured in detail. In the 'capital' zone the problem remains, however, of possible dissonance to the contemporary nation-building agenda of iconography inherited from the past (Tunbridge and Ashworth, 1996). Conversely, Queen Victoria's imperious gaze across the capital she nominally chose undoubtedly differentiates Ottawa's heritage from that of American cities from the perspective of foreign tourists puzzling over the nuances of more recent monuments.

The festival calendar, however, offers tourist attractions which are for the most part uncluttered by dissonant or confusing messages and provide seasonal activities of uncomplicated pleasure, perhaps the more so for visitors foreign to Canadian natural and cultural environments. It is here that the tourist pressure problem familiar to Europeans may arise, but in a quite different respect. In the urban tourist meccas most characteristic of the Old World it is the cultural environment which is at risk from trampling feet and other human overload factors; here it is the (quasi) natural environment. The severity of the Canadian climate limits the resilience of lawns, flower beds and trees and causes the NCC to monitor carefully the intensity and frequency of festival use of its open space, particularly Major's Hill Park facing Parliament (Figure 5.3). Fortunately the partial dependence upon indoor space (such as the CMC), the extent of NCC property and the economic and political desirability of expanding the benefits of inclusion leave a management problem which is mild by the standards of Venice or Florence and operates within an overall policy of tourism maximisation. (The management of pressure points in the 'green' environment is also an issue in the Gatineau Park, in which quasi-rural context it is more familiar to Europeans.)

A recent example of expanding festival space is the inclusion of the Casino de Hull in the Tulip Festival itinerary and events. More fundamentally, this new amenity represents a major geographical expansion of the Ottawa region's tourism resource base, promoting its capacity for tourism growth without negative environmental consequences (Figure 5.5). It emanates from the provincial and local governments in collaboration with private enterprise and the NCC. Locationally it capitalises upon an NCC-owned lake which, extended into a former quarry around the casino site, creates a scenic quasi-natural setting, outward waterfront views over the Ottawa skyline, and a means of water access from the city centre (Figure 5.3). The NCC's concern is the management and equilibration of uses of this environment. The Casino is designed to provide for year-round tourism, with winter-friendly underground access into a tropical interior environment containing fine dining and other recreational facilities. It thereby provides a permanent employment base for the relatively low-income population of Hull which has the necessary bilingual skills to service it; the predictable 'parasite' retail/service facilities which have appeared nearby magnify this desirable spin-off of tourism expansion. Whether the capture of tourism revenue outweighs the local social costs of gambling remains to be seen, a larger issue surrounding the diffusion of casinos which may never be quantifiable (see further in Carmichael et al., 1996).

As in most other urban tourism contexts, management is many-headed; it does not entirely address the national agenda, less still the international market. Locally fragmented jurisdictions create the further complication of local and regional priorities, which may be irrelevant or even contrary to the national priority or to each other. However, in practice, as often elsewhere, the common economic interest mutes any centrifugality and gives rise to a high degree of season-to-season cooperation. Discussion with the NCC and the local tourism authorities (1996) generated this response essentially from all; any dissension was not admitted. The NCC's Infocentre, notwithstanding its capital focus, provides encyclopedic computer-interactive guidance to the region's aggregate tourism resources, highlighting attractions such as the Casino de Hull without respect to their possibly equivocal impact upon others (in this case Ontario interests).

In terms of the management insights derived from the tourist–historic city discussion, Ottawa's expansionary tourism policy requires spatial growth and diversification of both its resource provision and its patterns of tourism consumption, to address its relatively minor concern of environmental pressure and its larger concern of multicultural equity. In both respects recent developments are positive,

Figure 5.5   Casino de Hull, in artificial/natural lake environment (John Tunbridge, 1997)

though not without tensions and dissonances. But the expansion of tourist–historic space magnifies the problem of potentially divergent jurisdictions, notably so in this case, although there is presently no major point to make concerning interjurisdictional conflict. The future is another matter, however, and to this unadmitted threat it is appropriate to turn in conclusion.

Conclusion: Ottawa tourism amid jurisdictional disintegration?

Local jurisdictional fragmentation is likely to be reduced as Ontario enforces municipal amalgamation as a cost-cutting measure, and Quebec may well follow suit. Paradoxically, however, the opposite applies at the provincial level, for the threat of Quebec separation hangs over the Ottawa region more than any other, because it threatens both metropolitan disintegration and partial or even complete loss of its national capital *raison d'être* and status. Neither the NCC nor other local officials are inclined to discuss the unthinkable, and discussion of consequences risks both self-fulfilment and futility given the unknowns involved. However, Boal (1993) and others have cogently discussed the growing self-sufficiency of the Quebec side, duplicating facilities for political reasons, and its disaffection on the fundamental ground of linguistic erosion as well as local opposition to federal 1970s *buldozage* of Hull's identity, in clumsy pursuit of its functional integration into the national capital. Irrespective of local sentiment (which remains understandably equivocal) the separation of Quebec, which must be presumed to be as a whole, would force a substantial divergence of interests between the two sides of the Ottawa River, which could very well extend to tourism now that Hull has developed potentially competitive facilities such as the casino. Ironically Hull's appeal was catalysed essentially by federal initiatives, the fate of which after separation is difficult to conceive.

The CMC is *par excellence* a celebration of Canadian diversity and could scarcely function in a Quebec essentially predicated upon a unicultural hegemony. More subtly, the Mackenzie King estate in the Gatineau Park would have difficulty continuing to function as a 1940s museum, in which King's alignment with the British wartime cause reconjures painful memories of Quebec's opposition to conscription; especially since Quebec extremists have long regarded the park as an 'English' colonial playground. More generally, the continuity of all the National Capital Region landscape nurturing would be broken.

However, there are global illustrations of tourist marketing of alien/colonial heritage for economic reward, typically the phenomenon of selling back to visitors their own heritage in a now-misplaced location (Tunbridge and Ashworth, 1996). Accordingly it cannot be assumed that future jurisdictional disintegration would destroy the national capital tourism in Quebec, particularly if economic desperation were to outweigh sociopolitical antagonism between the two sides. While this discussion is specific to Ottawa it has, of course, a wider resonance in a world substantially beset by factionalism and political centrifugality. As in Berlin, Nicosia, Jerusalem or other cities formerly, presently or potentially affected, the terms of separation are a critical input to the outcome for tourism.

There is a more subtle query with respect to the future efficacy of Ottawa's tourism jurisdictions, interconnected with the above. Government downsizing in response to the international problem of public insolvency has significantly reduced the profile of the federal government in the 1990s and, with it, the image of Ottawa as capital. In its place, the high-technology industry originally attracted by government has become the principal growth sector in the regional economy, disproportionately based in the perceived security and English linguistic environment of Ontario, and the image promoted of Ottawa is increasingly imprinted with its symbols (Wallace, 1997). Whether this could negatively affect the national capital's tourism remains unclear. City marketing is routinely segmented (Ashworth and Voogd, 1990) and the subsidy of Ottawa's tourist attractions by private industry (there are current examples) is likely to be self-serving in image terms. However, this creates a further uncertainty for Ottawa's tourism status and identity, including the degree to which a holistic vision of the region will remain in the long run.

At present the holistic marketing of regional Ottawa continues, under this name agreed for its promotional value. It was streamlined in 1997 into Futures Ottawa, a team effort led by the high-technology and life sciences private sector in which tourism and amenity interests play an important support role (Lemieux, 1997). Regional tourism opportunities have been targeted for expansive and better coordinated repackaging to reach newly evolving markets, untapped potential being recognised region-wide (such as waterfront development, wildlife/adventure and aboriginal tourism) but particularly in locations and respects which directly implicate Quebec (Franco Materazzi Consult/Corporate Research Group, 1997). However, political tension in Quebec could sour this positive approach, compatible with the national capital, into a narrower Ontario focus. In a worst-case scenario in which the capital of a truncated Canada moved elsewhere, the Ontario-side economy could contract into technological dependence, with tourism as whatever residual appendage could be sustained.

Ottawa at the turn of the millennium has become a highly sophisticated tourism resource in the hands of complex but successful expansionary management. The tourism economy may well continue to advance even if the circumstances and/or identity of the region experience significant change, since the multiple management and selling of cities to segmented markets is common. There remains a question, however, as to its future in an environment of potentially widening political and economic solitudes.

Should the capital-focused tourism product cease to be acceptable to the relevant political and economic interests, what new tourism focus and management ethos might replace it, and could it remain a holistic 'marriage of convenience' or would it disintegrate into rival components? In the absence of public discussion of the unthinkable it is the more difficult to predict its tourism outcome. However, the nurtured tourist–historic city would remain the logical focus: even though it would operate in an environment of intense global competition with its peers, in the absence of a 'trump card' and the likely presence of tension if not fragmentation. It would nevertheless be relatively well prepared by decades of meticulous grooming to compete in the dominant arena of contemporary tourism.

While Ottawa is a special case with an uncertain prognosis, as such it touches upon the broader issue of viability of tourism resources in environments of fragmented vision and divergent jurisdiction. In an unstable world other examples are not wanting.

Postscript on the fragile environment: the great ice storm of January 1998 destroyed or severely damaged an estimated 50 000 trees in the city of Ottawa alone, and regeneration is expected to take some thirty years. But meanwhile, industrial heritage reclamation is proposed for *both* sides of the Chaudière Falls.

Acknowledgements

In addition to individuals referenced above, the following representatives (in particular) of Ottawa-region tourism agencies are thanked for their information:
P. Levick, Director of Marketing, National Capital Commission; L. Crandall, Corporate Planning, Ottawa Tourism and Convention Authority; A. Massicotte, L'Association Touristique de L'Outaouais. Specific assertions and value interpretations, particularly in the Conclusion, are attributable to the author alone unless otherwise referenced.

Many thanks to Christine Earl, Department of Geography, Carleton University for the two maps used in this chapter.

References

Angelo, B. (1996) 'Hungry for theme dining', *Time*, 22 July, 30–2.
Ashworth, G.J. and de Haan, T.Z. (1985) 'The tourist–historic city: A model and initial application in Norwich, U.K.', *Field Studies Series*, 6, Groningen: GIRUG.

Ashworth, G.J. and Tunbridge, J.E. (1990) *The Tourist–Historic City*, London: Belhaven.

Ashworth, G.J. and Voogd, H. (1990) *Selling the City*, London: Belhaven.

Boal, F.W. (1993) 'One foot on each bank of the Ottawa', *Canadian Geographer*, 37 (4), 320–32.

Carmichael, B., Peppard, D.M. and Boudreau, F. (1996) 'Mega resort on my doorstep: local resident attitudes towards Foxwoods Casino and casino gambling on nearby Indian land', *Journal of Travel Research*, 34(3) (special issue on 'Casino gambling and tourism').

De Bres, K. (1994) 'Cowtowns or cathedral precincts? Two models for contemporary urban tourism', *Area*, 26 (1), 57–67.

Franco Materaazzi Consult Inc./Corporate Research Group Ltd (1997) Tourism Opportunities Study: Canada's Capital Region.
(http://www.inasec.ca/redo/publication/tourism—p2.html#VA)

Lemieux, C. (1997) Director, Futures Ottawa. Personal communication.

Mountain, J. (1994) 'Heritage Regions: Lanark County, Eastern Ontario', *Heritage Canada*, 1 (5), 9–10.

Taylor, J.H. (1986) *Ottawa: An Illustrated History*, Toronto: James Lorimer/Canadian Museum of Civilization.

Tunbridge, J.E. (1987) *Of Heritage and Many Other Things: Merchants' Location Decisions in Ottawa's Lower Town West*, Carleton University, Ottawa, Department of Geography Discussion Paper 5.

Tunbridge, J.E. (1998) 'The question of heritage in European cultural conflict', in B.J.Graham (ed.), *Modern Europe: Place, Culture, Identity*, London: Edward Arnold, 236–260.

Tunbridge, J.E. and Ashworth, G.J. (1996) *Dissonant Heritage*, Chichester: Wiley.

Waitt, G. and McGuirk, P.M. (1996) 'Marking time: tourism and heritage representation at Millers Point, Sydney', *Australian Geographer*, 27 (1), 11–30.

Wallace, I. (1997) Department of Geography, Carleton University, Ottawa. Personal communication: manuscript in preparation.

Worden, N. (1997), 'Contesting heritage in a South African city: Cape Town', in B.J. Shaw and R. Jones (eds), *Contested Urban Heritage: Voices from the Periphery*, London: Ashgate, 31–61.

6 Visitors to the world's oldest cities: Aleppo and Damascus, Syria

MYRA SHACKLEY

CHAPTER SUMMARY

Tourism in the Middle East has recently experienced rapid growth over the past decade with several countries (notably Syria and Jordan) developing significant cultural heritage tourism products competing with older-established destinations such as Egypt and Israel. Syria now receives over 2 million visitors a year, almost all of whom will visit its two major World Heritage cities of Damascus (the capital) and Aleppo. Both offer visitors a window on Syrian life through walking the markets (*suqs*), observing craft workshops, absorbing the atmosphere, shopping and visiting the many distinct religious and historical attractions located within the ancient city walls. However, both cities also have a series of urgent conservation and rehabilitation problems including decaying infrastructure, declining population due to out-migration, building disintegration and alteration. Tourism, if carefully controlled, presents a more sensitive basis for the future economies of Damascus and Aleppo than other industrial uses. It remains to be seen what role visitors play in proposed urban regeneration projects, how (and if) new tourism attractions should be developed within the Old Cities and how the necessary ancillary facilities could be developed, financed and managed.

Introduction

Tourism in the Middle East has recently experienced rapid growth as a direct result of increased political stability. Over the past decade several countries (notably Syria and Jordan) have developed significant cultural and heritage tourism products competing with older-established destinations such as Egypt and Israel. Syria presents an especially interesting case since, unlike Israel or Egypt which can offer beach holidays, its tourism is almost entirely heritage-based. Syria now receives

Managing Tourism in Cities. Edited by D. Tyler, Y. Guerrier and M. Robertson.
Copyright © 1998 John Wiley & Sons Ltd.

over 2 million visitors a year, almost all of whom will visit its two major World
Heritage cities of Damascus (the capital) and Aleppo. These walled cities are
extremely attractive to tourists, offering a unique window on Syrian life through
walking the markets (*suqs*), observing craft workshops, absorbing the atmosphere,
shopping and visiting the many distinct religious and historical attractions located
within the city walls.

Both cities, in common with Cairo, Isfahan, Tunis and Marrakech, have a series
of urgent conservation and rehabilitation problems typical of ancient walled centres. These include decaying infrastructure, declining population due to outmigration, building disintegration and alteration. Both are already major tourist
attractions and it could be argued that tourism, if carefully controlled, presents a
more sensitive basis for the future economies of both inner cities than other industrial uses (Law, 1993).

At present both urban centres are hosting major survey projects which are attempting to establish not just the extent of tourism usage but also its current and
projected impact, as well as producing accurate databases, fundamental to the
development of urban management strategies. Whether or not visitors can make a
positive contribution to the continuing life of these cities depends on a complex of
factors including public–private sector planning disputes, examining issues of real
estate pricing, employment generation and economic diversification into areas
which could not have been dreamed of when the urban centres were founded. It
remains to be seen what role visitors will play in these urban regeneration projects,
how (and if) new tourism attractions should be developed within the Old Cities and
how the necessary ancillary visitor facilities could be developed, financed and
managed.

Tourism in the Middle East

During 1995 the Middle East was the fastest-growing tourism destination in the
world welcoming some 11 041 000 arrivals (a growth of 11.8% over the previous
year, and increasing its tourism revenues by nearly 30% (WTO, 1995)). This rapid
growth reflected increased regional peace and political stability as well as a worldwide trend towards cultural tourism, since the tourism product of most Middle
Eastern countries is based around their built heritage and archaeological sites.
Within the Middle East Egypt remained dominant, increasing its revenues by a
massive 95% to US$2.7 billion. Large gains were also reported by Jordan, Bahrain
and Lebanon which made a strong comeback as an important destination attracting
402 000 people. It seems unlikely that the regional figures for 1996 will be quite so
optimistic, since the popularity of the area is closely related to perceived political
stability, yet the troubles of Israel may not impinge significantly on Syria, although
intra-regional tourism will certainly be affected.

As can be seen from Table 6.1, the number of visitors to Syria almost doubled
between 1990 and 1994; a growth rate in excess of 10%, meaning that Syria may
expect 3.7 million visitors a year by the end of the millennium. Almost all these
visitors will go to Damascus and/or Aleppo. Tourism earned Syria US$700 million
in 1993 (UN, 1995).

Table 6.1 Origin of visitors to Syria 1990–94

Region	1990	1991	1992	1993	1994
Africa	31 835	20 171	32 075	32 974	33 088
Americas	14 034	12 185	15 739	15 688	20 248
East Asia/Pacific	7 315	4 434	6 246	9 942	12 806
Europe	231 540	282 736	293 780	306 949	340 389
Middle East	922 848	1 095 355	1 184 427	1 357 097	1 435 222
South Asia	200 878	123 863	160 249	125 950	188 017
Other	33 991	31 417	47 368	61 316	71 312
Total	1 442 441	1 570 161	1 739 884	1 909 916	2 101 082

Source: WTO (1995).

Much of Syria's tourism features cross-border traffic, facilitated by easier border crossings between Syria and Jordan, Israel and Lebanon (Figure 6.1). However, the future of such developments depends on the political situation. The visitor experience in Syria is in many ways quite different from that of its competitors such as Egypt or north African countries, due partly to the country's relatively recent emergence as a cultural tourism destination and partly to low visitor numbers. Syrians are proud of their reputation for having a clean, safe and friendly country whose people welcome foreign visitors without harassment or exploitation. Syria has none of the religious extremism of Iran or reputation for hassle of Egypt and has an adequate infrastructure, good communications, a well-developed ground-handling industry and a reputation for wonderful shopping, particularly in its urban centres. Unlike Egypt, Syria is opposed to mass or beach-based tourism so the future of its international tourism seems firmly linked to a cultural/heritage product. This is placing increasing pressure on ancient urban centres.

Tourism in Syria

Tourism to Syria is primarily heritage tourism, with overseas visitors making more than 1.2 million trips to Syrian heritage sites (especially the four UNESCO World Heritage Sites of Damascus, Aleppo, Palmyra and Bosra) each year. No visitor surveys exist for historic sites but enquiries suggest that the majority of European visitors are French and German, with some Italians, British and a range of other nationalities. Another major category of visitors to Syria are Arabs from the Gulf States who come primarily for shopping or to visit friends or relations but may also visit World Heritage Sites which have special Muslim cultural or religous significance such as the Azzem Palace or the Omayid Mosque in Damascus. The vast majority of European visitors to Syria are on organised tours, and a well-established heritage site 'milk run' has developed whose itinerary varies with the length of the tour, price band and group objectives. Such tours are now available at levels varying from the most general introduction to Syria's heritage to detailed archaeological tours of major sites. Itineraries always include the major sites in Damascus (Omayid Mosque, Old City) and Aleppo (Citadel, Old City, pillar St Simeon Stylites), the Roman city of Palmyra, the theatre at Bosra and the great

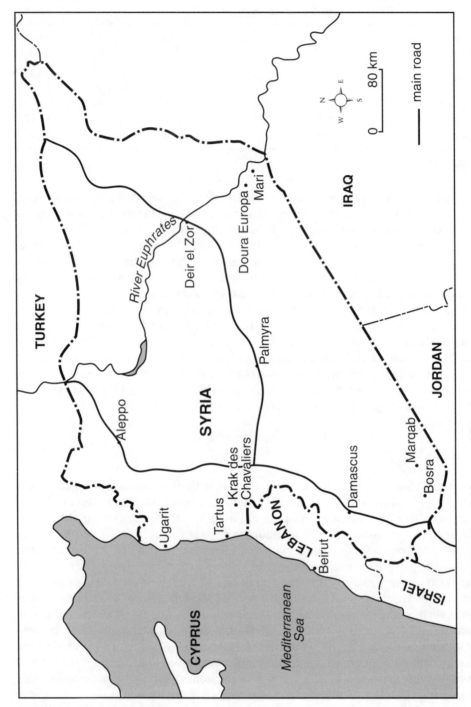

Figure 6.1 Syria, showing location of Aleppo and Damascus

crusader castle of Krak des Chevaliers (Figure 6.1). If time permits, an
may be made to look at the harbour at Tartus, Marqab and Sahyun Castles
Deir el Zor and Doura Europos, with other possibilities such as the aban
towns of Rasafa in the Euphrates valley or the site of Mari (Figure 6.1). Many
tours will be combining Syria with Jordan, continuing southwards to Jerash a
Petra. Some (particularly around Christmas and especially groups with a religious
orientation) may end their tour in Israel. Groups with specialised interests may be
accompanied by professional archaeologists or historians and all employ local
ground-handling operators and, generally, interpreters and guides.

Syria is a relatively expensive destination for the heritage tourist because of the
high cost of accommodation and ground transport. The air-inclusive price of a tour
from Europe, for example, may frequently exceed £1000/week, and very much
more from America or Japan. A recent innovation is the beginning of charter
heritage tourism to Syria (notably with the British company Voyages Jules Verne)
which brings in 180 visitors at a time, with varied itineraries, and manages to keep a
price as much as 50% less than other leading operators by utilising charter flights,
larger group sizes and hotels of lower standard. This produces pressure on heritage
sites visited and lowers the quality of the visitor experience since group sizes can
become unworkable, creating difficulties for guides and interpreters. Generally, the
more specialised the group, the smaller the group size is likely to be.

Tourism to Syria is seasonal with the majority of visitors coming between March–
April or September–November. A third peak exists around Christmas, generated
by tours which take in Syrian sites before moving to Jerusalem for Christmas.
During this time all Syria's international class accommodation is likely to be heavily
booked, with seasonal price rises and dense crowds at major sites. Very few visitors
are received during the months of June to August, which are regarded as being too
hot, and sites such as Palmyra attract few visitors in the depths of winter. Tourism
to urban centres such as Aleppo and Damascus is less subject to seasonal fluctuations due to high volumes of business visitors. Access and opening hours at heritage
sites may be erratic, depending on local conditions, and weekly variations apply.
For example, Fridays are popular times for families and schoolchildren to visit and
domestic tourists are offered reduced rates at all times, as are students and certain
other classes of visitor. Museums are generally closed on Tuesdays with the exception of the National Museum in Damascus.

Managing Syria's urban heritage

Syria's heritage sites include both complex ancient urban cities such as Damascus
and Aleppo and relatively isolated archaeological sites such as Palmyra. Both categories may have on-site museums and supplementary attractions. Syria has a very
active cultural resource management programme and since 1970 under the General
Directorate for Antiquities and Museums the number of registered archaeological
sites in Syria has increased from 795 to 3073. The number of museums increased
from seven to twenty-eight over the same period, resulting in a growth in potential
heritage tourism attractions. Domestic visitors to heritage sites are assisted by
schools policies encouraging such visits and a claimed literacy rate of nearly 70%.

tion in most developing countries, Syria's major historic
lustry and receive the bulk of its visitor impacts without
benefits. Renovation and conservation work at such
ry of Culture yet tourism revenues such as admission
f Finance. Although a proportion of this amount will
the Ministry of Culture as part of financial division
, there is no direct link between the popularity of a
unt of revenue allotted for its conservation and
interesting situation where heritage managers do
...crease in visitor numbers for whom they are obliged
...s and underwrite problems of site wear and tear.

Urban tourism in Aleppo and Damascus

Urban tourism and urban regeneration

Both Damascus, the capital, and Aleppo (in many ways Syria's cultural centre) include within their Old Cities a series of separate visitor attractions as well as the *suqs*, some of which are covered and consist of a maze of interconnecting lanes and passageways lined with shops, stalls and craftsmen's workshops. Individual historic monuments and locations of religious significance are found both within and on the periphery of the *suqs*. It is notable that visitor attractions (such as the National Museum in Damascus) located at some distance from these historic urban cores receive significantly fewer visitors than those within the walled cities, which act as magnets for the visitor.

The ancient city centres (Old Cities) of Damascus and Aleppo share many common problems including escalation of real estate prices due to tourism. A small shop at the entrance to Suq Al-Hamidiyyeh in Damascus now costs upwards of $50 000. Many of the residents are too poor even to maintain or repair their houses, and conservation efforts are hampered by a landholding system which may subdivide property among heirs, making it difficult to trace ownership. A Committee for the Preservation of The Old City of Damascus, which includes representatives from all relevant organisations, is attempting to develop a management strategy, and there are various individuals and voluntary organisations like the Friends of the Old City, who are trying to do the same thing. The city management is in the course of making a complete record of the buildings and their use, sector by sector, dividing the city on a grid basis. Several sectors have already been completely surveyed but the process will be lengthy. In Aleppo technical cooperation is being executed by the Municipality of Aleppo, the GTZ (German Technical Cooperation) and the Arab Fund to prepare a new development plan for the Old City of Aleppo and adjoining inner-city areas. This will provide guidelines for the management and control of building activities and develop recommendations for the promotion of appropriate economic and social developments.

Damascus and Aleppo are only two of the Middle Eastern cities causing international concern. Collaboration between the World Bank and UNESCO has resulted in six cities being earmarked for conservation funds, with three (Fes, Samarkand and San'a) sharing many of the problems of Aleppo and Damascus. All have a unique architectural heritage with an evolving economic base challenging the inner cities to provide jobs within a crumbling infrastructure and poor and overstretched social services. The management of tourism to the Old Cities of Damascus and Aleppo is closely connected with urban heritage conservation. Sudden floods of visitors put pressure on an already stressed infrastructure and a lack of local tourism research prevents visitors from being directed to specific attractions or areas of interest, with a negative impact on the quality of their experience. The conversion of historic buildings for tourist accommodation and restaurant use is frequently inappropriate and strains existing power, sewage and rubbish-disposal services as well as creating parking problems and traffic jams.

Not all tourism uses are compatible with traditional social life and, conversely, many aspects of traditional life potentially of interest to visitors are not being marketed. It is undeniable that the development of tourism has enormous (though little studied) economic and job-creation potential for the Old Cities with the possibility of remedying, at least in part, the outmigration of middle-class families to the newer housing of the suburbs. This process has resulted in partial ghettoisation of the Old Cities, which remain inhabited by poorer families who are unable to move and equally unable to maintain their crumbling houses. The development of new opportunities in tourism-related industries, particularly in catering and merchandising, could address many of these problems if properly supported within an integrated framework.

Since traffic within the Old Cities is pedestrian, at least within the core areas, increased volumes of visitors are causing parking problems on the periphery of the walled areas, particularly for coaches. Within the Old Cities themselves the standard of catering outlets is variable and there is little provision of information or other tourism services such as lavatories. The standard of tourism services is variable due to lack of overall planning control and effective quality policing, and not all specific attractions are easily accessible due to lack of signage. Since tourism forms an essential element in urban regeneration planning schemes for both cities future tourism developments must be compatible with the general strategic objectives of the rehabilitation projects. Lack of a central planning framework has led to the promotion of disparate private sector initiatives within a complex public sector framework.

Damascus

Visitor flows

Central Damascus has two major tourism accommodation areas, one with luxury hotels and supporting services and a second with budget hotels and hostels located near to the station (Figure 6.2). The main tourism axis is therefore the Shoukry al-Qouwatly/Al Shouhada streets which links the Old City with a secondary focus of visitor interest in the National Museum and Takieh Mosque complex. However, although the distance between these foci is not great (20 minutes' walk) most tour operators transport their clients between them by bus, creating parking problems outside both the National Museum and the Citadel, where most tours of the Old City begin. Almost all visitors to the Old City enter through the *suq*, generally via the Al Jabiya gate or Al Hamidiyah, leading directly to the covered *suq*. Behind the covered area the walled city is centred upon the Omayyad Mosque and Azzem Palace. Some visitors venture no further, whereas others follow Madhat Basha/Bab Sharqui (the 'Street called Straight') of the Bible which enters the Christian, rather than the Muslim, quarter of the Old City near St Mary's church and terminates at St Paul's chapel. The vast majority of visitors do not penetrate the lanes of the Al Quaimariyeh and Bab Touma quarters but remain in the western area.

Signage and interpretation

Visitors to the Old City also enjoy merely wandering the streets, shopping, watching the diversity of local people, and eating (sampling traditional foods such as pastries). The level of tourist hassle experienced by visitors is low, except at the entry to Souq al-Hamidiyah (Figure 6.2), and tourists are perfectly safe to wander wherever they like, even at night. However, because of its layout the Old City is confusing to the visitor making even well-known attractions difficult to find. Map coverage of the Old City is very poor and there are no waymarked routes and few signposts. Existing maps are often stylised and sometimes (especially in general guidebooks) on a very small scale. This makes them most difficult to follow through the confusing alleyways of the Old City and some tourists are reluctant to go off on their own for fear of getting lost.

Historic buildings and conservation

The conservation of Old City buildings and their conversion to tourism uses is an on-going process. Some historic buildings such as the magnificent Nizam House, occupied by the British Consul in the mid-nineteenth century, have been restored for tourism purposes but not yet opened to the public or given a designated function. The restoration of the eighteenth-century caravanserai Khan Assad Pacha, built in the same year as the Azzem Palace and located in the heart of the *suq*, is nearly completed but the City management has not yet decided on a function. Current plans include possible conversion into an hotel, although this seems likely to be rejected on the grounds of difficulties with parking and utilities. Other alternatives include developing the Khan as a museum of Natural History using Japanese sponsorship, although this would be a most inappropriate location for such a museum, or as a multiple-use centre combining handicraft workshops, traditional foodstuffs, eating places, simple accommodation and entertainment. There is therefore considerable potential for the development of additional visitor attractions within the existing Old City.

Pricing policies

The writer examined in more detail the pricing policy and visitation pattern to a single-visitor attraction in Damascus, choosing the Azzem Palace (Figure 6.2) since

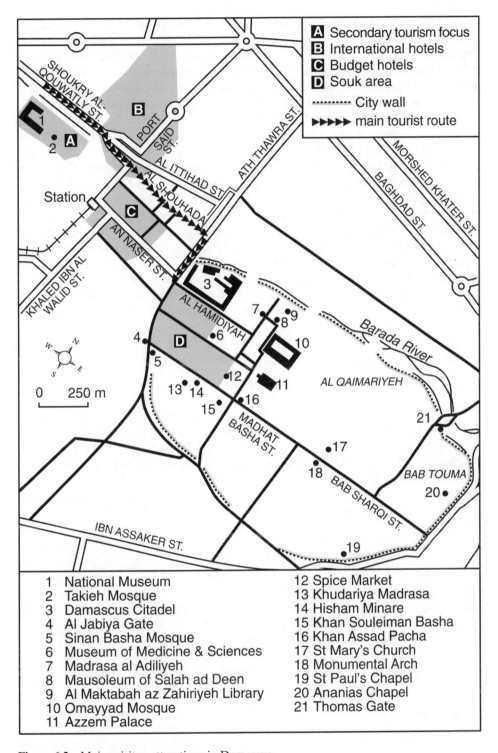

Figure 6.2 Major visitor attractions in Damascus

almost all visitors to the Old City go there at least once. The Palace is located just south of the Omayid Mosque and was built in 1749 by the then governor of Damascus, Assad Pacha. It is a splendid multi-courtyard building with pleasant gardens which currently houses the Museum of the Arts and Popular Traditions of Syria. These exhibits, mostly reconstruction models and case displays, are housed in rooms off the Palace courtyard but very little interpretation, even case labelling, is available. The Palace is open all year (except Tuesdays). An entry charge of S£200 is made per individual, although group entry is still being charged at the old rate of S£10. Around 300 000 tourists visit the Palace each year, and during high season it may receive 1700 visitors a day, dropping to 300 during the heat of summer. Revenue from visitors can be substantial – in peak season (August/September) 1995 the palace 'earned' more than S£1.5million, considerably more than the National Museum. Observations made by the writer suggested that the average dwell time for a group visit was 41 minutes, although individual visitors, generally going round with a guidebook, might stay twice as long. Visitors stayed between 30 seconds and 5 minutes in any one room, never longer, and some were heard to complain about the lack of interpretation and information. An independent visitor without a guidebook would be unable to make much sense of the displays, and no official guides are available for general visitors (as opposed to official parties).

Aleppo

History and topography

Aleppo was already the capital of a powerful kingdom by the eighteenth century BC. It is especially famous as a trading city, and today the labyrinth of 7 km of covered medieval *suqs* are probably the most spectacular in Syria, a 400-hectare area home to 200 000 residents. However, the delineation of the Old City in Aleppo is not so clear as in Damascus since most of its walls have been destroyed by earthquakes. The Citadel, a World Heritage Site, is located at the eastern end of the suq surrounded by a moat 30 m wide and 20 m deep, dug in the twelfth century. The impressive gateway was started in the twelfth century and finished under the Mamluks some 400 years later. Many buildings inside the citadel were destroyed during a great earthquake in 1822 which killed 60% of Aleppo's inhabitants although part of the Royal Palace, a heavily restored twelfth-century mosque and some smaller buildings still remain. The theatre has been reconstructed, rather unhappily, and in 1994 a new building was opened as a site museum, also heavily restored. The impressive entrance towers and fortifications remain the main reason for World Heritage designation (see Figure 6.3).

During the period January-September 1995 visitation to Aleppo was as shown in Table 6.2 and can be projected to give an approximate annual estimate.

Visitor flows and signage

Visitors generally start a tour of Aleppo at the Citadel (coaches being parked some distance away) and either walk or are driven to the Archaeological Museum and

119

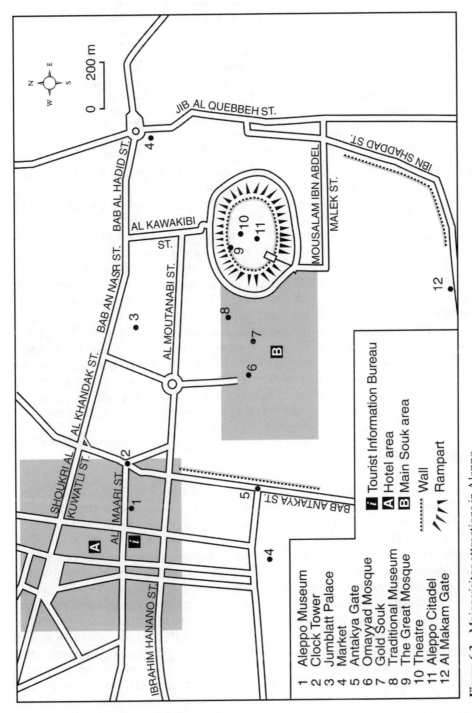

Figure 6.3 Major visitor attractions in Aleppo

Table 6.2 Visitors to historic sites in Aleppo during 1995

Location	Visitor numbers Jan.–Sept. 1995	Possible annual visitation
Museum	62 400	83 000
Citadel	263 730	350 000
Museum in Citadel	44 720	59 000
Ethnographic Museum	20 220	26 000
St Simeon Stylites	123 074	164 000

Source: Records in Aleppo Museum.

the entrance to the *suq* area. The main museum at Aleppo is far more visitor-friendly than Damascus or Palmyra, although the arrangement of its collections is confusing. An on-site museum and visitor centre is proposed for the Citadel, possibly funded by the EU. Not only does Aleppo have Syria's best *suqs* and museum but the Citadel also has a proper visitor guide, written by the curator of the Aleppo Museum and available for purchase both at site and museum. However, the map/plan that it contains is impossible to follow on the ground and none of the buildings are numbered or labelled. Buildings are also located on the map of the historical buildings of Aleppo 1260–1918, published and available from the same source. Although without a scale, this excellent map locates all Aleppo's major buildings by period. The manager of the Museum estimates that 50% of visitors to Aleppo buy some sort of a guidebook, which greatly enhances the quality of the visitor experience. The availability of adequate map coverage for Aleppo makes it far easier for visitors to form a cognitive map of the city (Pearce, 1977; Walmesley and Jenkins, 1992).Conversely, the lack of such a map in Damascus adversely affects the quality of the visitor experience since many visitors remain frightened of getting lost.

Historic buildings and conservation

The destruction of houses in the Old City was stopped by government order during the 1980s, and during the subsequent decade Aleppo has had a remarkable rehabilitation project, financed partly by the Arab League and partly by the German aid agency GTZ. The project involves a total survey and mapping of all buildings, together with associated archived material on building utilisation and occupation. The Aleppo Committee, composed of representatives from all relevant public and private sector organisations, has the power to grant or withhold planning permission for building conversions and also to assist poorer householders with the provision of grants, loans and technical expertise to restore their properties. Population densities in the Old City are high; up to 50 homes per 1000 m^2 with a total of at least 200 000 people inside the Old City. Here, tourism development (if carefully controlled) is seen as a potential solution to the Old City's problems. The conversion of older buildings to workshops, or their abandonment, are considered more harmful to the urban fabric than potential conversion for tourist restaurants or accommodation. Indeed, two of Aleppo's new luxury restaurants have been developed (with permission) in fine fifteenth-century houses incorporating many original features

(including underground access to the archaeological lev
tems) as extra visitor attractions. However, since tourism
rapidly the Committee is currently undertaking a system
and proposed future tourism developments with a view
tourism management framework.

Improving the quality of the visitor experience

The quality of the visitor experience in either Aleppo or
the match between expectations and reality. Within an
tourist is visiting discrete destinations linked together by a (frequently invisible)
network of infrastructural services and product marketing. The tourist visit is
merely a snapshot in time and the visitor may be frequently unaware of the many
issues which are affecting the nature of the urban environment through which he or
she is travelling. All, however, distinguish between different levels of service and
experience quality yet are powerless to affect these during their brief visit, a
powerlessness exacerbated by language difficulties. The role of the guide and inter-
preter becomes especially important, with the guide also acting in a large measure
as a culture broker. The range of factors which affect tourists image of destination
include ambience and safety, shaping the quality of the experience (Gilbert and
Joshi, 1992). Several major features adversely affect visitor experience quality in
Aleppo and Damascus including:

- Lack of visitor facilities (information, toilets), inability to find major attractions
  without maps or waymarking
- Diffidence when approached with cultural unfamiliarity (language, bargaining,
  lack of other tourists)
- Need to walk (unsuitable for disabled visitors)

  but not:

- Personal safety (except in a sense of overall political stability)
- Religious intolerance
- Vehicular traffic

Interpretative trails and visitor attractions

It would be a relatively simple matter to plan waymarked trails through both Old
Cities linking places of interest, requiring the development of plaques as waymarked points and the design and printing of leaflets. Such a plan has greatly
facilitated exploring the suqs quarter and Old City of Tunis. It is probable that this
idea will be financed by the EU during 1997/8, in addition to the possible construction of a purpose-built visitor centre in the Citadel of the Old City
(Damascus), with audiovisual presentations and an introduction to the Old City. A
waymarked trail will then lead the visitor directly into the *suq* to explore, with the

ific leaflets, a series of themed trails linking places of historical interest or
ar shopping areas, which could be followed on the map assisted by way-
ed signs. New attractions could easily be incorporated using this method. For
ample, the Medical Museum has interesting displays of traditional herbal medicines located very near the corner of the *suq* where such medicines are sold and
prescribed today. It would be easy to design a short themed route linking these
locations.

Guides and guiding

The quality of guides also affects visitor experience. Official Syrian guides are
graduates, trained and employed by the Ministry of Tourism, but they receive only
a small input from the Ministry of Culture not qualifying them to comment in detail
on historic sites. Many guides are utilised merely as escorts by European tour
operators, who bring their own specialist guide. It is quite difficult for guides to
obtain up-to-date technical information since the latest excavation reports and
books are unavailable in Syria, making specialist tourists better informed.

Conclusion: the future of urban tourism in Syria

Urban centres are foci of cultural and economic activities, meeting places, major
tourist gateways, accommodation and transportation hubs (Mullins, 1991). Although tourism in Aleppo and Damascus has not reached the pressured situation of
London, York, Florence or Venice it needs to be integrated into an overall development plan. Where overcrowding occurs at major tourist sites it has a negative effect
on visitors with low tolerance thresholds (Page, 1995). Additionally, walled cities
contain major tourist attractions supported by retail and catering outlets but without any kind of appropriate infrastructure (Jansen-Verbeke, 1986). The impact of
visitors within Syrian walled cities can be summarised as follows:

- Causing conversion of existing buildings (some residential or craft) to tourism
  use straining sewage, water, power services
- Creating new market for crafts
- Altering the traditional spatial structure of the *suq* where the entrance becomes a
  tourist zone diminishing in intensity with distance from the entrance. This has
  implications for real estate pricing (see above) but is a result of price competition
  between vendors
- Impetus for maintenance of existing historic buildings and rehabilitation of old
  ones
- Impetus for creation of new visitor attractions and links between them
- Creating employment (direct and indirect)
- Retention of households within Old City area

The most likely future developments in Syria include increased cross-border
heritage tours with Jordan, Israel and Lebanon, especially when further political

stability is ensured. Liberalisation of Syria's airline policy will certainly result in increased visitation. Other significant stimuli to the heritage tourism market include the lifting of the ban on reporting Syria by the US travel press, the permitting of faxes and improvement of the telephone and postal systems together with the implementation of the so-called Law 10 allowing hard currency to be available for certain imports.

Increased tourism has resulted in the fact that existing 5-star hotel capacity is frequently exceeded, especially at peak season. There are rumours that Syria intends to promote the building of 3-star hotels and encourage homestays and other alternative types of tourist accommodation (including some within the Old City providing a 'caravanserai experience'), but it is unlikely that such developments will appeal to the high-quality high-cost heritage tourism market. It is easy to see how easily Syria could achieve its target of doubling visitor arrivals over the next decade (all of whom will come to Damascus), but less easy to see how these visitors are to be accommodated. Existing accommodation capacity is estimated at 32 000 beds, hardly enough to accommodate 2.1 million tourists. Managed properly, this growth in Syrian tourism has the capacity to contribute the necessary economic power and impetus for rejuvenation and conservation of the Old City areas (Law, 1992). However, such developments require an integrated urban planning scheme involving complex private and public sector developments. The start of such a scheme can be seen in both Aleppo and Damascus, suggesting a bright future for the world's oldest cities.

References

Gilbert, D. and Joshi, L. (1992) 'Quality management and the tourism and hospitality industry', in C. Cooper and A. Lockwood (eds), *Progress in Tourism, Recreation and Hospitality Management, Volume 4*, London: Belhaven, 149–68.

Jansen-Verbeke, M. (1986) 'Inner city tourism; resources, tourists and promoters', *Annals of Tourism Research*, 13, 79–100.

Law, C.M. (1992) 'Urban tourism and its contribution to economic regeneration', *Urban Studies*, 29 (3/4), 599–618.

Law, C.M. (1993) *Urban Tourism: Attracting Visitors to Large Cities*, London: Mansell.

Mullins, P. (1991) 'Tourism urbanisation', *International Journal of Urban and Regional Research*, 15 (3), 326–42.

Page, S. (1995) *Urban Tourism*, London: Routledge.

Pearce, P.L. (1977) 'Mental souvenirs: a study of tourists and their city maps', *Australian Journal of Psychology*, 29, 203–10.

United Nations (1995) *Statistical Yearbook*, 4th edn, New York.

Walmesley, D.J. and Jenkins, J. (1992) 'Tourism cognitive mapping of unfamiliar environments'. *Annals of Tourism Research*, 19 (3) 268–86.

World Tourism Organisation (1995) *Handbook of Tourism Statistics*, Madrid.

7 Tourism management in Venice, or how to deal with success

JAN VAN DER BORG

CHAPTER SUMMARY

This chapter discusses the visitor management problems faced by Venice both as a result of its continuing popularity as a tourist destination and as a function of planned religious celebrations at the time of the millennium. The chapter considers the impacts of this position in relation to the type of visitor that Venice attracts. It takes a theoretical background of sustainable tourism management and within this presents various visitor management techniques that could be used to manage the capacity limits that are quickly being reached, including the use of new technology to manage visitor flows.

Introduction

Venice may very well be the world's number-one destination for urban tourism. Even before the days of the Grand Tour, the city was an important crossroad for travellers of different kinds. It should, therefore, not be surprising that Venice can be found on the front page of virtually every tour operator's guide dealing with city trips (Van der Borg, 1994). This, together with the sensitivity of Venice's urban environment in general (UNESCO, 1968), explains why so much attention has been paid to tourism development in Venice and the way it is to be managed.

This chapter provides the interested reader with the latest results of the ongoing research on tourism in Venice and in other European cities of art, undertaken by the University Ca'Foscari of Venice from the end of the 1970s onwards. Some of the results have been published in various forms elsewhere (see, for example, Van der Borg, 1991; Costa and Van der Borg, 1993; Van der Borg, Costa and Gotti, 1996). An important decision by the Vatican to declare the year 2000 a Holy Year, and recent developments in computer and information technologies that may successfully be applied to visitor management, are assumed to have major consequences for Venice's tourism system and thus fully justify this update.

Managing Tourism in Cities. Edited by D. Tyler, Y. Guerrier and M. Robertson.
Copyright © 1998 John Wiley & Sons Ltd.

This chapter has been divided into three parts. The first introduces the reader to the principal characteristics of Venetian tourism development and the city's experiences with excessive demand. Attention will be paid to the likely impact of the Holy Year, or 'Giubileo', on tourism demand. The second discusses the concept of sustainable tourism development and presents different, relevant dimensions of the upper limit to tourism development, better known as the tourist carrying capacity. Finally, the third part focuses on past tentative measures taken by the city of Venice to manage tourism flows, and then considers the new perspectives that are offered by technological progress.

Tourism in Venice

It is generally acknowledged that growing visitor numbers have positive effects for the local society, especially in terms of income and employment. However, should growth persist, then it is likely that the pressure of tourism on the destination becomes excessive. In Venice, tourism is causing permanent damage to the local environment, to the monuments, to the local population, and even to the quality of the visitor's experience.

It is beyond doubt that the city of Venice finds itself in such circumstances. Visitors, inhabitants and other urban functions, such as the university and the local administration, are competing for the 'use' of the historic centre of Venice, which at present has fewer than 80 000 inhabitants, and receives daily up to 47 000 commuters. In 1951, Venice boasted 175 000 inhabitants, a number which has been declining ever since. The 'exodus' of population and economic activities has been partly fuelled by a process of 'crowding out': tourism-related activities are suffocating residential and other city functions. In short, tourism development is no longer sustaining the local society but has become a menace for its continuity.

The historical centre of Venice, a gathering of small islands of about 700 hectares that are situated in the middle of a lagoon and constitute the unique 'forma urbis', still survives thanks to a series of special laws and the loving attention of the elite of the world. Although Venice may be seen as an extreme case, other studies – even those of former 'selling-the-city' prophets – have pointed out that its problems are not only shared by other European heritage cities but are expected to intensify in the near future as well. This makes Venice such an extremely useful case to study.

One of the most important aspects of the Venetian tourism market is the development of tourism demand in its centre. While in 1952 more than 500 000 tourists spent 1.2 million bed-nights in Venice, these figures have grown to 1.45 million tourist arrivals in 1995 and 3.23 million bed-nights spent in tourist accommodation (Van der Borg and Russo, 1997). At the same time, Venice has become a destination for a huge number of visitors that do not use accommodation (almost 7 million excursionists in 1996 alone).

 Growth in tourism demand has been more or less continuous, notwithstanding the sporadic stagnations in growth. In 1985 and 1986, for example, the massive renouncement of the American tourists, an important segment of the Venetian market, of any vacation in Europe, under the influence of an unfavourable exchange rate of the US dollar and of terrorism, caused a temporary setback in arrivals and stays. In 1991, the Gulf War generated a similar dip in demand.

Over time, the number of arrivals has grown somewhat faster than the number of stays, which has led to a decrease in the average stay of the residential tourist. On average, tourists tend to stay little more than 2 nights. The shortening of the average duration of the holiday is a phenomenon observed on a global scale, and certainly not typical for Venice. Most other destinations of city trips register an average duration of the stay similar to that of Venice (Van den Berg, Van der Borg and Van der Meer, 1995).

It has already been mentioned that Venice is visited not only by tourists but also by excursionists. In the absence of official statistics that document excursionism, the relative importance of excursionism for the centre of Venice has been established through specific surveys among visitors. The visitor flow to Venice in 1992 consisted of 31.1% of tourists and for the remaining 68.9% of excursionists.

Three types of excursionists may be distinguished, a distinction that has implications for management. The first visits Venice from its home and is called 'traditional' excursionist (26.3% of visitors and 38.2% of excursionists). Traditional excursionists visit Venice from the major cities in the north of Italy, the south of Germany and Austria. The second type of excursionist passes holidays close to Venice, on the Adriatic coast or in the Dolomites, for example, and visits the city from the vacation destination (which is not Venice). These 'indirect' excursionists account for 18.2% of the visitors and 26.4% of the excursionists. Last but not least, 'commuting' excursionists have chosen Venice as the destination of their vacation, but use accommodation elsewhere. Hence, 24.4% of the total number of visitors and 35.4% of the excursionists to Venice 'commute'.

The share of excursionists in the total number of visitor tends to increase steadily. Given the expansion of the global market for cultural tourism and the limited supply of hotel beds in the centre of Venice (slightly more than 11 000 hotel beds and 4000 beds in other types of accommodation), the share of excursionism is going to rise considerably. It is, therefore, not surprising that the local tourism industry is reorientating its supply towards excursionism.

The explanation for the growth of the market for commuting excursionism is easily found: they can save a substantial part of their holiday budgets locating close to but not in Venice. The price of a double room of equal quality diminishes smoothly with an increase of the distance from the historic centre of Venice (Rispoli and Van der Borg, 1988). The heritage cities of Padova and Treviso, both situated at about 30 miles from Venice, in particular, offer a valid alternative. There, a double room in a 4-star hotel costs much less (about 30% of the Venetian price of ECU 250 per room). Closer to Venice, hotels in Mestre and Marghera (part of the Municipality of Venice and situated just on the other side of the rail and road bridge that connects the island with the centre) allow for savings of up to 50%.

More recently, the beach resorts on the Adriatic coast have started to supply beds to excursionists during the low season. They offer favourable prices to international tour operators that organise group travel. For example, Jesolo, Italy's second destination for sun and sea vacations, attracts thousands of French and Spanish tourists in May, June, September and October (Figure 7.1).

Various forecasts of the development of tourism demand exist. Costa and Van der Borg (1993) have produced an estimation of future demand by means of an econometric model. This relates economic development to changes in demand for tourism

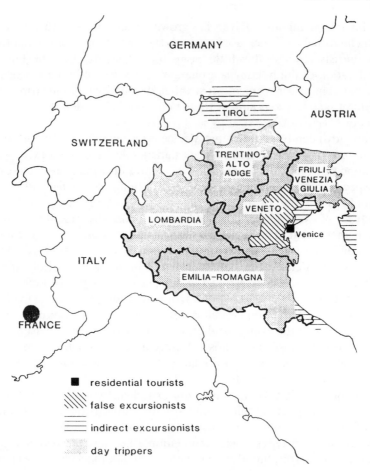

Figure 7.1 Regional catchment areas for different types of tourist

and excursionism, and assumes that an increase in disposable income has triggered the expansion of the tourism market. The model foresees, for the year 2000, a total of 1 540 000 tourist arrivals, generating 3 491 000 nights, and 5 261 000 excursionists.

More recently, new forecasts have been made in the light of the announcement of the 'Giubileo' (Consorzio Venezia Ricerche, 1997). These forecasts were produced by means of an autoregressive model that interprets future developments by looking at changes in the past. The results of this analysis partly confirm those obtained by Costa as far as tourism is concerned. The foreseen number of excursionists, however, is considerably higher: 8 million. In addition to this autonomous growth, the effect of the touristic–religious mega-event had to be calculated. Two extreme scenarios were formulated. A minimum scenario that assumed that the event is concentrated in Rome and the impact on Venice is going to be limited to indirect excursionism. The maximum scenario has reserved an active role for Venice in the event. In this case, Venice will attract not only additional excursionists (traditional, indirect and commuting) but also tourists. Additional tourism demand generated by the 'Giubileo' will thus range from about 3 to 8 million pilgrims.

Excursionists spend much less than residential tourists. This is true not only for Venice but for other heritage cities as well (Van der Borg, Costa and Gotti, 1995). A residential tourist spends on the average L120 000, about 60 ECUs, in the historical centre. Traditional excursionists spend L50 000 (25 ECUs), the indirect excursionist L100 000 (50 ECUs), while the commuting excursionist spends L115 000 (67 ECUs). A large part of the expenses of indirect and commuting excursionists is spent on accommodation not in Venice.

It is the excursionist that gets most of the blame for Venice's problems with excess tourism demand. From an economic point of view this preference for residential tourism seems more than justified: excursionists spend much less in Venice than tourists, and, as Van der Borg (1991) pointed out, their contribution to various social costs is slightly more negative than that of residential tourists. Apparently, residential tourists help a local economy earn more money than excursionists but at less cost.

However, the case of Venice demonstrates that the strictly economic dimension should not be the first and principal argument for discriminating against excursionists. It is the management dimension that makes excursionism such a threat for the urban tourism system. This can be easily explained. Residential tourism demand is, by definition, related to and thus controlled through the supply of beds. This means that the maximum number of residential tourists that the centre of Venice hosts per day is explicitly limited by the total number of beds that the centre of the city supplies. The market for hotel accommodation thus regulates residential tourism demand in the longer run. Furthermore, since many residential tourists book their hotel, information is available in advance concerning the pressure of residential tourism on the city. Peaks can thus be anticipated, and adequate measures taken.

Excursionists do not make use of a 'core' facility that might limit their number explicitly. Therefore, regulation by means of limiting supply or pricing is difficult. The facilities that may hinder their arrival to Venice, such as specific means of public transport and parking places, can always be avoided if necessary. And since excursionists improvise their visit, it is very awkward to anticipate their arrival.

Any visitor management strategy, therefore, needs to concentrate first on controlling the flow of excursionists. For them, mechanisms that automatically regulate demand are absent. The measures that need to be designed for the management of the excursionist flows should be substitutes for those mechanisms.

Sustainable tourism development and Venice's tourist carrying capacity

Having established which direction a visitor management strategy for Venice should take, a vision for the strategy should be developed. Sustainable tourism development, a trendy concept recently embraced by policy makers and the tourism industry alike but with solid roots in public economic theory (see, for example, Pearce and Turner, 1990), forms the basis for such a vision.

Developing tourism in a sustainable manner means using the scarce resources a destination possesses in an optimal manner for tourism purposes, safeguarding the interests not only of today's inhabitants, tourists and the tourism industry but also of tomorrow's. An optimal use implies that the net impact of tourism development for the local society is being maximised over the different stages of tourism development. Using Butler's life-cycle model, Van der Borg (1991) argues that a development process of the destination contains both sustainable and not sustainable stages. Van der Borg, Costa and Gotti (1996) develop this approach further with the help of cost–benefit analysis.

Typically, the first stage of tourism is hardly profitable: investment costs are huge and benefits meagre. Therefore, developing tourism only makes sense if one may expect that after having invested in attractions and facilities the number of visitors rises sufficiently. The saturation stage tends to generate a net loss for the local society: benefits no longer compensate for negative externalities, such as congestion and pollution.

In general, negative externalities appear when a limit to development has been surpassed. The limit to tourism development is called the tourist carrying capacity, that is, the maximum number of visitors a destination can host. Notwithstanding the criticism to which the carrying capacity as a planning instrument has recently been exposed (see, for example, Lindberg et al., 1997), it has proven its value for visitor management in Venice. It had already been shown by Glasson, Godfrey and Goodey (1995) that the carrying capacity of a tourist destination is a complex and dynamic instrument.

The carrying capacity can be measured on various territorial and functional levels, including the level of the individual attractions and of the destination as a whole. In practice, the specific character of the city determines which of the levels is the most relevant. Interviews with attraction managers in Venice has taught us that, since the majority of visitors do not visit any of Venice's attractions but just wander around in the centre, the attraction level does not seem of much relevance to Venice. A similar situation exists in well-conserved and well-restored heritage cities such as Bruges, Rothenburg and Salzburg, which are attractions in themselves. And since the attitudes and behaviour of inhabitants, tourists and the tourism industry change over time, the negative and positive effects generated by tourism will be valued differently over time. Hence, the relevance of the temporal dimension.

Moreover, the tourist carrying capacity has a multitude of dimensions. The number of visitors may be limited because the physical structure of a destination is compromised (e.g. the physical carrying capacity), because the local society loses its character (e.g. the social–anthropological carrying capacity) or because the local economy gets frustrated (e.g. the social–economic carrying capacity). Two different dimensions that have always worried Venetians are briefly discussed below: the social–anthropological and the social–economic carrying capacities.

Residents are an important part of the tourism system around a destination. They are an important ingredient of 'hospitality' of a destination. The reaction of the inhabitants of a tourism city to tourism in general, and to tourists and excursionists in particular, determines the social impact of tourism on the local society and thus the social–anthropological carrying capacity of the destination.

Following a survey among inhabitants of Oxford (for more details on the methodology see Glasson, Godfrey and Goodey, 1995), the University of Venice organised in 1993 a survey among the inhabitants of Venice. The results of this survey were quite surprising. It showed, among other things that Venetians did not have the negative perception of tourism in their city as might have been expected. The respondents were nevertheless very well informed about tourism development in general. They perceived the 'massification' of tourism and the diminishing quality and especially the growing weight of excursionists in total demand. However, the decreasing quality of life in the city is not so much blamed on excessive tourism demand but also on the poor management of the local government as a whole.

The social–economic tourist carrying capacity may be defined as the total number of visitors that can be allowed into a city without hindering the other functions that the city performs. This dimension is closely linked to the phenomenon of 'crowding out', described for the first time by Prud'homme (1986). Tourism in cities like Venice or Bruges tend to dominate the urban societies; they push other activities or functions from the centre to the outskirts. The price for centrally located land, and the diminished attractiveness of a city for families and firms due to congestion and pollution, explain the process of crowding out.

The problem of determining the social–economic carrying capacity for the centre of Venice has been formalised in Canestrelli and Costa (1991). They translated the conflict between tourism and other functions into a fuzzy linear programming model that maximises the income from tourism under capacity restrictions. These restrictions take into account, for example, the availability of accommodation, catering facilities, parking facilities, intra-urban transportation, waste disposal services and the space available in St Mark's Cathedral. The philosophy of the linear programming model is very close to the sustainability approach, namely that of the quest for the optimal use of resources. Until now, the model has been applied with success to different mature tourist resorts, such as Cambridge (urban environment), Crete and Capri (islands) and Cortina d'Ampezzo (mountain resort).

Canestrelli and Costa found that Venice can support about 25 000 visitors in one day, comprising some 15 000 tourists (60% of tourism demand) and 10 000 excursionists (the remaining 40% of the total number of visitors). Among the active restrictions are: the number of beds (the model tends to fill Venice first with tourists and then starts to look at whether there is still space available for excursionists); the availability of local water transport (which determines the number of excursionists); and, relaxing this restriction, St Mark's Cathedral.

Although the model lacks an explicit temporal dimension, the results are of great interest for visitor management. It teaches us first, that the 'optimal' visitor mix differs from the actual one. In fact, instead of a weight of 60%, tourists represent slightly more than 30% of the actual total tourism demand. Second, one may conclude that at present the overall pressure from tourism seems – at least in theory – compatible with the stress the city is able to support. In the absence of fluctuations in demand, the total carrying capacity of Venice is 9 million visitors, while the city is visited by 8.45 million people annually. This suggests that there may even be room for a slight increase in demand. Finally, an analysis of the distribution of demand over the year shows that demand is concentrated at weekends and in the spring, autumn and particularly summer months. During ten days of the year, total demand is more than 100 000 persons. Peaks of 200 000 visitors on special occasions are no exception. Two-thirds of the year, the number of visitors easily surpasses the social–economic carrying capacity.

Thus, at present, sustainability of tourism development in Venice depends, on the one hand, on the mix of the visitor flow, that is, the weight of tourists in total demand, and, on the other, on the fluctuations in tourism demand. In effect, the number of excursionists should be reduced and that of tourists enhanced. At the same time, peaks in demand need to be smoothed out and the low season utilised more intensively. These then become the two priorities of the visitor management strategy of Venice.

If the forecasts of tourism demand development are true, total demand will soon be incompatible with the carrying capacity, and Venice's problems will rapidly intensify. It is likely that the 'Giubileo' will worsen the situation even more. In any case, modelling shows that Venice should try not to get actively involved in any of the events organised for that occasion. This all makes the need for a sound visitor management strategy extremely urgent.

Visitor management in Venice

Designing policies that enable cities to control visitor demand is made difficult because of the need to ensure that the heritage city must be kept as accessible as possible for some categories of users, such as inhabitants, visitors to offices and firms located in the city, and commuters studying or working in it. At the same time, the heritage city needs to be kept as inaccessible as possible to other user categories, excursionists in particular.

'Hard' and 'soft' interventions can be distinguished. 'Hard' interventions physically impede visitors behaving as they want and often imply specific infrastructures. 'Soft' interventions aim at changing the visitor's behaviour, mostly through information campaigns and marketing. 'Hard' measures are believed to be far more effective than 'soft' measures, but the converse is usually true.

A possible 'hard' measure of visitor flow control would be to close the centre of the heritage city to private and touring cars, and to reserve the right to use central parking lots, and the right to stop at the relevant terminals, for inhabitants and commuters. This, in combination with the rationing of the capacity of the means of public transport that bring the visitors to the centre, would allow the local authorities to manage the volume of the visitor flow. Such a policy might easily lead to disappointment and frustration among those visitors that are not able to visit the city as they would have expected. On some occasions it may even become a challenge to enter, notwithstanding the limitations on access, as the island of Capri experienced in 1993 when it decided to abolish temporarily ferry boats to reduce car traffic connected with tourism. Fishermen immediately offered their services and the congestion was even more intense than before.

A 'softer' and probably more efficient way of avoiding excess demand, from both the city's and the visitor's point of view, would be the introduction of incentives that guide tourism demand. These incentives should recognise the fact that the destination is an asset with a limited capacity, the use of which should be rationalised also for the sake of the visitor experience. This should be communicated in advance to the market, either directly to the potential visitors or indirectly to the travel agents and tour operators.

This type of rationalisation policy would require an advanced booking system. Through the reservation of service packages, which could include, for example, meal vouchers, tickets for exhibitions and museums and discounts in souvenir shops, visitors could be stimulated to visit Venice at specific periods. The booking of such a package could be mandatory (a sort of entrance ticket) or optional. In the last case the potential users must be convinced of the advantages the package offers them, and hence accept advanced booking. Another incentive could be the introduction of a 'city currency card', serving as a credit card, valid for the length of the visit, and with which goods and services in the city could be paid. The card could be issued in different forms to different types of visitors, in numbers fixed in advance. The personal credit card furthermore could allow for price discrimination according to the hour or the day that it is used.

Both the city service package and the city currency cards can be seen as surrogates for the core service the tourist uses, the hotel bed. It would thus help to convince excursionists to plan their visit instead of improvising. Their reservation could be organised in the context of any telecommunication network which permits long-distance sales in real time, an immediate update of the availability, and the issue of relevant receipts, such as the systems developed by various airline consortia.

In this context, the Internet has some promising characteristics that offer very interesting possibilities if it forms the core of such a reservation system. In principle, the Internet reaches potential visitors at home before their trip, it is interactive and therefore allows for an eventual booking, it operates in real time, it is cheap, and, last but not least, it is selective. Yet its diffusion is still limited.

Venice is currently studying the possibility of requiring tourists to book visits to the city in advance through the Internet. The first step has been the creation of a specific site with the name WETVENICE. The subsequent introduction of the so-called 'Venice card', which is a combination of the two reservation policies mentioned above, might offer visitors an incentive strong enough to make them book their visits to the city well in advance. How would this Venice card work? Visitors would be invited to book their visit to Venice, and receive in exchange the 'Venice card' which would offer them a series of advantages and possibilities not accessible to visitors that do not book (the latter still having access to the city). The number of cards issued would be equal to the most restrictive of the different carrying capacities of the centre of Venice, which seems to be the social–economic one. Visitors spending the night within the Municipal boundaries would receive the card together with the reservation of hotel accommodation.

Ermolli and Guidotti (1991) describe the conditions which would have to be satisfied to guarantee a successful implementation of such a reservation system. They come to the conclusion that from a technical point of view, the monitoring and the control of the tourist flows in real time would not create any problems. What is essential, however, is that all the actors involved in tourism development are convinced that a reservation system brings them specific benefits. It seems that this condition is finally met in Venice, not in the least because the 'Giubileo' is threatening the entire tourism system.

Venice is not only studying ways to improve the spread of visitors over time, it has been working on improvements to the territorial distribution of the visitors once they are in the city. At present just a few areas of Venice are involved in tourism development. Tourism is concentrated in the area between the Rialto

Bridge and St Mark's Square. Alternative routes within the city may be introduced to rationalise the use of the city and its numerous unknown cultural
treasures.

Alternative routes are attractions linked through a route and sustained by complementary tourism facilities. Since tourism demand concentrates around the
'musts', an alternative tourism route might persuade the visitors to visit attractions
that have been less promoted and thus are less known to the public (which certainly
does not mean that they are not worth a visit; on the contrary), and thus relieve the
already congested attractions and areas. The alternative route may also involve the
surroundings of the city. It has already been said that mature destinations suffer not
only from excess demand but also from an unfavourable mixture of overnight and
same-day visitors. The route may therefore also constitute a strong incentive for the
visitor to stay longer in the city.

Not all cities are willing to spread tourism over the municipal territory. In some
cases the concentration of tourism is to be preferred, in order to keep certain areas
genuine. Furthermore, there is the danger that by introducing an alternative tourism route the quality of the overall tourism product would improve too much. If
total demand rises, congestion problems after spreading may remain the same as
before, especially if one realises that the 'musts' will be visited in any case. The
tourism development strategy should address these issues in particular.

Conclusion

Tourism might easily become a major source of well-being for many European
heritage cities. A necessary condition for sustainability is that tourism development
strategies succeed in respecting the limits that are inherent in the city's needs.
Sustainability of urban tourism development is more than just a trendy slogan, as
the results of our study have illustrated.

The case of Venice clearly shows that tourism generates considerable benefits,
but at the same time there are also huge social costs. Venice is at risk of losing its
appeal because of its immense popularity among tourists. Tourism demand for the
city is still growing, as well as the weight of excursionism, to the detriment of the
destination. The 'Giubileo', a religious mega-event that is going to be organised for
the year 2000, will enforce these tendencies. This means that the carrying capacity
of Venice, calculated to be 25 000 visitors a day, will be reached very soon.

Only through a proactive visitor management strategy can Venice protect itself
from the negative externalities that excess tourism demand generates. The principal
characteristics of this strategy were discussed in this chapter: stimulate residential
tourism, through the creation of new hotel beds in the centre, and control excursionist demand with the help of a booking system, which provides added value to
those willing to plan their visit to Venice with a package of services reserved for
them. Peaks in tourism demand are thus reduced. The implementation of such a
system benefits from the recent developments in telecommunication technologies
applied to tourism, the Internet in particular.

Moreover, Venice is trying to rationalise the use of its centre by creating alternative routes. These routes are combinations of lesser known attractions and facilities

that seek to reduce the pressure on specific parts of the historical centre, and achieve a better distribution of visitors in space.

With the continuously increasing interest in cities as tourist destinations, many European heritage cities may follow this example. They may experience the same dramatic growth in tourism demand, until local society starts to perceive tourism as a threat to their quality of life and of the business climate. The knowledge that these problems have been studied and partially solved in Venice may comfort and guide them.

References

Canestrelli, E. and Costa, P. (1991) 'Tourist carrying capacity. A fuzzy approach', *Annals of Tourism Research*, 2, 18, 295–311.

Consorzio Venezia Ricerche (1997) *Impatto del Giubileo su Venezia*, Venice.

Costa, P. and Van der Borg, J. (1993) *The Management of Tourism in Cities of Art*, Quaderni CISET, 2, Oriago di Mira.

Ermolli, B. and Guidotti, E. (1991) 'Un'ipotesi progettuale per il monitoraggio e il governo dei flussi turistici di Venezia', *Rivista Veneta*, 38, 103–14.

Glasson, J., Godfrey, K. and Goodey, B. (1995) *Towards Visitor Impact Management*, Aldershot: Avebury.

Lindberg, K., McCool, S. and Stanley, G. (1997) 'Rethinking carrying capacity', *Annals of Tourism Research*, 2, 24, 461–465.

Pearce, D.W. and Turner, R.K. (1990) *Economics of Natural Resources and the Environment*, London: Harvester Wheatsheaf.

Prud'homme, R. (1986) *Le Tourisme et le Developpement de Venise*, mimeo, Paris: Université de Paris.

Rispoli, M. and Van der Borg, J. (1988) 'Piu lontani, piu cari', *CoSES Informazioni*, 32/33, 57–64.

UNESCO (1968) *Report on Venice*, Paris.

Van den Berg, L., Van der Borg, J. and Van der Meer, J. (1995) *Urban Tourism*, Aldershot: Avebury.

Van der Borg, J. (1991) *Tourism and Urban Development*, Amsterdam: Thesis Publishers.

Van der Borg, J. (1994) 'Demand for city trips', *Tourism Management*, 15, 66–9.

Van der Borg, J. Costa, P. and Gotti, G. (1995) *Tourism and Art Cities, Venice*, UNESCO Venice Technical Report, No 20.

Van der Borg, J., Costa, P., and Gotti, G. (1996) 'Tourism in European heritage cities', *Annals of Tourism Research*, 2, 23, 306–21.

Van der Borg, J. and Russo, P. (1997) *Indicatori per lo Sviluppo Sostenibile del Turismo a Venezia*, Fondazione Mattei.

Section III
Tourists and space in the city

Introduction

This section looks at the way that tourists and the tourism industry use the spaces in and around the city. This can have profound effects upon not only the tourism product but also the city itself, the way that the various functions of the city are perceived by its residents, the perceptions of the historic city by tourists and also the power relations between various users of the city (Hall, 1997).

A knowledge of the use of space is useful both to those planning the tourism product and to other functions, such as residential communities, of the city. The way that the city, or sub-areas of it, are perceived by different groups is also useful to know when trying to establish mitigating measures (Evans, Chapter 10) to reduce inter-user group conflict, and when trying to re-image an area so that local users are not alienated from a destination within their own city (Dodson and Kilian, Chapter 8).

The section starts with a consideration, by Dodson and Kilian, of the effect of the dockland redevelopment in the City of Cape Town, South Africa. Tracing the history of the docks, they show how land uses have become redundant and how new uses for the land and water not only bring new people to the area but also change the whole nature of this quarter of a city, overlaying a post-modern land use of spectacle, commodification, modern culture and ambience on top of remnants of the old industries. This itself brings conflicts of use, but also heightens the profile of the area as it takes on new symbolic meanings for both the tourist and residents of the city. Dodson and Kilian give a clear profile of the processes that the city authorities went through in creating this post-modern space, and some of the consequences of such re-imaging.

Chapter 9, by Hughes, discusses how various areas of cities are adopted by tourist sub-markets. He takes as a case study the gay quarters of Amsterdam, describing how each quarter attracts a different type of gay tourist. More importantly, he analyses the qualities and characteristics of the city that have led to this phenomenon occurring, and clearly links the culture of the city and its reputation to the nature of the use of space. So far from tourism shaping the nature of the city, as in the Dodson and Kilian study, Hughes shows how the city and the political and social milieu of the city have helped to shape the tourism product.

It is known that the marketing arms of government and private enterprise project a particular image of a destination which they believe will attract the tourist.

However, image and reality often diverge on the tourist's arrival. Evans explores the relationship between expanding suburbs and the Giza Plateau, while Dodson and Kilian explore the changing perceptions of space by various sectors of the Cape Town community, some of whom have discovered the new post-modern lesiure space and others who feel excluded from it.

Finally, in Chapter 10 Evans considers how the city is used by different groups of tourist and residents. She takes the Giza Plateau, Cairo, as her case study and considers how a framework of primary and secondary uses (Burtenshaw et al., 1991) can help to identify potential conflicting uses and hence appropriate visitor management techniques. In cities where heritage and residential needs often sit cheek by jowl such techniques could be useful in assessing future management needs. Indeed Evans shows that Cairo, and the Giza Plateau in particular, are used in different ways by different groups. She questions, therefore, the wisdom of a UNESCO management plan whose sole purpose is to manage the site as mono-functional antiquities/heritage destination, without giving due weight to the needs of other users' requirements of that space. Evans calls for wider consideration of user group interests to help develop more sensitive and sustainable plans for such sites of world importance.

Little research has really been undertaken to establish how tourists use, perceive and interact with city space, or what it is that they are looking for in the physical and psychological fabric of the city. These three chapters, each taking a different perspective on the issue of space, help to develop key ideas of ownership, perception, sub-group use, user conflict and space manipulation.

References

Burtenshaw, D., Bateman, M., and Ashworth, G.J. (1991) *The European City: A Western Perspective*, London: David Fulton.
Hall, C.M. (1997) 'The politics of heritage tourism: place, power and the representation of values in the urban context', in P. Murphy (ed.), *Quality Management in Urban Tourism*, Chichester: Wiley, 91–103.

8 From port to pl...
the redevelopmer...
Victoria and Alfred
Cape Town

BELINDA DODSON and DARRYLL KILIAN

CHAPTER SUMMARY

The global phenomenon of waterfront redevelopment is one manifestation of contemporary spatial restructuring. Wider processes of capital accumulation and maritime technological change as the key driving forces behind the transformation of waterfront places in countries around the world form the context to an understanding of the revitalisation of Cape Town's historic Victoria and Alfred Dockland. Together with a model developed by Pinder, Hoyle and Husain (1988), these theoretical constructs assist in explaining the factors that resulted in the establishment, evolution, redundancy, abandonment and eventual renewal of the Victoria and Alfred Waterfront (V&AW). Commodification and spectacle-isation are identified as the key forces underpinning the planning, design, development and operation of the V&AW. The creation and continual consolidation of a carefully styled post-modern harbourscape catering to the leisure tastes of locals and tourists alike are shown to be at the heart of the Victoria and Alfred Waterfront's success – effectively placing the development at the forefront of South Africa's tourist industry. The redevelopment has, however, not been entirely uncontroversial. Tensions and conflicts have arisen over the use of space and meaning of place in the Waterfront.

Introduction

One of the symptoms of the contemporary restructuring of geographical space is the phenomenon of waterfront redevelopment. Historic dock areas, once scenes of bustling harbour activity, later obsolete and neglected, have recently been transformed into multi-purpose centres of consumption and leisure. Such a development

Managing Tourism in Cities. Edited by D. Tyler, Y. Guerrier and M. Robertson.
Copyright © 1998 John Wiley & Sons Ltd.

...ertaken in Cape Town's Victoria and Alfred Basins (V&A) ...rder to elucidate the processes underlying and driving this world-...menon, along with their particular manifestation in Cape Town, this ...first examines the history of Table Bay harbour in the context of economic ...d technological change. This analysis helps to explain the processes which resulted in turn in the establishment, development, redundancy, abandonment and recent redevelopment of the Victoria and Alfred Waterfront (V&AW) – now a well-established destination on the South African tourist route. Once this historical context has been established, discussion turns to a theoretical account of the phenomenon of waterfront redevelopment before looking in detail at the Cape

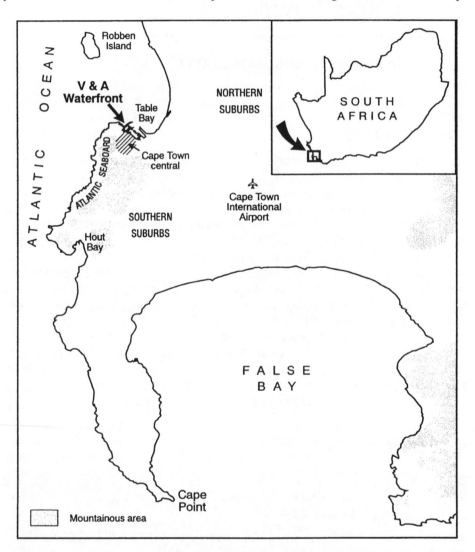

Figure 8.1 Map showing the position of the Victoria and Alfred Waterfront in Table Bay Harbour and the adjacent Cape Town city centre with its surrounding suburban districts at the southern tip of Africa. Reprinted with permission

Town case. The chapter concludes by considering the users (or consumers) of the waterfront today, questioning whether it is indeed a 'people-friendly destination'.

Tracing the morphological and functional development of Table Bay Harbour: from primitive port to modern harbour complex

Table Bay has been a port of call ever since the African continent was first circumnavigated by the Portuguese navigator Bartholomew Diaz in 1488, but it was not until 7 April 1652 that an expedition under Jan van Riebeeck went ashore at Table Bay to establish a replenishment base for Dutch East India Company (DEIC) ships. Despite the obvious importance of this settlement to Company operations, Table Bay long remained a primitive port, the DEIC proving unwilling to invest capital or labour in the construction of any significant port infrastructure (Figure 8.2, frame 1). Following losses of ships, people and cargo to winter storms, the DEIC eventually sanctioned the construction of a 'mole' in 1743 (Anon., 1967). It was 1831, 25 years after the British takeover of the Cape, before further harbour works were implemented. The sharp increase in the number of vessels calling at the Cape necessitated the construction of further jetties in 1838, 1842 and 1850, and eventually, in 1857, the construction of a 'safe, accessible and quiet harbour' was considered warranted (Anon., 1967 : 1). As Van Rooyen (1991 : 7) explains:

> It took two centuries and the loss of more than 2000 lives to shipwrecks in Table Bay before a concerted effort was made to protect ships in the bay – even then it was due more to the economic realities of the day than to humane considerations that the decision to build a breakwater was taken.

The governor, Sir George Grey, 'anticipated objections to the cost of the breakwater from Queen Victoria and ingeniously invited her second son, Prince Alfred, to inaugurate the scheme' (Van Rooyen, 1991 : 7). The tipping of the rocks for the construction of the breakwater was duly carried out on 17 September 1860 by Prince Alfred (V&AW Company, 1992a : 4). On 11 July 1870, ten years after construction commenced, the Alfred Basin was ceremonially opened, Prince Alfred again doing the honours (Van Rooyen, 1991) (Figure 8.2, frame 2). Although a major civil engineering feat for its time (Petersen, 1978), the adequacy of Alfred Basin was already being eclipsed by the dramatic changes in shipping technology with the conversion from sail to steam. With this conversion came a reduction in sailing time and a growth in economies of scale, making steam-driven vessels more competitive than sailing ships. By 1880, the Alfred Basin was unable to accommodate the large iron steam vessels which were increasingly being used on the Asian and African trade routes. Together with the growing number of ships calling at the Cape, this required the further enlargement and elaboration of harbour facilities.

Temporarily postponed due to a slump in trade, work on the new (outer) Victoria Basin started in 1886 (Figure 8.2, frame 2). Its construction represented a massive financial investment over a period of 19 years. Work progressed slowly until the discovery of gold in the Transvaal, but as the gold boom increased the flow of people and supplies through Cape Town, the pace of construction was stepped up. The commencement of the Anglo-Boer War in October 1899 had a similar

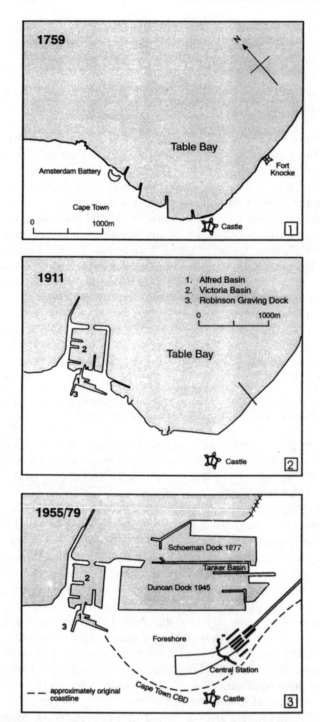

Figure 8.2 The spatial development of Table Bay Harbour showing the establishment, evolution and functional segregation of the Victoria and Alfred Dockland. (Source: adapted from Wiese, 1981 : 88–9)

effect, placing a strain on the already overburdened harbour facilities. Completed in 1905, the Victoria Basin, together with its predecessor the Alfred Basin, constituted the core of the current redevelopment and was called the Victoria and Alfred Waterfront.

Despite the additional quayage and sheltered water, the Victoria Basin was soon unable to meet the ever-increasing demand of shipping at the Cape. Yet given that a great deal of capital had been invested in its creation, the state was not willing to finance immediately the construction of larger harbour facilities. By the 1930s, expansion in the size and number of ships made existing port facilities inadequate, and in 1939 construction of the Duncan Dock commenced. To achieve the required depth and dimensions, the Duncan Dock was built nearly a kilometre out to sea (V&AW Company, 1993/4). This involved the reclamation of 480 acres of land between the old sea wall and the new extended quay (Pinnock, 1989) (Figure 8.2, frame 3). Development of a tanker basin and the Ben Schoeman Basin, a deep-water container terminal (Figure 8.2, frame 3), made the Victoria and Alfred Basins increasingly peripheral to harbour operations.

Redundancy and revitalisation

The spatial realignment of capital investment in the construction of the Table Bay port complex inevitably accelerated the underdevelopment of the V&A Docks and the adjacent maritime quarter. Unable to offer adequate facilities for the rapid throughput of cargo and accommodation of large modern vessels, the V&A port nucleus became functionally segregated from the expanding port system (Figure 8.2, frame 3). These shifts profoundly affected the traditional utilisation of space in the urban waterfront precinct. A functional 'vacuum' steadily developed, whereby land and water areas, customs sheds, warehouses and transport facilities formerly essential to the Table Bay port and its city became increasingly underutilised. Nevertheless, the V&A Docks remained important to the fishing industry which began to expand into the largely vacant Victoria Basin from the mid-1970s onwards (Sturgeon, Ward and Schwartz, 1990).

Continued V&A port underutilisation, coupled with a decline in the number of vessels calling at Table Bay during the early 1980s, provided the impetus to re-development initiatives. 'Commercial development and privatisation', writes Worden (1992 : 2), 'was now [mid-1980s] seen as a desirable way of developing state and municipal land [as] the working areas of the Victoria and Alfred Basins were in a greater state of decline'. Encouraged by successful port redevelopments elsewhere in the world, and with pressure from the media, the public and the Cape Town City Council (CCC) (1985a), the Minister of Transport Affairs established a committee under the chairmanship of Arie Burggraaf, then Inspecting Engineer – Harbours, to make proposals for redevelopment (V&AW Company, 1992a). Completed in 1987, the Burggraaf Report made 'bold and imaginative recommendations for the development of the Waterfront', causing 'ripples of excitement throughout the Cape tourist industry when ... released a year later' (Schafer, 1992 : 3). It supported the CCC proposals for a staged process of redevelopment, to include the restoration of historic harbour buildings and the creation of restaurants, a fish

market, an exhibition centre, shops, offices, hotels and a leisure boat marina, all
supported by parking facilities.

   The establishment in November 1988 of a wholly owned subsidiary of South
African Transport Services (SATS), called the Victoria and Alfred Waterfront
(V&AW) Company, signified the start of a public sector initiative to attract capital
back to the underdeveloped dockland areas of Cape Town (De Tolly, 1992) (Figure
8.3). Before going on to discuss in detail the nature and history of the redevelopment, it is necessary first to set out the theoretical foundation on which that discussion is based.

Theorising waterfront redevelopment: from uneven development to flexible accumulation

In many respects, the phenomenon of waterfront redevelopment is a classic example of the uneven development characteristic of capitalism. Attempting to overcome the immobility of the built environment, capital uses complete mobility as a
'spatial fix', 'see-sawing' geographically from a developed to an underdeveloped
area, and later switching back to the first area, now underdeveloped due to lack of
investment (Smith, 1984). In this way, capital uses uneven development to stave off
the crisis of dropping profits.

   This see-sawing action is clearly evident when assessing the process of port-land
redundancy and revitalisation, as modelled by Pinder, Hoyle and Husain (1988).

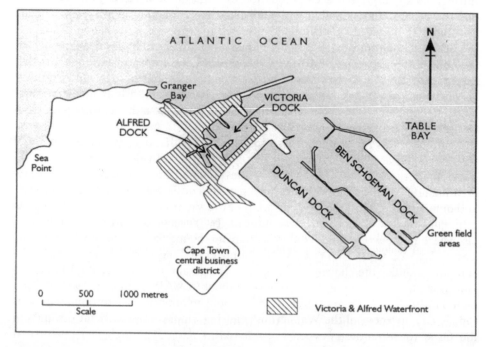

Figure 8.3   Layout of the Table Bay port complex indicating the location of the Victoria and
Alfred Docklands. (Source: adapted from V&AW Company, 1989 : 3)

Their model is represented in Figure 8.4. As the model indicates, global competition and de-industrialisation, together with maritime technological forces, have resulted in a retreat of capital from traditional waterfronts and in consequent maritime-quarter decline. With the subsequent dereliction and employment decline comes an eventual recognition by the port and city authorities of the problem of redundant and underdeveloped space. Their response to this recognition is often a 'spatial fix' – the revitalisation of underutilised harbour precincts. Given that local authorities are responsible for the cityport's urban fabric, in many ports the scale of dereliction, coupled with a lack of commercial enthusiasm, has demanded that cityport authorities place port decline on their agendas.

As a result, cityport authorities have attempted to reverse private sector apathy towards investment in the underdeveloped dockland areas. This has generally been achieved with the help of provincial and governmental grants (Pinder *et al.*, 1988). 'The state', explains Tweedale (1988 : 190), ' "primes the pump" by putting forward grants to cover aspects of the schemes which are unprofitable, enabling derelict industrial land to be cleared and serviced'.

> The contemporary international phenomenon of waterfront redevelopment, wherever it occurs and whatever form it takes, nearly always involves some form of public expenditure by local, regional or central government. In fact, the internationally prescribed model for waterfront redevelopment used in Australia, the United States, Canada, the United Kingdom and other European countries is for public-sector money to be used as a stimulus for private-sector investment (Church, 1988 : 199).

By accepting the risk and initiating development, cityport authorities have been instrumental in getting commercial interests to view redundant urban land not simply as exhausted assets but as areas with great profit potential (Pinder *et al.*, 1988). The initial investment by the local authorities in, for example, site clearance and preparation (Church, 1988), as well as the preservation and conservation of historic buildings (Pinder *et al.*, 1988) has greatly contributed to the dissipation of negative perception barriers. Thus private entrepreneurs and developers, in partnership with cityport authorities, have actively begun to speculate in derelict inner-city and port areas (Clark, 1988), turning them into sites of tourism and cultural consumption.

Another role taken on by cityport authorities has been the formulation of the broad strategy and framework for waterfront redevelopment:

> Public authorities have also frequently been instrumental in initiating the search for appropriate revitalisation strategies. Typically, this role has entailed fostering a local dialogue between potential actors in the revitalisation process . . . a learning process based on the emergent strategies of other (sometimes foreign) cityports. There is no shortage of reports by delegations despatched to investigate other cities' strategies . . . (Pinder *et al.*, 1988 : 253).

Commonly, '[t]he planning assumption is that this early framework is essentially a starting point to be revised and developed in the light of changing circumstances, such as rising commercial interest, assessments of past achievements and changes in the supply of unused waterfront land' (Pinder *et al.*, 1988 : 256). As a result, many

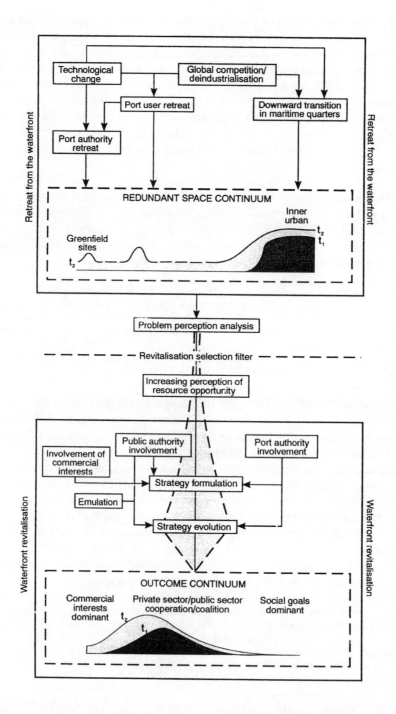

Figure 8.4   A model depicting the forces and trends which typify waterfront retreat, redundancy and revitalisation. (Source: Pinder, Hoyle and Husain, 1988 : 249)

redevelopment programmes are based on flexible 'incremental' planning rather than a 'rational-comprehensive' approach (Pinder *et al.*, 1988).

In order to understand fully the motives for port redevelopment, we need to return to the heart of capitalism, namely the process of capital accumulation. In addition to the forces and processes of uneven development outlined above, waterfront redevelopments can also be viewed as a manifestation of the regime of flexible accumulation (Harvey, 1989). Increased flexibility of capital has resulted in dramatic shifts in the patterning of uneven development, both between sectors and between geographical regions. In consequence, as Britton (1991 : 468) elaborates:

> Urban-region managers, in alliances with corporate, labour, and citizen groups have been anxious to position their territory to attract [a] mix of corporate, services, leisure, and consumption functions. Where this strategy has been taken, it has coincided with, or been legitimated by, other vital urban issues of urban management: the revitalisation of downtown areas in the face of competition from large suburban shopping malls; . . . to . . . large inner-city transition zones of derelict warehouses, ports, and factories rendered obsolete through changing technology . . .

Increasingly, therefore, an entrepreneurial ideology has directed urban governments to create a favourable environment that would attract capital to their respective cities. Given the intense inter-urban competition for position as centres of consumption, waterfront renewal projects, convention centres, sports stadia and Disneyworlds have emerged in rapid succession in cities across the world (Harvey, 1989). The 'leapfrogging' of these consumer-based developments from city to city has not only assisted the transition to flexible accumulation but has also helped to establish a post-modern urban culture in which eclecticism and spectacle are the hallmarks of both design and lifestyle.

The commodification and 'spectacle-isation' of place

Within this regime of flexible accumulation, certain places and sites (such as derelict waterfront areas) have increasingly become the target of urban managers, and more recently capital, because of their physical, social, cultural, and commercial attributes (Britton, 1991). And it is through 'the use of a particular place', assert Logan and Molotch (1987 : 18), that capital 'creates and sustains access to additional use values'. As a result, the material, spiritual and psychological aspects of places and sites have, to a greater or lesser extent, become commodities to be developed, exchanged, and ultimately exploited through a process of commodification. Britton (1991 : 462) identifies two generic forms of commodification:

> . . . first the legal recognition or transfer of commercial property rights involving ownership or lease of a site itself (a building, recreation site, or beach); or second, where the attraction cannot be privately appropriated directly, the inclusion of the touristic experience or attributes of place into saleable commodity (a tour, the ambience of a hotel in close proximity to a significant site, souvenirs, or symbolic image with recognisable connotations).

Both forms of commodification allow places, by virtue of their unique qualities, to provide opportunities for urban authorities and capital (either separately or in partnership) to capture rent and profits (Britton, 1991). To take advantage of new, flexible accumulation opportunities, and pursue and corner the spending power of the affluent middle classes (Harvey, 1987, 1989), places have increasingly been transformed into what Lefebvre (1976) refers to as 'leisure spaces'.

This trend is clearly evident in revitalised historic waterfront sites. The 'commercialisation of these historical areas and replacement of "authentic" lifestyle' is, according to Pistorius (1994), an obvious attempt to 'attract tourists with a superficial display of tradition'. By investing in aesthetic (symbolic and cultural) aspects of place, urban governments and capital, in the form of large commercial property speculators and corporations, have been able to sustain and strengthen the rents and value of local property (Logan and Molotch, 1987). In turn, this has meant the ideological reinforcement of capital's commitment to (re)development and (flexible) accumulation (Harvey, 1989). In several instances, therefore, the demand for symbolic and cultural capital has done much to transform prevailing inner-city built environments and their predominant economic and social relations. Britton (1991 : 470) captures this transformation in the context of inner-city gentrification, as in the case of urban renewal projects and the rehabilitation of old dockyards:

> The retail base is transformed and complemented with outlets serving demand from buyers of art and culture as well as tourists attracted by boutique shops and preserved architecture. Property values soar and draw new rounds of investment. . . . In the end, the enhancement and rejuvenation of the architectural environment in combination with the transformation of the social and economic milieux, creates a coherent space of consumption which signals both the appropriation of the inner city by the upper classes, and a particular interpretation of what constitutes fashionable symbolic and cultural capital . . .

The appropriation and 'mystification' of symbolic and cultural capital has resulted in 'the recuperation of "history" . . . and of "community", and the need for embellishment, decoration, and ornamentation' (Harvey, 1989 : 269). As it is impossible to separate subjective symbolic and cultural meanings from their physical contexts, the co-option of symbolic and cultural capital has inevitably meant the further commodification of place. In most instances, places have been assimilated into the flexible accumulation process as tourist commodities. Advertising, packaging, and marketing are the primary mechanisms employed in the 'production' of tourism. 'The purpose,' argues Britton (1991 : 464), 'is to persuade the consumer, the tourist, that by purchasing a particular product (a stay in a certain hotel, visit to a destination, taking a tour), she or he will receive more than the product is capable of delivering'. Thus by marketing places as desirable products, public-private sector alliances are able to 'package and sell' (to the post-modern tourist) place-specific sensations, feelings and perceptions (Feiffer, 1985). The commodification of place represents one of the most recent and flexible avenues whereby aesthetic aspects of place are integrated into the overall system of capitalist accumulation (Jameson, 1984).

We turn now to a consideration of the second manifestation of flexible accumulation: the mobilisation of place as spectacle. For Britton (1991 : 471), the urban spectacle or festival is 'designed to attract not just local residents, but domestic and especially international tourists' for the purposes of post-Fordist consumption. The process of 'spectacle-isation' has been effected through the use of post-modern architecture employed to enhance the display of a particular tourist attraction or place. Indeed, post-modernism as both style and attitude has become central to the success of the spectacle or festival. Due to the ability of these spectacles to attract crowds, entire built environments have been transformed into 'centerpieces of urban spectacle and display' (Harvey, 1989 : 271).

As one of the most 'recent development[s] in the integration of tourism with [post-Fordist] consumption' (Britton, 1991 : 471), redeveloped waterfronts such as those in London, Sydney, Toronto, Baltimore and Hong Kong have become common phenomena. The proliferation of these waterfront spectacles attests to the fact that tourists (be they local or international) want to spend their money in a place that offers not only pleasure and entertainment (Harvey, 1989), but a post-modern urban landscape of pavilions and plazas, shopping malls and leisure centres. Thus, rather than exhibit an outdated and discredited modernist architectural style, cities' downtown areas are increasingly imbued with images of festival and spectacle, performing in essence the well-tried formula of 'bread and circuses' (Cloke *et al.*, 1991 : 183). 'It is on this terrain of the spectacle,' writes Harvey (1989 : 71), 'that the break into the post-modern urban culture . . . has partially been fashioned', effectively drawing the distinctive qualities of place into the centre of a regime of flexible accumulation. As we now go on to demonstrate, the recent (and ongoing) structural transformation of the Victoria and Alfred Waterfront provides a perfect example of these processes in operation.

The redevelopment of the Victoria and Alfred Waterfront

From its very beginnings, the V&A development epitomised the planning context and strategies modelled by Pinder *et al.* (1988): maritime-quarter decline; selective 'filtering' of redundant dockland space; public sector investment initiative leading to private sector involvement; and flexible and incremental physical planning. With a management team headed by David Jack (a former town planner for the Cape Town City Council) and a board of directors representing a cross-section of public interests, the V&AW Company was able to galvanise public sector involvement in the formulation of the development strategy. The establishment of a liaison committee by the Minister of Transport Affairs on 11 August 1989 ensured the participation of key public and commercial institutions. These new alliances not only fostered greater interest in the underdeveloped Victoria and Alfred Docklands, but enhanced capital's flexibility with respect to future private sector investment.

The development framework (V&AW Company, 1989), a strategy formulated in conjunction with the Cape Town City Council, outlined the company's planning *modus operandi*, providing a general overview of their intentions regarding the development of the Waterfront. It formed part of a hierarchy of plans, the 'package of plans', established to 'guide the planning, services and financial matters . . . [jointly] agreed to by the Waterfront Company and the CCC' (V&AW Company, 1989 : 3). Modelled on the Planned Urban Development (PUD) approach of the

United States, the 'package of plans' provided a systematic approach by which to undertake flexible and incremental (and thus post-modern) planning. The 'package of plans', together with the Legal Succession to South African Transport Services Act allowing for the re-zoning of land use in the 83.2-hectare development site from April 1990 onwards (V&AW Company, 1993/4), gave the V&AW Company the planning and regulatory tools required to transform the V&A Docklands.

The development framework enabled the identification and resolution of broad development objectives at the precinct plan scale. The aim of identifying precinct plans was to break away from the existing monofunctional use of land, and to establish a mixed-use development which included retail, hotels, entertainment, museums, offices and restaurants, thus typifying post-modern planning. The central tenet of development flexibility underscored the company's planning ethos: 'To make the historic harbour a very special place for Capetonians and visitors' (V&AW Company, 1989 : 1). This ethos points to the V&AW Company's intention to commercialise the harbour's existing aesthetic and historic attributes (collectively referred to as symbolic capital) to create an environment for touristic consumption and urban spectacle.

With the precedent of a great number of successful port redevelopments around the world, Cape Town's city and port authorities decided to emulate the post-modern planning strategies applied in these international waterfront schemes. Local representatives visited various waterfront schemes in North America and Europe to familiarise themselves with their planning strategies and architectural styles. David Jack, Managing Director of the V&AW Company, led many of these information-gathering excursions. For him existing waterfronts were an admitted model for the Cape Town development:

> I have been interested in waterfronts and marinas for about 20 years now, since my final project at UCLA which was on a marina. Since then, and particularly over the last four years I have visited a number of waterfronts each year. . . . There are two groups that are emerging in America that have the management expertise: the Rouse Company and the Enterprise Development Company. The centres developed by these two groups are still doing very well because they have an intimate knowledge of waterfronts and an attitude to these that is quite different from other commercial developers. . . . We noted the key factors that we considered to be responsible for the success of these two groups . . . (Jack, 1991 : 5).

Determined to ensure the success of the Victoria and Alfred redevelopment, the V&AW Company set about implementing a combination of globally established, post-modern planning strategies. Incremental planning allowed for the phased and flexible development of the dockland site, while the existing harbour structures were retained to add the necessary 'authenticity'. Most dockland revitalisation schemes have, to a greater or lesser extent, emulated the development strategies of earlier redevelopments, resulting in the physical and functional replication of waterfront redevelopment projects worldwide. The physical similarity of maritime port structures (warehouses, sheds, quays, cranes, bollards, etc.) further reinforces this sense of sameness. As Basil Davidson, African National Congress (ANC) spokesperson on planning, remarked: 'the V&A doesn't have a Cape Town flavour. Its Victorian architecture could be anywhere' (personal communication, 1992).

In its attempts to co-opt existing symbolic and cultural capital, the V&AW Company began to restore and market buildings of historic significance. Its restoration of the historic buildings in the vicinity of the Pierhead – the Harbour Master's Residence (1860), Clock Tower (1887), Port Captain's Office (1903), and Union-Castle House (1918) – aimed to attract those 'businesses who wanted buildings with character' (Jack, 1991 : 5). The company, as part of its overall post-modern planning package, was thus able to commodify the sensations and feelings evoked by the Pierhead's historic buildings. Not surprisingly, therefore, one of the first site-development projects involved the renovation of the 1904 North Quay warehouse, a building in close proximity to these symbolic sites. Completed by the end of 1990, this renovated building was leased as a hotel (the Victoria and Alfred Hotel), restaurant and speciality shopping complex – a mixed-use complex typifying the form and style of the evolving post-modern waterfront. Since its opening, visitors staying in the hotel have been afforded the opportunity of experiencing the excitement and energy of a constantly changing working harbour environment. Thus, in a further manifestation of the process of commodification, the symbolism evoked by the working elements of the V&A Harbour (e.g. the ships, graving dock and synchrolift) have also become commodities for touristic consumption.

To attract private sector pecuniary backing, the V&AW Company (with SATS's financial help) continued to invest in the aesthetic, symbolic and cultural attributes offered by the Pierhead. As in the case of the heritage industry, the V&AW Company actively sought to retain (and enhance) the 'historic and cultural context of the waterfront' (V&AW Company, 1989 : 10). To this end, the company carefully recreated a historical maritime ambience of romance and spectacle. This is clearly evident in the Waterfront's award-winning audiovisual presentation at the visitor information centre:

> The city was the sea – the sea was the city. The city left the sea – it crept inland, it left the harbour to itself . . . it left behind some of the most beautiful buildings, romantic places . . . left behind the slap of water, the creak of rope, the groan of wood . . . Yet today a clock is being carefully turned back.

Through these processes of commodification, the V&AW Company has been able to appropriate 'symbolic capital', thus attracting both large numbers of visitors and much-needed entrepreneurial investment:

> Traders who opened their doors at the end of 1990 were visionaries; they identified with V&AW's goals and saw beyond the squalor and the chaos of construction. Those who adopted a wait-and-see attitude were convinced by the success which followed – seven million visitors in the first year (V&AW Company, 1992b : 27).

Encouraged by the success of initial developments and having acquired further funding from Transnet (formerly SATS), the company awarded a 112 million Rand contract for the construction of a new 26 500 m^2 shopping and entertainment complex (V&AW Company, 1992c), completed in October 1992 (Figure 8.5). Overlooking Quay 5 and the Victoria Basin, the Victoria Wharf building was orientated to best exploit 'the spectacular views of the docks and (gothic style) clock tower' (Karol, 1992 : 25). Designed to resemble a nineteenth-century Victorian transportation terminal, this 'post-modern' complex succeeded in 'spectacle-ising' the surrounding Victoria and Alfred Docklands. Its extended balconies allow people to observe the waterfront spectacle below and beyond (to the Pierhead), while the large promenade, with its multi-purpose amphitheatre situated in front of the Victoria Wharf, provides visitors with space to enjoy and, in most instances, to become part of the surrounding spectacle or festival (Figure 8.6). In testimony to the 'copy-cat' nature of waterfront developments, the complex bears a more than passing resemblance to Baltimore's Harbor Place (Figure 8.7). Extensions completed in 1996 have effectively doubled the provision of retail and entertainment space, and a large up-market hotel – its architecture a veritable model of post-modern pastiche – has recently opened on an adjacent site (Figure 8.8). These new structures dwarf the buildings of the historic Pierhead precinct that formed the original nucleus of the redevelopment.

Figure 8.5 Spaces of consumption: interior of the Victoria Wharf shopping centre. (Source: V&AW Company)

Figure 8.6 Spaces of spectacle: African cultural performance at the amphitheatre. (Source: V&AW Company)

Figure 8.7 Form and function at the post-modern waterfront: Victoria Wharf shopping centre, Cape Town. (Source: V&AW Company)

Figure 8.8 Merging and expanding of tourism and consumption: extension to the Victoria Wharf shopping complex and construction of the Table Bay Hotel. (Source: V&AW Company)

With public sector backing, the V&AW Company has been able to build the momentum needed to ensure private sector speculation in the V&A Docklands. Today, private entrepreneurs and developers in partnership with city and port authorities continue to develop ever-larger areas of underdeveloped dockland. Consistent with the dictates of flexible accumulation, the V&AW Company is spearheading further expansion, forging in the process a site that is at once a postmodern tourist centre of international significance and a leisure and retail centre for the residents of Cape Town. This dual market is no coincidence, reflecting the Waterfront's status as a nexus between the local and the global; a site where the global is localised and the local globalised. The Victoria and Alfred Waterfront, like so many other docklands across the world, has been refashioned into an environment of promenades, pavilions, shopping malls and leisure facilities, catering to the lifestyle tastes of the new middle classes.

Place and consumption

The discussion above has focused very much on the Waterfront as site, along with the structural forces controlling its physical and functional redevelopment. In this final section of the chapter, we turn to the consumers of the Waterfront, the tourists and local residents who go there to shop, partake in the range of available leisure activities, or simply 'hang out'. Once again, some theoretical exposition is necessary before the details of the local case study can be adequately explored.

Particularly pertinent to this discussion is the notion of the consumption of place. Long neglected in geographical (and sociological) research, the study of consumption has experienced a recent surge (e.g. Miller, 1995; Sack, 1992; Urry, 1995). In geographical terms, places are increasingly viewed as being consumed:

> First, places are increasingly being restructured as centres for consumption, as providing the context within which goods and services are compared, evaluated, purchased and used. Second, places themselves are in a sense consumed, particularly visually . . . Third, places can be literally consumed; what people take to be significant about a place (industry, history, buildings, literature, environment) is over time depleted, devoured or exhausted by use. Fourth, it is possible for localities to consume one's identity so that such places become literally all-consuming places. This can be true for visitors, or for locals or for both (Urry, 1995 : 2).

These intellectual developments are grounded in a changing reality, bound up in the global shift to a post-modern era, with its underpinnings of flexible accumulation and commodification (see the discussion above). Post-Fordist consumption, rather than Fordist industrial production, has become the driving force behind much urban development. But who are these 'post-Fordist consumers'? Jackson and Thrift (1995 : 207) note the 'symbiotic relationship between this new stage of commodification and particular social groups', with 'the new middle classes . . . as the cheerleaders for new forms of consumerism as they follow lifestyles that convert symbolic capital into economic capital and vice versa'. Yet the geographical outcome in the form of the consumer landscape, with its recycled buildings and postmodern architecture, is easier to identify and describe than the human agents whose lifestyles and consumer behaviour give it form and purpose.

Indeed, as Jackson and Thrift (1995 : 210) contend, 'geographers have tended to ignore the active roles of consumers in shaping contemporary consumer cultures'. Sack (1992 : 10), too, seeks to place consumers in a more central position in geographical analysis:

> Virtually everyone in the modern world, no matter how reluctantly and disdainfully, is of necessity a consumer and aware of the consumer's world, even if not inhabiting it fully. Moreover, as consumers of mass-produced goods, we all share the fact that we are (unwitting) agents jointly transforming the world.

Thus not only do people consume in places, but also, by the very act of consumption, they make and alter places, playing 'an active role as creative agents before, during and after the moment of purchase' (Jackson and Thrift, 1995 : 218). Actual consumers bring to the process and site of consumption different practices, values and perceptions, along with their different (and contested) identities. A place of consumption such as a shopping mall or redeveloped waterfront can be at once 'dynamic and liberating, an image of paradise, and also shallow and disorienting, an inauthentic pastiche' (Sack, 1992 : 221); the pleasures of consumption for some are countered by others' agoraphobia (literally 'fear of the marketplace'). Tourism, in some ways the most pure and complete form of consumption, contains similar, even exaggerated ironies, contradictions and ambiguities. But it is these 'very ironies and ambiguities that give contemporary consumer culture so much of its power and dynamism' (Jackson and Thrift, 1995 : 220).

Despite their centrality to an understanding of the consumption process and its geography, the voices of 'real' consumers are only now beginning to be heard in geographical and sociological studies of consumption (Jackson and Thrift, 1995). And if the 'target market' of the post-Fordist consumption-driven economy has received so little academic scrutiny, then how much less the people it excludes, marginalises or displaces; the 'old' classes who cannot afford to buy in to the gentrified post-modern city. What are their options for resistance to the rampant commodification of the urban landscape? Goss (1993 : 41–2) lists a number of tactics by which people can resist or reclaim spaces of consumption, from the passive resistance of simply not making any purchases to the more active reappropriation of space for purposes that exceed or conflict with those of the designers:

> Third is the struggle to open the shopping center to all activities consistent with public space, even those that may affront the sensibilities of the consumer or disrupt the smooth process of consumption . . . By confronting the rights of exclusion, encouraging the presence of undesirable activities, and challenging the legality of such rights in court, we can expose the ersatz and profoundly undemocratic nature of public space and the controlled carnival manufactured in the contemporary retail environment.

Far from being unproblematic reclamations of derelict space, therefore, gentrified inner-city and waterfront areas should be seen as places of contested meaning: sites of control and resistance; of inclusion for some and exclusion for others; of 'exploitation and empowerment . . . desire and dread' (Jackson and Thrift, 1995 : 221). As demonstrated in the discussion below, the Victoria and Alfred Waterfront represents just such a collection of contradictions and conflicts.

Consuming the post-modern waterfront: Who's consuming what? A survey of visitors to the Waterfront

The chapter now turns to an analysis of the V&AW Company's annual visitor survey undertaken between November 1996 and January 1997 (Douglas Parker Associates, 1997). Although visitors were interviewed at different times of day at sites throughout the Waterfront, the fact that the survey was conducted during peak tourist season means that results may not be truly representative of visitor profiles and consumption trends at the V&AW. They nevertheless provide important clues to the Waterfront's popularity as a centre of leisure and consumption.

The survey clearly showed that the V&AW attracts local residents as well as domestic and international tourists. It revealed an increase in 8% since 1993 in the number of foreign tourists visiting the Waterfront (16%). These originate mainly from continental Europe (22%) or the UK (32%) and account for 16% of visitors sampled. Of the 193 foreign tourists interviewed, almost half (47%) indicated that they were visiting Cape Town and the Waterfront for the first time. This together with the high incidence of repeat visits (with 26% of foreign tourists having visited the Waterfront before) supports V&AW Company claims of being an international tourist destination. In line with the company's express mission to establish a facility for locals as well as tourists, the survey also found that almost two thirds (or 66%) of the 1204 visitors interviewed were resident in Cape Town.

Respondents were mainly English speaking (67%) and single (55%), principally between the ages of 24 and 34 years. The survey highlighted some interesting gender and age differences between locals and tourists (domestic and international). A high percentage of tourists were male (55%) and above the age of 34 (46%), while 55% of the locals surveyed were female and 75% of locals were under the age of 34. Thus, in a clear example of flexible accumulation, the V&AW Company has created a multi-use leisure and retail environment, where older, wealthier leisure seekers from other parts of South Africa or abroad can rub shoulders with younger socially mobile Capetonians, who are in turn attracted by the cosmopolitan nature of the Waterfront. Visitors surveyed represent unambiguously the new middle classes to whom Jackson and Thrift (1995) refer. This is true almost by definition of the tourist market; but the profile of local visitors also locates them within this group. Some 40% of the locals interviewed were found to reside in the upmarket suburbs of the city bowl and Atlantic Seaboard (Figure 8.1), many of them (60%) indicating weekly visits to the Waterfront. They reported low average household size (under 3.5 people) and a decidedly white-collar career profile (management, professionals, students, etc.).

But why do people visit the Waterfront? Certainly, a prime attraction is the diversity of experience on offer – whether taking in and forming part of the spectacle or consuming the host of available goods and services (Figures 8.5 and 8.6). The greatest proportion of respondents (68%) stated that they visited the Waterfront to walk around the development browsing through the shopping area and craft markets, or merely to sit observing the comings and goings of other visitors and harbour activities. Apart from browsing, people were also attracted by leisure activities (18%), entertainment (34%) and shopping facilities (24%). The 1996 extensions to the Victoria Wharf shopping centre, apart from altering the geography of the Waterfront, have had a substantial economic impact, contributing to the marked increase in the number of visitors reporting shopping as an attraction (from a figure of 14% in 1994). Indeed it was earlier consumer surveys, reporting shopping as a major activity of Waterfront visitors, that motivated the developers to expand retail facilities. The ongoing process of redevelopment is thus very much consumer-driven and -shaped. Different groups of consumers have differing motives for coming to the Waterfront. Whereas visitors from city and Atlantic Seaboard suburbs were most likely to visit the Waterfront for the purpose of 'serious' (including household) shopping, other locals, mainly from the Northern and Southern suburbs (Figure 8.1), were more likely to be attracted by entertainment and leisure facilities such as cinemas, restaurants, cafés and bars. This can be ascribed to the existence of large multi-purpose shopping complexes in these latter areas, catering to the everyday needs of suburban residents.

Tourists, while also focusing their activities on the Victoria Wharf as the centre of consumption in the V&AW, were found to visit a wider spectrum of facilities and activities than in the past, when the Waterfront was smaller in extent with a less extensive range of facilities. Key attractions include: the IMAX Theatre complex (31%), Two Oceans Aquarium (25%), boat trips (21%), pubs and taverns (20%), craft market (36%) and Alfred Mall (34%). This diversification of the leisure and retail experience lies at the heart of the V&AW's success. Offered a choice of shopping and entertainment facilities within a post-modern harbourscape, visitors (be they locals or tourists) are almost certain to find something on which to spend their money and time. Other attributes, too, make the V&AW a visitor-friendly place. Apart from the appeal of its numerous promenades, plazas and other open spaces, the V&AW's success is based on factors such as service in shops and restaurants, safety, cleanliness and easy access. Respondents were asked to rate – on a scale of 1 (poor) to 5 (excellent) – the Waterfront's performance and standards in terms of each of these criteria. All received ratings of 4 and above, thus revealing why the redevelopment attracted over seventeen and a half million visitors in 1996 (V&AW Company, 1997).

Resisting consumption at (by?) the post-modern Waterfront

Despite (or perhaps because of) its patent commercial success, a number of con-flicts have arisen over the use of space and meaning of place in the Victoria and Alfred Waterfront. While some of these conflicts were essentially inevitable as one form of land use replaced (or displaced) another, other forms of competition, some specific to the social order of post-apartheid South Africa, have also led to tensions and dispute.

One of the primary sources of conflict has been the fundamentally geographical one over competition for use of land and water space. A claim of the developers, right from the earliest proposals, was that the Victoria and Alfred Basins were to continue to operate as a working harbour (Kilian and Dodson, 1996). Although this remains one of the selling points in the V&AW's publicity, the reality is rather less straightforward, for as the redevelopment has gained in momentum and prof-itability, it has expanded well beyond redundant space into what were the func-tional domains of an active fishing industry. So threatened were the various fishing companies operating in the area that they formed the Port of Cape Town Fishing Industry Association (POCTFIA) in order to enhance their bargaining power in negotiations with the developers. The utilisation of existing harbour space and, more specifically, questions of security of tenure and affordable rentals, remain points of dispute between the fishing industry and the V&AW Company. Although there is a transactional commitment to co-existence, the working harbour remains, at best, indifferent to the commercial development.

A second source of tension and conflict has been competition for consumers. The V&A Waterfront is widely perceived as having drawn customers away from two areas in particular: the Central Business District (CBD) and Atlantic Seaboard. Although little quantitative research has been undertaken to prove this perception, the success of the Waterfront has undeniably been contemporaneous with a decline in the CBD and Sea Point retail and restaurant precincts (Figure 8.3). Shopowners and restaurateurs from these areas are openly hostile towards the V&AW for having 'stolen' their customers, and in the early days of the waterfront redevelop-ment T-shirts bearing the spoonerised slogan 'Duck the Fox' were a common sight on the streets of Cape Town. With the combination of shops, restaurants, cinemas and other leisure facilities, the Waterfront provides a wider range of consumer experience than almost any part of Cape Town of comparable size and accessibility. The added attractions of its dramatic setting, maritime ambience, cleanliness and (especially significant) security make the Waterfront a consumer magnet drawing both local residents and tourists. In terms of the types of 'place consumption' identified above, the Waterfront combines at least two, being both centre of consumption and a place that is itself consumed, particularly in the sense of the 'tourist gaze' (Urry, 1990). The CBD and Atlantic Seaboard, plagued by problems such as litter, crime, prostitution and street children, have been hard pressed to compete.

Questions of racial and class exclusivity have dogged the redevelopment since its inception. For instance, while Worden (1992) challenged the V&AW Company's oversimplified, 'white' reading of the Waterfront's history, the press criticised the sanitised, middle-class character of the redevelopment itself (*South*, 1992). More recently, *The Argus* newspaper labelled the Waterfront a 'rip-off'. 'While overseas visitors don't yet seem to mind parting with their powerful yen, marks, dollars and pounds, many locals have begun to shun the Waterfront, disgusted by the huge discrepancy in prices there and other parts of the city' (*The Argus*, 16 January 1997).

In order to dispel perceptions of exclusivity, the V&AW Company has set about implementing strategies aimed at greater race and class inclusiveness. In addition to bussing in underprivileged children from the townships for entertainment and educational activities, the company has also erected information boards relating the stories of some of the convicts, sailors, slaves and dockworkers who represent the 'real' history of the waterfront (Bickford-Smith and Van Heyningen, 1994). Somewhat lost within an overpowering environment of conspicuous consumption, these boards are an interesting (if incomplete) addition to the Waterfront experience. There is particular irony in two components of the redevelopment when related to their past meaning and use. Near what was the site of some of the first racially segregated accommodation in South Africa, the black dockworkers' hostel, an upmarket marina housing development is to be constructed. Nearby, the Breakwater prison, 'home' to convicts whose labour built much of the structural fabric of the harbour, is now the University of Cape Town's Graduate School of Business. Clearly, commercial rather than social considerations are paramount.

A recent twist to these various tensions and contradictions has been the expression of anti-Waterfront sentiment by factions of the Muslim community of Cape Town. An anonymous flier, signed 'a few decent, militant unapologetic muslims' and distributed to a number of Cape Town households, denounced the 'zionist bourgeois media, zionist corporate/business/Waterfront sector', going on:

> Many people who live in townships like Khayelitsha, Manenberg, Guguletu etc. never have the time nor the money to visit the Waterfront. They either do not have the money to visit the Waterfront, and/or they are too preoccupied with bread and butter issues i.e. they work their backs off so that they can provide sustenance for their hungry children. This so-called demise of Apartheid and the promise of a land of milk and honey has unfortunately not reached them yet – it has only reached the zionists and their allies – it is no mystery who they are (A few decent, militant unapologetic muslims, 1997 : 2).

Part of the anti-Waterfront feeling among the Muslim community stems from a specific incident in late 1996. The predominantly Muslim organisation People against Gangsterism and Drugs (PAGAD) held a march at the Waterfront to protest at the lack of official response to gang-related crime in the largely coloured townships of the Cape Flats. The very selection of the Waterfront as a site of protest action is significant. Disrupting the smooth operation of consumption in a setting purposely isolated from the crime and poverty encountered in other parts of Cape Town was a deliberate strategy, designed to force a response from civic authorities and to focus public attention on PAGAD's cause. The strategy trag- ically misfired. A PAGAD marcher was fatally shot during the march, and although PAGAD claims that the shot came from the police, it seems more likely that it came from the weapon of another marcher. Far from attracting sympathetic atten- tion from the wider Cape Town community, the march served to enhance anti- PAGAD sentiment on the part of both public and police.

The PAGAD incident can be read as an example of the 'reclaiming' of a space of consumption for activities consistent with public space yet antithetical to the pur- poses of the designers (Goss, 1993). Certainly it 'affront[ed] the sensibilities of the consumer [and] disrupt[ed] the smooth process of consumption' (Goss, 1993 : 41). So alarmed was the V&AW Company at this threat to its profitability that it included questions on the PAGAD incident in its annual user survey; but any disruption to holiday-season leisure and consumption appears to have been both minimal and short-lived. Nothing, it seems, can seriously disrupt the 'controlled carnival' (Goss, 1993 : 42) that attracts both local and overseas visitors to the Wa- terfront in ever-increasing numbers.

Conclusion

The Victoria and Alfred Waterfront is undoubtedly one of the great economic success stories of South Africa. In the context of Cape Town, the redevelopment signifies the most recent step in a process of harbour evolution spanning three centuries. Whereas wider processes of capital accumulation and technological change were the key driving forces behind the rise and fall of the historic V&A Dockland, its current refashioning, consistent with the dictates of more flexible regimes of capital accumulation, is underpinned by processes of commodification and spectacle-isation. In keeping with global trends, the V&AW Company has systematically commodified the area's aesthetic, symbolic and cultural attributes – thus transforming Cape Town's old dockyards into a landscape of consumption and spectacle. This has been achieved using the flexible and incremental planning strategies that have proved so successful at other waterfront redevelopment schemes around the world. The underdeveloped harbour area has been transformed into a neo-Victorian pleasurescape which, however inauthentic, attracts locals and tourists alike. Yet the Waterfront's redevelopment has not been without tension and dispute. In addition to conflict with the working har- bour over the use of land and water space, the V&AW Company has had to face charges of social and racial exclusivity. Such problems notwithstanding, the Wa- terfront continues to draw large numbers of visitors – Capetonians and tourists, buyers and browsers, gazers and gazed upon – to its quintessentially post-modern ambience.

Acknowledgements

Earlier versions of parts of this chapter were published in the *South African Geographical Journal*: Kilian, D. and Dodson, B.J., (1995) 'The capital see-saw: understanding the rationale for the Victoria and Alfred redevelopment', *SAGJ*, 77(1), 12–20, and Kilian, D. and Dodson, B.J. (1996) 'Forging a postmodern waterfront: urban form and spectacle at the Victoria and Alfred docklands', *SAGJ*, 78(1), 29–40.

Our thanks go to Sue Sayers for preparing the illustrative material for this chapter and to the Victoria and Alfred Waterfront Company for the use of their slides and the results of their 1996/1997 visitor survey.

References

Anon. (1967) *The History of Table Bay Harbour*, publisher and place of publication unknown.

Bickford-Smith, V. and Van Heyningen, E. (1994) *The Waterfront*, Cape Town: Oxford University Press.

Britton, S. (1991) 'Tourism, capital, and place: towards a critical geography of tourism', *Environment and Planning D: Society and Space*, 9, 451–78.

Cape Town City Council (1985a) *Development Potential of Cape Town's Historic Waterfront*, Cape Town: City Engineer's Department.

Cape Town City Council (1985b) *The Development Potential of Cape Town's Historic Waterfront*, Cape Town: City Engineer's Department.

Church, A. (1988) 'Demand-led planning, the inner-city crisis and the labour market: London Docklands evaluated', in B.S. Hoyle, D.A. Pinder and M.S. Husain (eds), *Revitalising the Waterfront: International Dimensions of Dockland Redevelopment*, London: Belhaven.

Clark, M. (1988) 'The need for a more critical approach to dockland renewal', in B.S. Hoyle, D.A. Pinder and M.S. Husain (eds), *Revitalising the Waterfront: International Dimensions of Dockland Redevelopment*, London: Belhaven.

Cloke, P., Philo, C. and Sadler, D. (eds) (1991) *Approaching Human Geography*, London: Paul Chapman.

De Tolly, P. (1992) 'Cape Town's central waterfront', *Architecture SA*, 3, 23–6.

Douglas Parker Associates (1997) *Annual Study: Victoria and Alfred Waterfront*, Cape Town, February.

Feiffer, M. (1985) *Going Places: The Ways of the Tourist from Imperial Rome to Present Day*, Chicago: Macmillan.

Few decent, militant unapologetic Muslims (1997) 'An important message', flier distributed to Cape Town households.

Goss, J. (1993) 'The "magic of the mall": An analysis of form, function and meaning in the contemporary retail built environment', *Annals of the Association of American Geographers*, 83(1), 18–47.

Harvey, D. (1987) 'Flexible accumulation through urbanisation: reflections on "postmodernism" in the American city', *Antipode*, 19, 260–86.

Harvey, D. (1989) *The Urban Experience*, Oxford: Basil Blackwell.

Jack, D. (1991) 'Waterfronts in perspective', *Environment, Planning and Management*, 2, 5–13.

Jackson, P. and Thrift, N. (1995) 'Geographies of consumption', in D. Miller (ed.), *Acknowledging Consumption: A Review of New Studies*, London: Routledge.

Jameson, F. (1984) 'Postmodernism, or cultural logic of late capitalism', *New Left Review*, 176, 53–93.

Karol, L. (1992) 'Getting the very best', *The Waterfront Review*, 2, 23–6.

Kilian, D. and Dodson, B. (1996) 'Between the devil and the deep blue sea: functional conflicts in Cape Town's Victoria and Alfred Waterfront', *Geoforum*, 27(4), 495–507.

Lefebvre, H. (1976) *The Production of Space*, Oxford: Basil Blackwell.

Logan, J.R. and Molotch, H.L. (1987) *Urban Fortunes: The Political Economy of Place*, Berkeley: University of California Press.

Miller, D. (ed.) (1995) *Acknowledging Consumption: A Review of New Studies*, London: Routledge.

Petersen, S.T. (1978) *The development of the Table Bay Harbour 1860–1870*, Unpublished honours thesis, Department of History, University of Cape Town.

Pinder, D.A., Hoyle, B.S. and Husain, M.S. (1988) 'Retreat, redundancy and revitalisation: forces, trends and a research agenda', in B.S. Hoyle, D.A. Pinder and M.S. Husain (eds), *Revitalising the Waterfront: International Dimensions of Dockland Redevelopment*, London: Belhaven.

Pinder, D.A., Hoyle, B.S. and Husain, M.S. (eds) (1988) *Revitalising the Waterfront: International Dimensions of Dockland Redevelopment*, London: Belhaven.

Pinnock, D. (1989) 'Ideology and urban planning: blueprint of a garrison city', in G.J. Wilmot and M. Simons (eds), *The Angry Divide: Social and Economic History of the Western Cape*, Cape Town: David Philip.

Pistorius, P. (1994) 'Postmodernism and urban conservation', *Architecture SA*, 5, 28–35.

Sack, R.D. (1992) *Place, Modernity and the Consumer's World*, Baltimore, MD: Johns Hopkins University Press.

Schafer, P. (1992) 'The man who saw it all', *On the Waterfront*, 2, 3.

Smith, N. (1984) *Uneven Development: Nature, Capital and the Production of Space*, Oxford: Basil Blackwell.

South (1992) 'Waterfront: yuppie themepark – or plek for all people', 20–24 June.

Sturgeon, K., Ward, S. and Schwartz, N. (1990) *The Fishing Industry in Table Bay Harbour Victoria and Alfred Waterfront*, Cape Town: MLH Architects and Planners.

The Argus (1997) 'The unfairest Cape', 16 January.

Tweedale, I. (1988) 'Waterfront redevelopment, economic restructuring and social impact', in B.S. Hoyle, D.A. Pinder and M.S. Husain (eds), *Revitalising the Waterfront: International Dimensions of Dockland Redevelopment*, London: Belhaven.

Urry, J. (1990) *The Tourist Gaze*, London: Sage.

Urry, J. (1995) *Consuming Places: A Review of New Studies*, London: Routledge.

V&AW Company (1989) *Development Framework Report III*, Cape Town: MLH.

V&AW Company (1992a) 'The essence of the waterfront', *The Waterfront Review*, 2, 4–5.

V&AW Company (1992b) 'Waterfront update', *The Waterfront Review Supplement*, 2.

V&AW Company (1992c) 'Development news', *The Waterfront Review*, 3, 7–9.

V&AW Company (1993/4) 'The first five years', *The Waterfront Review*, 4, 1–12 (section one).

V&AW Company (1997) *The Waterfront – the visitors' guide 1997*, Cape Town: V&AW.

Van Rooyen, G. (1991) *The Waterfront: Cape Town*, Cape Town: Belmor Group.

Wiese, B. (1981) *Seaports and Port Cities of Southern Africa*, Wiesbaden: Franz Steiner Verlag.

Worden, N. (1992) 'Unwrapping history at the Cape Town waterfront', paper presented at History Workshop Conference: Myths, Monuments and Museums, University of the Witwatersrand.

Personal communications

Davidson, B. (1992) Regional Executive of the African National Congress (ANC) and the Development Action Group (DAG), August 1992.

V&AW Company PR and Marketing Division (1997) May.

9 Sexuality, tourism and space: the case of gay visitors to Amsterdam

HOWARD L. HUGHES

CHAPTER SUMMARY

Amsterdam is a very popular centre for gay visitors though those visitors are a minority visitor group. The consequence is a number of distinctive gay leisure clusters. This use of space is, in part, a means of confirming sexuality for gays and has transformed the physical appearance of parts of the city. This spatial transformation also contributes to the 'alternative culture' image of the city adding to its general tourism appeal even though its tourist assets are ostensibly cultural and historical. The case study investigates the attributes of Amsterdam that make it appealing to this group of tourists, and how different parts of the city have been adopted by different sub-sets of the gay tourism market.

Spatial transformation

The focus of this chapter is the appropriation and use of space by male homosexual tourists to Amsterdam. (The discussion is limited to males, also referred to as 'gay' men.) The aim is to determine the form and extent of this spatial transformation and the implications both for tourism in the city and for gay life. Tourist motives and activities are diverse and this study will contribute towards an understanding of the heterogeneity of tourism.

In using the space of urban areas tourists transform that space in both the material and symbolic sense (Ashworth and Dietvorst, 1995). The physical presence of the tourist alters the atmosphere and appearance of a location (material transformation); the very act of being there means space is being appropriated, sometimes resulting in overcrowding and wear and tear. In addition, certain places become regarded as 'tourist' places through interpretation by tourists (symbolic transformation). There is, however, little research about activities of the tourist that enables study of this transformation process to occur; 'cities can make accurate estimates of numbers and nature of visitors but only have the vaguest idea of what

Managing Tourism in Cities. Edited by D. Tyler, Y. Guerrier and M. Robertson.
Copyright © 1998 John Wiley & Sons Ltd.

they actually do in the city' (Ashworth, 1989 : 44). The actual behaviour of any one tourist or category of tourist over the duration of a trip is not well researched. Such analysis requires complex research techniques (Ashworth, 1989) and must deal with mixed and changing motives of tourists. Cooper (1981) and Debbage (1991) attempted to determine 'tourist activity space' – the spatial pattern of facilities used, activities undertaken, and the order and duration of these – through the monitoring of tourist behaviour. Data collection has usually relied, at least in part, on self-completion diaries; this requires the active cooperation of the tourists.

All tourists transform the space they occupy but, in the case of gay tourists, transformation is the consequence of a group of people who are marginalised in society. The transformation thus has the potential for alienating other tourists. The transformed space may, however, enhance the tourist resource base of the destination both in terms of visits to such space by the 'curious' general tourist and by contributing to a 'disreputable' part-image that some cities cultivate. Such an analysis is fraught with added problems associated with a particular 'squeamishness about exploring these connections' (Knopp, 1995 : 150); there is a 'sensitivity' about researching matters relating to sexuality (Binnie, 1994).

Urban space is, however, recognised as having particular significance in (*inter alia*) studies of sexuality. Gays and lesbians, for instance, use space to adopt separate identities. The gay identity is often adopted away from home and the workplace. Discrimination against gays has encouraged them to find their identity in the leisure sphere. Urban areas facilitate the assumption of a gay 'self' in many ways not least through the number and concentration of gay leisure places available. The gay identity is represented and formed by activity outside work in a space that is 'not of our own choosing' that is defined by business (Dyer, 1992); it is formed in a 'space of consumption' through the purchase of leisure activities and the usage of space for leisure purposes. Such leisure-related freedom has been widely embraced as a validation of gay identity if only as a reaction to a more general powerlessness (Binnie, 1994). The very use of space may have the effect of transforming that space so that it becomes coded as gay (Knopp, 1995). Tourism by gays and lesbians may be the ultimate manifestation of the use of space in order to separate identities.

The tourist activity space of gay men may seem to centre around sexual encounter, thus influencing the spatial transformation in a particular way. Examination of the gay press generally and its advertisements confirms this impression of a sex-holiday relationship. The copy of operator's brochures reinforces the sex aspect with references to nudist beaches, cruising (pick-up) places and the like. The best-known gay travel guide, *Spartacus*, is explicit in including sections on places in individual destinations where other men can be 'picked up'. Sexual encounters are, however, infrequently commercial and most are consensual encounters with locals or other visitors without payment. In this respect most sex aspects of gay travel are unlike 'sex-tourism' associated with prostitution. For Evans (1993) the defining characteristic of gay tourism is sexual activity but the reality remains under-researched. There is a strong body of opinion and some evidence to suggest that when on holiday, sexual norms of heterosexuals are relaxed (Clift and Page, 1996; Hall, 1994; Ryan and Kinder, 1996) but 'there are surprisingly few research studies concerned with gay men, travel and sexual behaviour' (Clift and Wilkins, 1995 : 44). In some respects this is of little consequence as 'the significance of holidays for gay men lies in their contribution to the process of establishing identity' (Hughes, 1997 : 4).

Tourist clusters

Tourism in a city is related to a combination of its primary (or core) and secondary elements (see Table 9.1). The primary elements, those which constitute the major attractions have, in turn, two components: 'activity place' and 'leisure setting' (Jansen-Verbeke, 1986). The 'activity place' is composed of the attractions that characterise most cities such as museums, art galleries, historic sites and buildings and theatres whereas the leisure setting is the physical and social–cultural context within which the attractions are set: the overall spatial structure of the city and its ambience. The urban attraction can often be character and atmosphere that amount to more than simply the physical structures. Jansen-Verbeke's secondary elements include shops, cafés, restaurants and bars, hotels and entertainment. Primary elements that are proximate to each other, as clusters, may have a greater appeal to the tourist than do non-proximate elements (Jansen-Verbeke, 1994). Several tourist clusters, spatially separate and with distinct features, may exist in a city to give it 'polycentricity' (Ashworth and Tunbridge, 1990). Often these clusters are associated and interconnected spatially and functionally and together constitute a critical mass as 'tourist recreation complexes' (Dietvorst, 1995). It is a relatively easy prospect to 'catalogue' and describe such tourist resources though there are conceptual and operational difficulties associated with this (Ashworth, 1989).

The identification of clusters ultimately depends on tourist use, usually by analysing particular elements and assessing tourist activity in each. The elements themselves are usually used by both tourists and local residents. This multi-use adds to analysis problems – few facilities are exclusively tourist – as does the fact that tourists are multi-motivated.

Suppliers of tourist services may also cause a city, in whole or in part, to be transformed, both materially and symbolically. The existence of bars, hotels, restaurants and the like 'code' the city as tourist and alter its image; it is subject to symbolic transformation as well as material transformation. Places become positioned and constructed as 'sites of pleasure' (Shields, 1991). A place imperceptibly

Table 9.1 Tourism products of Amsterdam

Primary (core) elements	*Secondary elements*
Historical	Shopping
including buildings, canals and	Cafés
urban morphology	Bars
Cultural	Coffee shops
including museums and lifestyle	Restaurants
Outdoor recreation	Hotels
including parks	Entertainment
	Red-light District

Based on Jansen-Verbeke (1994)

becomes a 'place-for . . .'. A visitor's image of a city is likely to be restricted to a few marked sights and the 'tourist city' is likely to correspond to a limited area of the city (Burtenshaw *et al.*, 1991).

Tourism in Amsterdam

Amsterdam, with a population of about 720 000, is the largest city in the Netherlands. It is a port-city whose development during the seventeenth century owed much to trade. The tourist-city is only a small part of the whole metropolitan area and is bounded to the north by the waterfront from which it is now isolated by the railway station and tracks. Its spatial morphology is semi-concentric shaped by the canal system linking the interior of the city to the waterfront.

As a tourist city, Amsterdam ranks as of one of the major destinations in Europe, although a second-tier one (Bywater, 1994). A study by van den Berg *et al.* (1994) identified the city as a 'classic' or 'best-selling' city. This was on the basis that the city was one of only 19 cities (out of 92) that were offered in travel brochures in six or more European countries. In terms of tourist arrivals it ranked fourteenth in Europe in 1991 with 1.7 million.

Amsterdam plays a major tourist role in the Netherlands: it has about 17% of all visitor beds in the country, though a much higher proportion of hotel beds. The Netherlands and Amsterdam appear to be particularly attractive to UK tourists. The city is the second most popular city-break destination (after Paris) (Carr, H., 1995). Amsterdam is served by a major international hub airport and there are scheduled flights to Amsterdam from 22 British cities. An added attraction for UK visitors is that English is widely spoken.

Amsterdam's tourist product is related to its 'historical image and the compactness of the urban morphology' (Jansen-Verbeke, 1994 : 356) (see Table 9.1). The old city centre has been preserved and within this setting 'a number of public attractions have developed into an urban cultural product' (Jansen-Verbeke and van de Wiel, 1995 : 137). A wide range of museums, art galleries (particularly associated with Rembrandt and van Gogh) and historic monuments are part of the primary elements. The 'historic' city is largely represented by the area around Dam Square with a cultural quarter to the south of the city centre. The unique canal network and canal-side houses (tall, narrow and gable-fronted) are themselves a major core attraction. It is this 'urban ensemble' as a whole rather than any impressive individual building that is the attraction of the city (Ashworth and Tunbridge, 1990). The view of Amsterdam as a cultural and historical centre but with an abundance of restaurants, bars and entertainment is affirmed in the brochures of UK tour operators. Amsterdam is a relatively small city, it is spatially compact and the major attractions are within walking distance of each other.

Amsterdam has a reputation for being a free and open city. It has great cultural diversity and considerable tolerance has been extended towards different ways of life from around the world and towards alternative lifestyles. 'It has an image as an entertainment and fun place' (O'Loughlin, 1993 : 59) derived from the 1960s sex and drugs culture. Possession of drugs is illegal but personal consumption of marijuana is tolerated in designated coffee-shops. This all makes it an attractive place to live and to visit, especially for younger people.

Amsterdam's reputation for liberalism is, in part, responsible for it being in a 'precarious position in the big league' (Ashworth and Tunbridge, 1990 : 181; see also Jansen-Verbeke and van de Wiel, 1995). This liberal reputation is one that the tourist boards are anxious to dispel. A poster of a joint-smoking van Gogh, part of a Eurostar campaign, was withdrawn after protests from the Netherlands Board of Tourism (NBT) (Lowing, 1996).

The more notorious aspects of Amsterdam, especially the sex industry, do feature as an attraction in some tour operators' brochures. The Red-light District is very close to Dam Square and makes a significant contribution to an image of 'excitement' for tourists whether or not they use its services (Ashworth et al., 1988). It is not, however, referred to at all in the NBT brochure. The availability of drugs is rarely mentioned by tour operators or in guidebooks though the latter are rather more likely than tour brochures to refer to the sex and drugs culture, especially guidebooks aimed at the young independent traveller.

Reference to gay and lesbian life in Amsterdam is limited in conventional brochures and guidebooks though it is cited as evidence of the vitality and freedom of the city in some. There is no reference at all in the brochures of the main operators nor in the NBT brochure. It is similarly ignored by travel writers and by academic commentators and researchers: see Jansen-Verbeke's model. The *Insight Guide* does, however, describe the city as 'second only to San Francisco in its social acceptance of homosexuality . . . The city has a number of recognisable gay districts' (Catling, 1991 : 151).

A number of approaches for collecting material for this chapter were considered. Despite the 'sensitivity' of issues relating to sexuality, approaches such as interviews, questionnaires and self-completion diaries are commonly used (see, for instance, Coxon, 1996). For this case it was considered more appropriate to derive data by observation and from primary 'documents' such as brochures and guidebooks and secondary material such as research papers and research reports.

Gay tourism in Amsterdam

Brochures and guides

There are a number of guidebooks and brochures which relate specifically to gay and lesbian tourism and to Amsterdam in particular. Destinations covered in brochures of UK tour operators catering for the gay men's market are mainly associated with sun, sea and sand. Several also offer city destinations such as Paris, Prague, Barcelona and New York but the most frequently offered is Amsterdam.

In one such brochure (*Sensations*) Amsterdam is referred to as 'a mind-blowing city' with reference to the attractions of the gay scene but none to the conventional attractions of Amsterdam. *The Man Around* brochure also refers to little else other than 'the scene' which is described as 'excellent and will cater for all of your needs'. It is rated as 'the number one gay and lesbian city break destination'.

The other conventional attractions of Amsterdam are, however, mentioned in the *Uranian* brochure; the city is also described as 'the gayest city in Europe . . . (with) . . . a red hot nightlife which is world renowned for wild and free expression'.

Gay Times, a monthly 'serious' news and lifestyle magazine (stocked by W.H. Smith), has regular features on gay destinations. The tone and content of the last report on Amsterdam (Carr, J., 1995) reflects the preoccupations of tour operators' brochures. 'It is extremely hard not to pick people up . . . Offers a whole network of the sort of sex-oriented venues that we still lack at home . . . The city's scene is still hot'. *Gay Times* also, in its advertising section, devotes a permanent section to Amsterdam. This is the only foreign destination treated in this way with the obvious implication regarding the city's popularity with British gays.

Travel guides aimed at gay travellers invariably identify Amsterdam as an important gay destination. One of the most comprehensive gay guides to Amsterdam is the *Best Guide* (Crawford, 1994). About half is devoted to extensive general information. The remaining 100 or so pages provide gay information including listings and descriptions of accommodation, bars, clubs and discos, saunas, brothels, escort services and cinemas. Here the tone is frequently on sexual activity; the availability of condoms at particular venues is clearly identified. Various facilities are described as having 'a cruisy reputation', as having 'a notorious cellar'. Visitors are advised that they can 'enjoy a little action in the back seats' of a cinema and 'further adventures in the dimly-lit showers' may be sought in a sauna.

A gay tourist map of Amsterdam (published by the health education organisation SAD-Schorerstichting) is widely available in the city and identifies gay venues such as bars, discos, coffee-shops, hotels, restaurants and shops. The names of venues where 'condoms for anal use are available' are printed in bold lettering. The same group also publishes a small booklet *Gay Tourist Information* in which is the statement: 'the city has cannabis, 24 hour saunas, plentiful back-rooms, wild leather parties, heavy pornography and legal brothels. Naturally you'll want to try at least one of the above during your stay . . . Play safe!'

There would appear to be, in gay-oriented material, a definite association of Amsterdam with gay sex; it is claimed by Duyves (1995 : 60) that 'the international interest of gay tourists in Amsterdam's gay life is intense but limited and directed at satisfying their needs immediately'. It is clearly difficult to demonstrate that sexual encounter (commercial or otherwise) is or is not a significant reason for the visit to the city but the Netherlands undoubtedly has a more liberal approach to homosexuality than have many countries. Unlike the UK, for instance, there are no gay-specific sexual offences and the age of consent is 16. There is, ostensibly, greater toleration of gay life-styles resulting in Amsterdam having 'one of the most sophisticated and developed lesbian and gay communities and commercial scenes of any city of its size anywhere in the world' (Binnie, 1995). A letter in the Dutch *Gay News Amsterdam* (September, 1996, p.2) from two English visitors summarises the attraction of Amsterdam for many: 'we did something we've never done before . . . We walked down the street holding hands'. There is also a significant number of gay amenities reflecting the liberal attitude towards homosexuality. This liberal atmosphere combined with the ease of access to the city from the UK accounts for the popularity of the city as a gay tourist destination.

Gay tourists

The number of gay tourists is not known precisely but it has been estimated that
there were about 55 000 (male) gay visitors in Amsterdam over the year 1992–3
(staying visitors only) (Meershoek *et al.*, 1996). This represents about 4.4% of the
total number of tourists in the city. This figure was derived in an indirect way; a
comprehensive visitor study was undertaken by the Amsterdam Tourist Office
(VVV Amsterdam, 1994) and gay respondents were 'identified' as those who were
male and who had visited a gay 'attraction' or place during their stay. (There is also
a significant economic dimension to gay tourism. The city tourist office has estimated that about 12% of the jobs in Amsterdam's tourist sector can be attributed
to gay tourism: Meershoek *et al.*, 1996.)

Some key characteristics of these gay tourists are shown in Table 9.2. The gay
tourist is apparently younger, better educated and a more frequent visitor to
Amsterdam than is the 'average' visitor. There is a higher proportion of gay visitors
from 'GB and Ireland' than is the case for other visitors. These are the 'single' most
important source of gay visitors to the city.

The gay visitor is apparently less of a cultural tourist than is the general visitor
and is more a hedonist (see Table 9.3). He is more likely to go to discos, bars,
coffee-shops, theatres and less likely to visit museums and galleries than is the
average visitor. A (limited) hotel survey confirms that the gay scene was the main
reason for the visit (Meershoek *et al.*, 1996). In particular, evening activities were
likely to be focused on gay venues and space.

Gay space

Gay space exists throughout Amsterdam but there are a number of 'gay clusters'
which are the outcome of both residents' and tourists' behaviour. Although it is
estimated there are about 21 500 gay and bisexual adult men in Amsterdam

Table 9.2 Characteristics of tourists to Amsterdam

	All staying visitors	*Gay staying visitors*
Appreciation of visit (max. score 10)	7.9	9.2
Number of visits in last 3 years (average of 'repeat' visitors)	10.1	16.3
	% of each category of visitor	
	All staying visitors	*Gay staying visitors*
Age 21–40	62.9	75.2
From 'GB and Ireland'	18.9	22.4
Higher education completed	59.6	66.1
Visit alone	21.7	36.2

Sources: Meershoek *et al.*(1996); VVV Amsterdam (1994)

Table 9.3 Activities of tourists to Amsterdam

| | % of each category of visitor engaging in each activity | |
	All staying visitors	Gay staying visitors
Dining out	73.5	72.4
Shopping	68.0	78.4
Sightseeing	67.0	62.9
Museums, galleries, etc	64.0	56.0
Dancing, discos, cafés, bars	42.0	69.8
Coffee-shop (soft drugs for sale)	28.0	40.5
Theatres, concerts	16.8	31.8
Visit to Red-light District	36.0	44.8

Sources: Meershoek *et al.* (1996); VVV Amsterdam (1994)

(Duyves, 1995) it is likely that these gay amenities would not exist in present numbers if not for the tourists to the city. There is not a gay residential concentration in Amsterdam such as there is in San Francisco. There are, though, spatial concentrations of gay amenities around four centres (see Figure 9.1): Warmoesstraat, Reguliersdwarsstraat, Amstel and Kerkstraat. Each has its own distinct character, performing a different function and being frequented by a different 'clientele'. These spaces are leisure-spaces and are on the margins of the 'conventional' centres for entertainment: Zeedijk (and Red-light District), Leidseplein and Rembrandtplein.

The gay cluster that general visitors are most likely to encounter is at Warmoesstraat (see Figure 9.2). This 'scene' is the one most likely to be associated by heterosexuals with homosexual activity. It is close to the Red-light District and visitors will invariably come across it in making their way to that District. Its proximity to the District codes it in a particular way, possibly as a place to pass through rather than to dwell too long. The street is narrow and in one of the oldest districts of the city. It is not entirely 'leather' but is predominantly so; there are a number of leather bars and leather shops and also hotels, cinemas and sex shops. The street is explicitly and specifically gay – with almost a 'ghettoish' feel. The cluster is possibly the most isolated of the four and has less relationship with the others and the rest of the city; this in itself may be an attraction. There is limited gay activity during the day and a rather unwelcoming air with some places shut and shuttered. It is busy with pedestrian tourist traffic and not too threatening, however. At night it can appear more 'threatening' in part because of the traffic of leather-clad men. Bars and clubs are frequently open all night and have dark-rooms for sexual activity.

A second cluster, the Amstel cluster, comprises gay bars and hotels on the Amstel waterfront and around Rembrandtplein. This square has a number of non-gay hotels, bars and restaurants and is a focus of considerable general tourist activity. Gay space tends to be off the main tourist cluster rather than on the square itself. The gay cluster is much less readily identifiable as gay than is Warmoesstraat. The cluster is virtually indistinguishable from the rest of the city and is well integrated into the city fabric (see Figure 9.3). It is patronised by general tourists who are

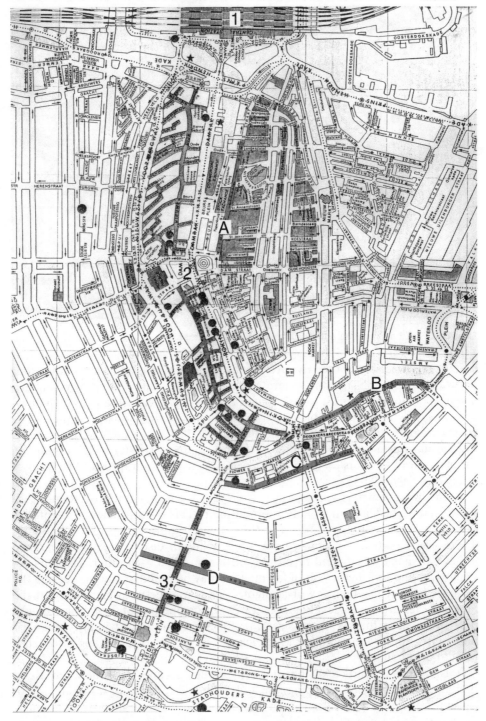

Figure 9.1 Amsterdam and its gay tourism clusters: A Warmoesstraat, B Amstel, C Reguliersdwarsstraat, D Kerkstraat

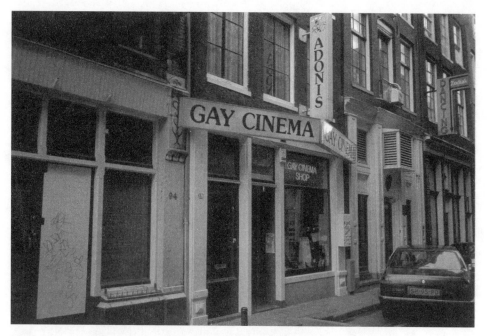

Figure 9.2   Adonis cinema and bookstore, Warmoesstraat

seeking the experience of the riverfront and associated views and some of the older
bars of Amsterdam. The atmosphere in the gay bars is summed up by comments
about 'foot-stomping sing-a-longs' though this is not the case in all bars. The bars
are open, friendly, comfortable and traditional and attract a mixed clientele. The
clients are more likely to be aged over than under 30. There is, in addition to these
bars, a 'sub-cluster' of two or three bars which are more sinister with a reputation
for 'predatory hustlers . . . waiting to be ogled by their prospective clients'
(Crawford, 1994 : 223).

A further distinct gay cluster exists in the western stretch of Reguliersdwarsstraat which leads off from Rembrandtplein. This is a much newer manifestation of gay space. It tends to serve the younger, more fashion-conscious gay.
There are a number of bars, coffee-shops, cafés, a disco and underwear and
swimwear shops, all situated favourably with respect to each other. The bars are
minimalist and stylish, the sort of facility that may be found in any city serving the
younger market whether gay or straight. This is a direction which many of the
latest gay leisure space developments through Europe have taken. The whole is
much more open than Warmoesstraat; the frontages are large windows and glass
doors integrating street and bar (see Figure 9.4). Decor, external and internal, is
bright but subdued.

It is not on a particular tourist route though it does lead between Rembrandtplein and a main shopping street (Leidsestraat). It is not a threatening or
sinister area and is particularly open and has a youthful and modish air about it.
There are no sex shops or gay cinemas. It is a fairly narrow street and vehicular
traffic is restricted so that in fine weather, in particular, the street becomes very
much gay space.

Figure 9.3 Amstel Taverne, the oldest gay bar in Amsterdam

The fourth cluster, Kerkstraat, is also off Leidsestraat but further south, close to Leidseplein. Leidsestraat is a shopping street heavily patronised by tourists; Leidseplein is similarly a significant general tourist leisure space: cafés, bars, restaurants, hotels, and on-street entertainment. Kerkstraat is a pleasant open street which, like Reguliersdwarsstraat, is not particularly frequented by general tourists. It is a mixture of Reguliersdwarsstraat-type coffee-shops and the Warmoesstraat-type sex shop, gay cinema, bars and a 'night' sauna. (There is 'day' sauna a few blocks away.) There are also four gay hotels here including the oldest gay hotel in the city. A number of buildings are of the older front-gabled narrow Amsterdam style and are generally discreet but some street frontages make explicit the gay orientation of the street. The sauna is completely anonymous and its presence would not be noticed by the unknowledgeable. Some gay tourists are believed to spend little time elsewhere but Kerkstraat, staying in a gay hotel, visiting day or night sauna and gay cinema and bar (Meershoek *et al.*, 1996). There is a clear functional relationship between these venues.

Amsterdam is polycentric with respect to gay leisure facilities but the spatial connectivity, in terms of proximity, between the gay clusters is generally good. With

Figure 9.4   April Bar, Reguliersdwarsstraat

respect to function it appears that the clusters are more isolated and many gay visitors confine themselves to one of the clusters during the visit. The outcome of the hotel survey referred to earlier was that gay tourists to Amsterdam could be classified into three groups each representing about a third of the total: 'leather', 'atmosphere' or 'sex' tourists (Meershoek *et al.*, 1996). The 'leather' tourist was predominantly from North America and was interested in the Warmoesstraat leather scene. The 'sex' tourist, mainly from the UK and Ireland, was the most frequent visitor to Amsterdam and was interested primarily in finding sexual activity in the Kerkstraat area. The 'atmosphere' tourist was more likely to be from Germany, was younger and his interest was around the Reguliersdwarsstraat area, though he was the least spatially focused of all. The 'leather' tourist appeared to be the least integrated and the 'atmosphere' tourist the most integrated into Amsterdam city life.

A number of other gay services are scattered throughout the city. Two brothels, for instance, are outside the four clusters but are within easy walking distance of them. The long-established Blue Boy is situated on a broad boulevard almost directly across from the Holiday Inn Crowne Plaza Hotel. This is not a tourist leisure area but is a main traffic thoroughfare. The frontage, while discreet, is unmissable. The Boys Club 21 is close, above the Man to Man cinema, and offers a similar range of services. It is advertised as being 'just around the corner from the Renaissance Hotel and the Holiday Inn Crowne Plaza' (*Gay News Amsterdam*, September 1996, p.10). 'Escort services' contactable by phone are also widely advertised.

Outside the clusters there are a number of other gay-run and gay-friendly bars and restaurants and several gay bookshops which stock a large number and variety of fiction and non-fiction works. A significant non-commercial focus of gay attention is the Homomonument. This is a memorial dedicated, in 1987, to all homosexual men and women over the world who have been oppressed or persecuted. It is striking, without being prominent or obvious, and is in a highly public place en route to the major tourist attraction of Anne Frank's house. The development in Amsterdam of an international exhibition and information centre on homosexuality has been suggested to strengthen its position as a gay centre (Meershoek *et al.*, 1996). This, linked with further developments on Utrechtsestraat, could result in a 'Gay Circle' (Amstel, Reguliersdwarsstraat, Kerkstraat and Utrechtsestraat) a concept that could be used in promotional activity.

The gay scene in Amsterdam includes events many of which are likely to have a tourism dimension, especially the annual Roze Wester Festival on the Queen's birthday. Recent events have included Europride 1994 and, in 1996, the Gay Pride Weekend and Leather Pride. The former was promoted by the Gay Business Association, itself only formed in 1995 in order to revive flagging tourism in the city. The 5th Gay Games, last held in New York in 1994, are to be held in Amsterdam in 1998 and are expected to attract 12 000 participants and up to 100 000 visitors (Meershoek *et al.*, 1996).

Conclusions

Amsterdam is a popular tourist destination for gay men. The city has been both materially and symbolically transformed by gay attention. There is no gay residential concentration as such but there are a number of distinct gay leisure clusters that are strongly associated with tourism. The city is materially transformed by the existence of these concentrated clusters of gay facilities and by the usage of these facilities and of public space by gay men. The facilities are, generically, little different from any other leisure or tourist facility – bars, cafés, restaurants, saunas, brothels, discos, etc. – but their particular form is occasionally distinct (such as leather bars). The clusters are clearly 'signed' as gay though some are more obviously gay than are others. There is no attempt to obscure the gay orientation; all clusters have, at least, a number of rainbow flags flying. Most of the clusters, and other individual elements of the gay scene, are indistinguishable components of the urban leisure fabric. There is little that is out of character; the material manifestation of gay life is occasionally 'sleazy' but this is confined to those parts of the city where it is to be expected. Activities rarely conflict with the rest of the city life, either of residents or tourists; most occurs 'inside'. When it does become external (on-street social life or street events) this is regarded as no more than a part of the liberal atmosphere of Amsterdam. Most gay venues, as leisure venues, are night-time oriented. This adds to the vibrancy and animation of the city's night scene though as a consequence the clusters are 'dead' areas during most of the day.

Symbolic transformation is evident in the labelling of Amsterdam as the 'Gay Capital of Europe' (Duyves, 1995). The city is identified by gays worldwide as a centre for gay life and is perceived as a gay-friendly place where gay life-styles go unremarked. As a consequence, it has a strong appeal to many from outside the country and is a popular place to visit. The content of *Gay Times* and tour operators' brochures suggests that it is a centre for urban tourism by gay men from the UK. Gay tourists from 'GB and Ireland' are also the most important 'single' category of gay visitor to the city.

The existence of gay tourism in Amsterdam illustrates the diversity of tourism and diversity of motives and activities of tourists. The core elements of the Amsterdam tourist product for the gay tourist do not coincide with the core elements identified by Jansen-Verbeke. The secondary elements of her model become the core elements of the gay tourism model (see Table 9.4). Additionally, there are elements which do not feature in Jansen-Verbeke's model. Space is used by gays to fulfil needs and for activities that are different from those of general tourists. Amsterdam performs a vital role in validating gay identity, enabling gays to be themselves and in providing opportunity for sexual encounter. Gays are empowered through the consumption of leisure and appropriation of space. The opportunity for encounters and the experiencing of a liberal atmosphere are core elements of the gay tourism product of Amsterdam. The sexual encounter element may seem, from a consideration of the content of published material in particular, to be especially dominant.

Attempts by the tourist boards to promote Amsterdam as a gay centre have faltered. A number of advertisements were placed by VVV Amsterdam and NBT in upmarket gay journals in the United States during 1992. This campaign encouraged the view that gays would be welcomed in Amsterdam: the advertisements included copy such as the locals were people 'who respect your choices' (see the US magazines: *QW* 19 July 1992 and *Frontiers* 14 August 1992). Reference to nightlife, clubs and bars was discreet and there was an emphasis on the historical and cultural attractions of the city. This limited campaign was apparently successful in raising the 'visibility' of Amsterdam and in promoting a view of the city as a potential tourist destination (Meershoek *et al.*, 1996). It has not, however, been repeated. The idea of Amsterdam being promoted as a gay destination was not universally welcomed by tourist interests in the city (Binnie, 1995). Jeroen Saris, the Amsterdam Alderman responsible for gay and lesbian policy, has commented that 'we have to be careful about promoting Amsterdam as a purely gay destination. . . The average family tourist stays away' (Crawford, 1994 : 11).

Table 9.4   Gay tourism products of Amsterdam

Primary (core) elements	*Secondary elements*
Cafés	Historical
Bars	Cultural
Restaurants	Outdoor recreation
Discos	
Coffee-shops	
Entertainment	
Saunas	
Brothels	
Hotels	
Shopping	
Lifestyle	
Toleration	
Sexual encounter	

This failure to acknowledge the reality of Amsterdam as a gay centre leads Duyves (1995 : 64) to believe that 'the touristic promotion of the city threatens to mimic a city lying in state'. He considers that the opportunity to meet other people is one of the great attractions of Amsterdam; ways of life are as much reasons for visits to the city as are history and culture and should therefore be reflected in 'official' promotion.

There is nothing to suggest that spatial transformation by gay tourists has adverse effects. The resident population of Amsterdam has long had a reputation for tolerance (though there is less willingness currently to tolerate some of these freedoms). General tourists are, in large part, unaffected by the material manifestations of gay tourism – bars, clubs, etc. These are not dominant features of most mainstream tourist activity space. Additionally, tourists are not given the opportunity to be affronted by a gay image of the city even though they may be aware of the reality. There is not the same willingness, in promoting the city, to recognise its gay aspect as there is to acknowledge even its 'sex and drugs' culture (however constrained that may be). The gayness of the city is not referred to in general promotional campaigns nor in mainstream tour operators' brochures or guidebooks. There may well, though, be widespread actual knowledge among general tourists of the gayness of Amsterdam and it may be an important implicit contributor to the city's overall image of 'excitement'.

Amsterdam is apparently a significant gay tourist centre and its related transformations are congruous with overall Amsterdam life and image; a number of research issues remain, however. Assertions about the relative importance of the city as an urban tourist destination for gays are not firmly based and reasons for and activities during the visit are known only hazily. The perceptions, knowledge and reactions of general tourists to the Amsterdam gay scene are not known with any accuracy and the consequences for general tourism of the existence of the gay clusters are unclear. The views and policies of VVV Amsterdam, NBT and the municipal government could be explored further. Gay tourism in Amsterdam is not actively encouraged or acknowledged by official bodies and its form, extent and significance for gay men are underresearched. It is a hidden aspect of Amsterdam's tourism; to misquote Lord Alfred Douglas, it is 'the tourism that dare not speak its name'.

References

Ashworth, G. (1989) 'Urban tourism: an imbalance in attention', in C. Cooper (ed.), *Progress In Tourism, Recreation And Hospitality Management*, Vol. 1, London: Belhaven, 33–54.

Ashworth, G. and Tunbridge, J. (1990) *The Tourist Historic City*, London: Belhaven.

Ashworth, G., White, P. and Winchester, H. (1988) 'The redlight districts of the West European city', *Geoforum*, 19, 2, 201–12.

Binnie, J. (1994) 'The twilight world of the sadoMasochist', in S. Whittle (ed.), *The Margins of The City: Gay Men's Urban Lives*, Aldershot: Arena, 157–69.

Binnie, J. (1995) 'Trading places, consumption, sexuality and the production of queer space', in D. Bell and G. Valentine (eds), *Mapping Desire: Geographies of Sexualities*, London: Routledge, 182–99.

Burtenshaw, D., Bateman, M. and Ashworth, G. (1991) *The European City: A Western Perspective*, 2nd edn, London: David Fulton.

Bywater, M. (1994) 'Netherlands', *International Tourism Reports*, Economist Intelligence Unit, 1, 45–64.

Carr, H. (1995) 'Setting the right pace in Amsterdam', *Travel Trade Gazette*, 24 May.

Carr, J. (1995) 'Amsterdam's quaint freedom', *Gay Times*, June, 96–98.

Catling, C. (ed.) (1991) *Insight Guide: The Netherlands*, APA Publications Ltd.

Clift, S. and Page, S. (1996) *Health And The International Tourist*, London: Routledge.

Clift, S. and Wilkins, J. (1995) 'Travel, sexual behaviour and gay men', in P. Aggleton, P. Davies and G. Hart (eds), *AIDS: Safety, Sexuality And Risk*, London: Taylor & Francis.

Cooper, C. (1981) 'Spatial and temporal patterns of tourist behaviour', *Regional Studies*, 15 (5), 359–71.

Coxon, A. (1996) *Between the Sheets*, London: Cassell.

Crawford, B. (ed.) (1994) *Best Guide To Amsterdam And The Benelux*, 5th edn. Amsterdam: Bookscene.

Debbage, K. (1991) 'Spatial behaviour in a Bahamian resort', *Annals of Tourism Research*, 8, 2, 251–68.

Dietvorst, A. (1995) 'Tourist behaviour and the importance of time-space analysis', in G. Ashworth and A. Dietvorst (eds), *Tourism and Spatial Transformations*, Wallingford: CAB International, 163–81.

Dietvorst, A. and Ashworth, G. (1995) 'Tourism transformations: an introduction', in Ashworth, G. and Dietvorst, A. (eds), *Tourism And Spatial Transformations*, Wallingford: CAB International, 1–12.

Dyer, R. (1992) *Only Entertainment*, London: Routledge.

Duyves, M. (1995) 'Framing preferences, framing differences: inventing Amsterdam as a gay capital', in R. Parker and J. Gagnon (eds), *Conceiving Sexuality: Approaches To Sex Research in a Postmodern World*, London: Routledge.

Evans, D. (1993) *Sexual Citizenship: The Material Construction Of Sexualities*, London: Routledge.

Hall, C.M. (1994) 'Gender and economic interests in tourism prostitution', in V. Kinnaird and D. Hall (eds), *Tourism: A Gender Analysis*, Chichester: Wiley, 142–63.

Hughes, H. (1997) 'Holidays and homosexual identity', *Tourism Management*, 18, 1, 3–7.

Jansen-Verbeke, M. (1986) 'Inner-city tourism: resources, tourists and promoters', *Annals of Tourism Research*, 13, 1, 79–100.

Jansen-Verbeke, M. (1994) 'The synergy between shopping and tourism: the Japanese experience', in W. Theobald (ed.), *Global Tourism: The Next Decade*, Oxford: Butterworth-Heinemann, 347–62.

Jansen-Verbeke, M. and van de Wiel, E. (1995) 'Tourism planning in urban revitalisation projects: lessons from the Amsterdam waterfront', in Ashworth, G. and Dietvorst, A. (eds), *Tourism and Spatial Transformations*, Wallingford: CAB International, 129–45.

Knopp, L. (1995) 'Sexuality and urban space: a framework for analysis', in D. Bell and G. Valentine (eds), *Mapping Desire: Geographies Of Sexuality*, London: Routledge, 149–61.

Lowing, G. (1996) 'Amsterdam's unorthodox culture', *Travel Trade Gazette*, 22 May.

Meershoek, C., van den Broek, B. and Dankmeijer, P. (1996) *Gay Capital Of Europe: Homotourisme In Amsterdam*, Amsterdam: Empowerment Lifestyle Services.

O'Loughlin, J. (1993) 'Between Sheffield and Stuttgart: Amsterdam in an integrated Europe and a competitive world economy', in L. Deben, W. Heinemeijer and D. van der Vaart (eds), *Understanding Amsterdam*, Amsterdam: Het Spuihus, 25–68.

Ryan, C. and Kinder, R. (1996) 'Sex, tourism and sex tourism: fulfilling similar needs?' *Tourism Management*, 17, 7, 507–18.

Shields, R (1991) *Places on the Margin: Alternative Geographies Of Modernity*, London: Routledge.

van den Berg, L., van der Borg, J. and van der Meer, J (1994) *Urban Tourism*, Rotterdam: Erasmus University.

VVV (Vereninging Voor Vreemdelingenverkeer) Amsterdam (1994) *Bezoekers In Amsterdam: Omnibusonderzoek 1992 – 93*, Amsterdam: VVV Amsterdam.

10 Competition for heritage space: Cairo's resident/tourist conflict

KATIE EVANS

CHAPTER SUMMARY

Cairo faces problems typical of many cities in developing countries, namely pressure on resources exacerbated by a rapidly growing population. The development of a tourism industry, however, brings with it new demands on resources. This chapter examines the conflicting demands evident in Cairo, comparing the requirements of international tourists with those of local residents.

Introduction

Cairo is the largest city in Africa and the two local names for it reflect a diverse history. The title 'Masr', meaning both the capital and the land of Egypt, is rooted in pharaonic civilisation and reflects the fact that this part of Africa has an ancient urban tradition. The other, more recent name 'El Qahira' (the conqueror), dates from the times of Islamic conquest in 969. The El Qahira district on the east bank of the Nile is now just one of the governorates of Cairo, the other two being the massive El Giza (containing about 80 towns and villages) on the west bank and the Qalyubiya area that stretches almost 40 miles to the north, well into the Nile Delta.

The impressive history of Cairo is represented by the many ancient monuments that are promoted as touristic landmarks, most famously the Pyramids at Giza but also the great Mosque of Mohammed Ali and many Coptic (Christian) buildings. Cairo bears witness to major cultures in its legacy of built heritage.

Despite an impressive history, Cairo is presently struggling with many of the problems facing Third World cities and is, in the words of Morris (1989), 'almost overwhelmed by its own fertility', with a population currently estimated at 15 million (Adley, 1995) as well as a daily in- and outflow of one million commuters from the Nile Delta. Rural urban drift is as evident in Cairo as elsewhere in the developing world and this, combined with a population growth rate of 3% per annum (EIU Report, 1991), puts great pressure on the urban resources.

ains how the country's economic growth rates have fallen way
increase in population. The per capita income has fallen from
pproximately $610 in 1994, while inflation has been rampant. In
population lived below the poverty line; by 1994 the figure was
f the whole population considered destitute. As many as 1.8 million
ollege graduates are unemployed and there is much underemploy-
a shortage of adequate housing. At present 30% of households lack
and 25% have no sewers (Adley, 1995).

d room for the growth of shanty towns the population of Cairo has
moved into any available space. Approximately one million Cairenes live in the
Northern Cemetery and Southern Cemetery, the infamous Cities of the Dead.
These gigantic graveyards on the eastern outskirts of the capital have formed a new
suburb within El Qahira, whose local governorate has resigned itself to the inevitable and laid on water and electricity supplies, as noted by Thoreaux (1993).

Other options for the poor of Cairo include rooftop dwelling or living in crudely
adapted houseboats on the River Nile. The south-west of the city has seen the growth
of shanty towns which have spread to the edge of the Giza Plateau.This represents an
immediate and obvious example of the competition for resources that can occur
between the host population and tourism, as discussed by Brunn and Williams (1983).

The lack of living space in Cairo is evidenced by a population density of at least
75 000 people per square mile (Thoreaux, 1993), and only an estimated 13 cm² of
green space per person (Adley, 1995). One consequence of this intense pressure is
that the Giza Plateau is treated as an urban park (Mabbitt, 1994) by the population
of Cairo. The city also suffers from lack of space for waste disposal and an overwhelming air pollution that poses a threat to both the local population and ancient
monuments. The pressure on resources evident in Cairo is exacerbated by both the
growing population and the development of tourism.

This pressure on resources is typical of historic cities, subject as they are to the
legitimate demands of their population for modern infrastructure such as transport,
water supply and electricity. Levin (1995) notes that historic buildings undergo
adaptation as residential needs change. In Cairo these needs are intense and present a major challenge to any conservation effort in historic areas of the city. For the
tourist these buildings and monuments are potential attractions but, unlike museum
collections, they cannot be isolated from use.

As a consequence the Egyptian capital today is coping with conflicting demands
from the host population and tourists. This chapter aims to consider both these
groups, examine the differences that exist between them and analyse the influence
they exercise on the demand for and supply of resources for tourism in this urban
context. The resulting conflicts over resource usage are identified and possible
management responses to these problems are considered. This discussion begins
with an overview of tourism in Egypt, before moving on to the case of Cairo itself.

The development of tourism in Egypt

The Egyptian government actively supported the development of tourism from
1974 onwards, encouraged by President Sadat's 'Open Door Policy'. Tourism was

identified as a source of much-needed foreign exchange and employment. To support its development, measures were introduced to increase investment in tourism from local and foreign sources. This took the form of construction of usually 4- or 5-star hotels, the majority of which were in Cairo. The government gradually withdrew from its previous practice of setting standard rates for hotel rooms, allowing a more competitive sector to develop. Other supportive moves were the simplification of exchange rates in 1987, with the introduction of the free banking system and the lifting of restrictions on charter flights. These measures stimulated the growth of international travel to Egypt in the 1970s and 1980s, allowing the country to develop a substantial industry at a time when international tourism was increasing.

The tourism product

A country as extensive as Egypt and with such an impressive history inevitably has a range of resources that can be promoted as tourism products. Rich in both natural and cultural attractions the country now offers a wide range of activities to the prospective visitor. Diversification has occurred in recent years with the development of resorts along the Red Sea Coast and the opening up of Sinai. Egypt's more established tourism products are those based on cultural heritage, particularly antiquities from the pharaonic era. This period in the history of Egypt has left a legacy of ancient monuments and a wide range of artefacts that still fascinate people today. Of the built heritage, the Pyramids and other burial monuments and temples attract tourists. Urban Cairo now extends to the edge of the Giza Plateau where are found the largest of the the Pyramids (the Great Pyramid of Khufu) and the Sphinx. The most famous of the ancient artefacts, the treasures of Tutankhamun, are to be found on display in the Museum of Egyptian Antiquities in Cairo, which is usually referred to as the Egyptian Museum. Egypt's pharaonic civilisation was dependent upon the River Nile and the most-visited sites are concentrated along the Nile Valley. Visits to Cairo, Luxor, Aswan and Abu Simbel are usually packaged as an organised tour that includes a Nile cruise. Travel patterns have been altered recently to avoid areas thought to pose a threat to tourists but the two main gateways are still Cairo and Luxor.

Visitors from the Arab world are interested in Islamic culture both past and present. Spiritually Cairo's Islamic centre is the so-called 'historic city', in the governorate of El Qahira, the ancient quarter lying at the foot of the Citadel. Here the Mosques, the Khan el-Khanili bazaar and the Citadel form a potentially attractive area for all tourists. Its current appeal, however, is limited to the more dedicated visitor such as Morris (1996), who was enthralled by the fact that the area is basically the same shape as when it was founded as a fortified palace compound in 969. She revelled in the district's jumble of cramped squares and narrow alleys choked with traffic, seeing an elegant simplicity in the design of what is now an area of poor housing. The district suffered severe damage during the earthquake of 1992, due, it has been suggested by Pugh (1993), to the lack of proper maintenance. Attention should have been paid to the clay mortar foundations that have been washed away by lakes of waste water. It is thought that the Egyptian Antiquities Office had not intervened in this case because it is densely inhabited by the poor and so no longer considered worth saving. For similar reasons the area known as Old Cairo, the predominantly Coptic quarter to the south of the city, which is rich in evidence of the pre-Islamic Christian era, is not currently visited by many tourists.

By way of contrast the newer waterfront developments of 4- and 5-star international hotels and facilities such as the Cairo Opera House are to be found in the geographical centre of Cairo on the island of El Gezira and the banks of the River Nile opposite. Close to the Egyptian Museum of Antiquities and Tahir Square, this district provides many of the amenities normally associated with international tourism such as nightclubs, restaurants and high-quality shops. It is these facilities, typical of many major cities, that are of particular appeal to many Arab visitors, for whom Cairo is the most cosmopolitan of Islamic cities. The only other part of Cairo with such a notable concentration of these amenities is the Pyramids Road, in the south-west of the city, which leads to the Giza Plateau and its famous monuments. A cluster of higher-class hotels is to be found in this district, forming a satellite tourist zone.When assessing the tourism products of Cairo it is apparent that the most successful to date are those based on the legacy of the pharaonic era and those representative of a modern Arab culture.

Tourism trends and visitor numbers

Egypt has seen a increase in foreign visitor arrivals from 500 000 in 1970 to 2.5 million in 1989. Growth in the 1990s has been initially less consistent but has made a strong recovery with international tourist numbers rising to 3.1 million in 1995. The structural changes introduced in the 1970s produced an economic situation that was favourable to the development of international tourism and visitor numbers grew accordingly. Disruptions to growth were caused by the Gulf War in 1991 and thereafter by the increasing number of random attacks on tourists and tourist sites as discussed by Aziz (1995), although she points out that the majority of violent acts were against Egyptians. Table 10.1 illustrates the trend in international tourist arrivals in Egypt from 1985 onwards and shows the impact of political events in the 1990s.

Table 10.1 International tourist arrivals in Egypt

Year	Number of tourists	% change
1985	1 518 246	−2.70
1986	1 311 250	−13.60
1987	1 794 955	36.90
1988	1 969 493	9.70
1989	2 503 398	27.10
1990	2 600 135	3.80
1991	2 214 277	−14.80
1992	3 206 941	44.80
1993	2 507 762	−21.80
1994	2 581 988	3.00
1995	3 133 461	21.40

Sources: Tourist arrivals taken from Ministry of Tourism (1995); unpublished report prepared by the Egyptian State Tourist Office

Within the overall tourist visitor numbers lies an important and distinct division between tourists from OECD countries and those travelling from the Arab States, as identified in the EIU Report (1991). Of the OECD countries, Germany, the UK, Italy and the United States are the leading generators of tourists while from the Arab States the nearby countries of Saudi Arabia, Libya and the Palestinian territories are the most important. Tourism from Israel has also become significant. These two groups complement one another in terms of seasonality with the majority of OECD tourists arriving in the winter months while Arab tourists prefer to visit in the summer.

These broad groupings can be classified as market segments or tourist typologies, two of which form the basis for most urban tourism in Cairo. The two segments exhibit the following features:

The antiquities tourist
- Travel as part of a package tour
- Length of stay 14 nights
- Travel in the winter season
- Based in Cairo and Luxor
- Predominantly in the middle-aged/retired age group
- The tour including a Nile cruise
- The tour accompanied by a guide
- Accommodation in 4- or 5-star hotels
- Travel to Egypt by charter or scheduled flight

This group is drawn almost exclusively from the OECD countries. Cairo is seen as both a convenient gateway and a base from which to view the pharaonic antiquities, especially the Giza Plateau site and the Egyptian Museum. The presence of the international airport to the north-east of Cairo and approximately 80% of the country's 4- and 5-star hotels in the city contributes to the concentration of tourism in the capital.

The other segment, drawn from the Arab world, reflects the fact that Cairo is not only the leading Arab business centre but is also seen as an important place for the development of Arab culture and recreation. Since the decline of Beirut it has been unchallenged in this role and has become a major destination for the emerging Arab middle class. Characteristics of this market are:

The Arab tourist
- Professional people who usually visit Cairo with their families
- Accommodation in 4- or 5-star hotels
- Cairo's entertainment, eating facilities and shopping the main attractions
- Mostly repeat visitors
- The majority of visits are during the summer months
- Many visits are for an extended period of time

Thoreaux (1993) has attributed to different nationalities particular preferences when they visit Cairo. He notes that Gulf Arabs enjoy the freedom and nightlife, that the Lebanese respect Egypt as a fellow ancient culture, that Palestinians see it as a refuge on the other side of Sinai and that for rural Sudanese and other Africans, visiting Cairo is the ultimate city experience. In the context of urban tourism both the antiquities and the Arab tourist segments exist alongside the host population and utilise, to a greater or lesser extent, the same resources. This multiple usage of the same resources can be analysed by examining the demand and supply sides of the tourism system in Cairo against the needs of the host population.

Demand and supply analysis

It has been acknowledged by many authors that various user groups or market segments make different demands on the resources available in urban areas (Jansen-Verbeke, 1986; Ashworth and Tunbridge, 1990; Burtenshaw et al., 1991). The user groups analysed in this study are those previously identified, as the antiquities tourist, the Arab tourist and the host population. It has been demonstrated that in Cairo, as elsewhere, the host population is struggling to find resources for living space, parks, water supply and other basic requirements. This pressure inevitably influences the way in which resources are perceived and the use to which they are put. When considering the people of Cairo as a user group, it is important to remember that they are not homogenous and that a number of subpopulations exist. They tend to value and use the resources in different ways usually reflecting their economic status.

On the demand side of the analysis, the antiquities tourist, the Arab tourist and the local population all inhabit the city of Cairo at certain times but with differing priorities in relation to how they intend to use local resources. The antiquities tourists have seen Cairo presented as a city of awe-inspiring monuments and fascinating museums. Great care is taken, in the case of British tour operators at least, to use brochure photographs that show the Pyramids in an idealised state, free of any activity or indication that they are a suburb of urban Cairo (Stocks, 1994). For Arab tourists Cairo is presented as the cosmopolitan centre of the Islamic world, one that promises the features of modernity in an appropriate context. For the local population it is simply the place where they live.

The instrument selected to clarify this situation and to relate the expectations on the demand side with resources on the supply side is an adapted framework based on that originally presented by Burtenshaw et al. (1991). This framework allows for the consideration of functional links between user groups and the different resources found in a city. It also introduces a spatial perspective by identifying particular areas within a city such as the historic city, culture city or night-life city. The information presented below in the application of the framework is based on data collected by the author on a field visit in May 1995 and material published both before and after that date. The framework shown in Figure 10.1 has been adapted to illustrate the situation in Cairo, classifying the functional links (between users and resources) as primary, secondary or non-existent. Primary links are the most important, and indicate that the use of a resource is a priority for a particular user group. Secondary links show that a user group uses the resource, but that it is not as important to them as other resources in the city. This approach allows for the identification of the priorities of each group in relation to a particular resource. For

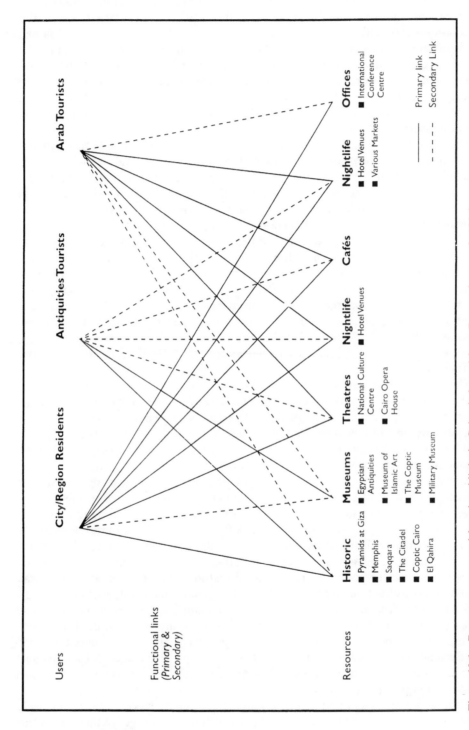

Figure 10.1 Resource usage and functional links in Cairo (adapted from Burtenshaw *et al.*, 1991)

example, when we examine the functional links between user groups and the historic monuments of Cairo, it can be seen that primary links exist between the antiquities tourist and the host population in respect of the Giza Plateau. Although the links are primary in both cases, the usages are different, which explains the degree of conflict that can arise when a resource is highly valued by different user groups. The framework can also be used to identify those resources which are unique and cannot be replicated, such as the Giza Plateau and the Citadel, which are by their nature fixed in location and are subject to the greatest pressures as different user groups seek to utilise it.

The Giza Plateau is currently struggling with the different demands made upon it and concerns have been expressed about the long-term survival of the Pyramids and Sphinx by Mabbitt (1994). Fowler (1996) has noted that the many and varied activities that take place there detract from the sense of the place. These concerns are not unfounded, as the case of the El Qahira district, the 'historic city' of Cairo, demonstrates. Once a tourist attraction, it has been unable both to cope with an increasing population and still maintain an appeal to tourists. As a result this potential tourist resource is now the preserve of the local population and a few dedicated tourists such as Morris. The Coptic part of Old Cairo has suffered a similar fate, overwhelmed by the demands of the local population. In these cases it is apparent that the resources have been used by Cairenes to meet their immediate needs for housing and that multiple usage is no longer a possibility. Despite this general decline, isolated attractions such as the Citadel have survived but many tourists travel directly to and from them, spending little time or money in the surrounding area.

The pressures that have created this situation are not unique to Cairo. In the case of the Walled City of Lahore, well documented by Wigg (1994), the main threat has been from uncontrolled urban growth, with some 300 000 people living inside the Walled City and fifteen times as many outside the walls in the larger city. The density proves attractive to businesses because they have a ready supply of cheap labour and a concentration of local customers but this only adds to the overcrowding. In Lahore the original city walls are being reconstructed, a mammoth task disrupting the lives of people living in the old city. Attitudes to the reconstruction have been mixed, members of the conservative Muslim party feeling that priority should be spending on building multistorey flats and a technical training institute for the poor masses living in the Walled City, thus addressing the immediate problems of overcrowding and unemployment. Other groups, including local architects, sympathised with the desire to restore local features in their original style. It was noted that conservation received support when it went alongside measures to improve the infrastructure. Fauzia Qureshi, a local architect, was quoted as saying that 'It's a living city. It shouldn't be preserved purely for touristic purposes. The people there aren't actors. They're living people' (Wigg, 1994 : 46). In the case of Lahore it would appear that tourists are not the only user group to have been considered and that the provision of local services has reduced some of the opposition to the conservation of the City Walls.

Other resources identified in the adapted Burtenshaw model such as theatres, nightclubs, restaurants and shops also experience multiple usage. In these cases the functional links with the Arab tourist users are primary, these being the main attractions for this group of visitors. These facilities will also be used by some antiquities tourists and members of the local population. The pressures on these resources are not as great as those placed on the ancient monuments or areas of historic architecture. Shops, nightclubs and restaurants are not tied to set locations and can be located in the places where they best serve a particular user group. The facilities are not unique and can be replicated, varying in function and location to meet the needs of different groups. In Cairo the exclusive restaurants, nightclubs and shops are often to be found within hotel complexes, while more traditional amenities flourish, as they always have, around the bazaars of Cairo.

Using the framework has demonstrated that in a city such as Cairo it is those resources that are unique, fixed in location and perceived to have different uses by the respective user groups that are most likely to suffer from multiple usage. It has been demonstrated that some of those uses are mutually incompatible, as in El Qahira and Old Cairo, where the population pressures were overwhelming. Another tourist site that is currently facing similar conflicts is the Giza Plateau.

The Giza Plateau case study

Figure 10.1 shows that in this case it is apparent that the same resource experiences the pressures of multiple usage. Some of the functional links have been identified as primary indicating the importance of the resource to a particular user group. The different groups have different expectations, among them the desire for a tourist experience, the need for living space, employment and the demand for an informal public leisure space. This semi-urban site is facing pressures similar to those experienced elsewhere in Cairo. The conflicts typify those evident in resource usage in cities in developing countries that have a sizeable tourist industry. The existing impacts and conflicts at the Giza Plateau site have been well documented in the report prepared by Mabbitt (1994) and more recently in investigations made by the author (Evans, 1995a). The findings discussed below are drawn from these studies.

For the antiquities tourist the location of this site may be the main factor that influences a decision to spend time in Cairo. The Giza Plateau Pyramids are world-famous and the only remaining Wonder of the Ancient World, often being presented as touristic symbols or icons adorning brochures and guidebooks alike (Selwyn, 1990) (Figure 10.2). The Pyramids and the Sphinx are presented as monuments in isolation, the importance and fragility of the Plateau itself being rarely commented upon. It is not surprising therefore that the main priority for antiquities tourists is to view the monuments as easily as possible. For the Arab tourist the Giza Plateau is not a major attraction and a primary functional link does not exist, but those who do visit often wish to experience it in a different way from the antiquities tourist, preferring to ride through the desert on horseback towards the Giza Plateau and Pyramids.

In contrast, the local residents view the site very differently. For them it is an integral part of urban Cairo and is treated as such. Some of those residents of Cairo who are living on the margins of society view the site as an economic and residential opportunity. People in this group have built shanty towns, Nazlet el Semmane and Kafret el Gabal, at the base of the Giza Plateau, one of the few spaces still available in Cairo (Figure 10.3). Not only do these Cairenes live close to the Plateau but the majority derive some form of income from it by providing unofficial services to the tourists such as guiding and horse or camel rides. A range of tourist souvenirs and related items, such as soft drinks and camera films, are sold unofficially on a very small scale.The other local group using the site is the middle class of Cairo who perceive the Giza Plateau as a leisure facility. The lack of green areas in the city means that any open space is highly valued and every evening, as the *son et lumière* performance begins at the Sphinx, hundreds of Cairenes promenade through the Pyramids (Evans, 1995b). For them, it is an open space, relatively free of traffic and is treated in effect as an urban park.

Estimates suggest that annually some 1.25 million international tourists visit the site (figures not being available for local usage). The needs of these tourists are served by the local tourism industry that operates formally and informally. The types of service offered to tourists have created problems at the Plateau, which is

Figure 10.2   Tourist usage of the Giza Plateau: camel rides around the tourist icon

Figure 10.3 Residential encroachment to the edge of the Plateau

archaeologically very sensitive. Official activities include the transport of tourists to and around the site by coach, taxi and trail bike. A network of tarmac roads currently runs over the Plateau and vehicles drive to the Pyramids and then off the road to park on the Plateau itself. Roads are not the only modern structures built on the site; there are also banks of lighting, old fences and modern buildings. As well as being visually disruptive these structures threaten the unexcavated archaeology of the site. Other inappropriate activity occurs as a consequence of the informal tourism sector (operated mostly by shanty town residents), who offer horse and camel rides across the Plateau. It has been suggested that untrained local guides might encourage inappropriate behaviour on the part of tourists, such as climbing monuments and taking souvenir pieces.

The shanty towns that house these Cairenes are thought to pose a threat to the Giza Plateau. As well as creating a visual disruption, the attempts to dispose of sewage have allowed polluted water to leak into the limestone Plateau, eroding the very foundations of the Sphinx. Solid waste disposal from both humans and animals has resulted in the emergence of unofficial rubbish dumps at the base of the Plateau. Local usage of the site as a park results in what are deemed by Mabbitt to be inappropriate activities such as family picnics and outdoor games on the Plateau itself.

Many of the activities identified above cause environmental damage to the Plateau and its monuments, and the UNESCO-appointed consultants felt that some of the uses were inappropriate for a World Heritage Site. A management plan has been devised to resolve some of the conflicts of interest and to protect the resource. The plan, while recognising the needs of local people, places the main emphasis on conserving the remaining archaeology of the Plateau and controlling further deteri-oration of the site, whether caused by tourist pressure or other usages. It identifies tourism as the only legitimate use on-site and states that other activities should be located elsewhere.

The plan aims to remove all activities identified as inappropriate from the Plateau. Vehicular access will be banned and the Plateau ringed by a tourist access road that will link three visitor centres, given the working title of 'gates'. Illustrated in Figure 10.4, the name of each gate indicates the attraction to which they are located closest. This infrastructure would formalise access to the site and tourists would walk to the monuments from these visitor centres, thus preventing vehicular access and discouraging the use of unofficial guides. The sale of goods and animal rides would also be removed to the centres, reducing damage to the Plateau and formalising this aspect of the economy. It is proposed in the plans to restrict access to the site to ticket holders only, so those Cairenes wishing to promenade through the site have to pay to do so or use a specially identified free picnic area near the Desert Gate. Another proposal is to clear the shanty towns from the Plateau's edge and rehouse the residents elsewhere, but anecdotal evidence suggests that there is local opposition to this proposal. Shanty town residents are fearful that the prom-ised housing will not materialise and, perhaps more importantly, that they will be relocated away from the Plateau, their current source of income.

It can be seen in this case that protection of the resource has taken priority and if that were not the case Egypt might witness the urbanisation of the Pyramids, removing what remains of their desert location. This protection may improve the way tourists experience the site but will not serve the other user groups so well. Those living next to the Plateau and selling goods and services informally are likely to be squeezed out of both their housing and opportunities to earn income, al-though the latter deprivation could be addressed by the establishment of a tourist market area that did not carry with it the sort of overheads associated with formal visitor centres. The issue of the shanty towns is a more difficult one to deal with, particularly as the residents are very reluctant to move. Moreover, for the other Cairenes looking for an open space to treat as a park, a picnic area in the desert will not be sufficient. A more flexible approach could be considered and local residents given free or reduced price entry to the site. This scheme could operate on specific days or at particular times, for example after 5 pm, but it would be contentious to demand payment for or restrict the right to walk in one of the few open spaces traditionally accessible to all.

It has been demonstrated in this case that the adapted Burtenshaw framework has identified the importance of a particular resource (the Giza Plateau) to

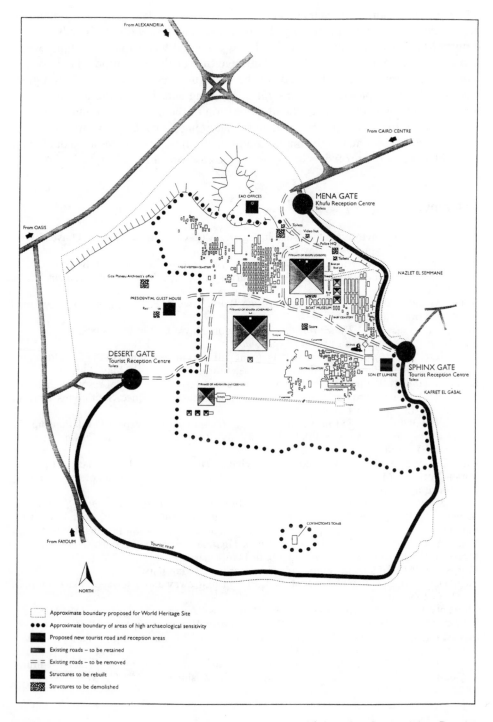

Figure 10.4 Proposal for the Giza Plateau Masterplan (after the *Conservation Practice*, Mabbitt, 1992)

different user groups. The management plan proposed to deal with the problems is mainly concerned with protecting the resource and less with the needs of the different local user groups, which would be expected when the consultants were asked to produce a plan for a World Heritage Site of this magnitude. However, a more flexible approach to the needs of the other user groups may result in a plan that is easier to implement and sustain in the long run. Use of the adapted Burtenshaw model would allow for the identification of the needs and requirements of different user groups at an early stage in the planning process. This would allow for a more flexible approach to the management of city-based resources and could help to avoid some of the problems identified in the case of Cairo.

References

Adley, E. (1995) 'Environmental issues in Egypt', Med-Campus Workshop, University of Alexandria, Egypt, 13–15 May 1995.

Ashworth, G.J. and Tunbridge, J. (1990) *The Tourist–Historic City*, London: Belhaven.

Aziz, H. (1995) 'Understanding attacks on tourists in Egypt', *Tourism Management*, 16, 2, 91–5.

Brunn, S. and Williams, J. (1983) *Cities of the World – world regional urban development*, New York: Harper Row.

Burtenshaw *et al.* (1991) *The European City*, London: David Fulton Publishers.

Economist Intelligence Unit (1991) *Egypt Report No.1*, London: EIU.

Evans, K. (1995a) 'Concepts of site management with specific reference to the Giza Plateau', Med-Campus Workshop, University of Alexandria, Egypt, 13–15 May 1995.

Evans, K. (1995b) 'Pyramids, mosques and museums – resolving issues of resource management', Urban Environment and Tourism International Conference, South Bank University, 11–12 September 1995.

Fowler, P. (1996) 'Heritage tourism, tourism heritage – towards a respectful relationship? in M. Robinson, N. Evans and P. Callaghan (eds), *Tourism and Cultural Change*, Sunderland: BEP Ltd.

Hirst, D. (1995) 'Poised between control and chaos', *The Guardian,* 11 February, p.15.

Jansen-Verbeke, M. (1986) 'Inner-city tourism: resources, tourists and promoters', *Annals of Tourism Research*, 13, 1, 79–100.

Levin, J. (1995) 'Historic structures & cities', *Conservation The GCI Newsletter*, X (III), 20.

Mabbitt, R. (1992) 'The Masterplan for the Giza Plateau', Conservation Practice/UNESCO.

Mabbitt, R. (1994) 'Progress report – the Giza Plateau', Conservation Practice/UNESCO.

Ministry of Tourism (1995) *Egypt – Tourism in Figures*, unpublished report.

Morris, J. (1989) *Destinations*, Oxford: Oxford University Press.

Morris, J. (1996) 'In a family embrace', *The Guardian*, 9 March, p.29.

Pugh, D. (1993) 'Egyptian "Venice of the East" washing away under sewage', *The Guardian*, 15 October, p.11.

Thoreaux, P. (1993) 'Cairo – clamorous heart of Egypt', *National Geographic*, 183 (4), 38–58.

Selwyn, T. (1990) 'Tourism as anthropology', *Tourism Management*, 11, 1, 68–9.

Stocks, J. (1994) *The Image of Egypt in Tour Operator's Brochures*, unpublished postgraduate Report, University of Derby.

Wigg, D. (1994) 'Of mosaics and mosques – a look at the campaign to preserve cultural heritage', *World Bank Development Essays (3)*, Washington, DC: The World Bank.

Section IV
City events and the national tourism product

Introduction

The impact of events on such issues as re-imaging are touched upon in this book (Hall, Tunbridge, van der Borg) as well as elsewhere (Getz, 1991, 1997; Hall, 1992). What this section does is to consider the role of events in the shaping of the national tourism product, and the long-term city product. It looks particularly at the reasons why and the ways in which cities are becoming entrepreneurial, competing with each other in a global market using 'imagineering' and events to do this.

In Chapter 11 Mules explores the way that the major cities in Australia have gone about administering their events programmes and how these have either been coordinated through special corporations or taken forward through more conventional tourism departments. Mules particularly explores the need for the cities to be enterprising in the face of increasing competition between cities to attract events. He considers the importance of formulating a coherent strategy at national and state level. In the second part of the chapter he explores how Expo '88 went to Brisbane as part of the national bicentennial celebrations. He investigates the national and international processes of its designation and the processes that led to post-event site redevelopment leaving a legacy to the city of new leisure and tourist spaces.

In Chapter 12, Robertson and Guerrier look at how Spain used three major international events (Olympics, European City of Culture, and Expo '92) to help remodel the national tourism product. At a time when international competition, and falling standards, were taking their toll on Spain's beach product, these events were planned to help to diversify the tourism product in terms of both seasonality and product type. The chapter discusses the ways in which a new image, both for the cities and nationally, was designed and deployed through this trilogy of events. However, while Spain has been successful in shedding most of its old negative tourism images, the chapter questions how much each of the three cities have gained, in the long term, from their hosting of the events.

References

Getz, D. (1991) *Festivals, Special Events and Tourism*, New York: Van Nostrand Rheinhold.
Getz, D. (1997) *Event Management and Event Tourism*, New York: Cognizant Communications Company.
Hall, C. M. (1992) *Hallmark Tourist Events: Impacts, Management and Planning*, London: Belhaven.

11 Events tourism and economic development in Australia

TREVOR MULES

CHAPTER SUMMARY

Special sporting and cultural events have emerged as major tourism policy instruments for governments keen to boost local business from the spending of visitors to the events. In Australia the state governments compete in a quest to attract visitors to events in their state, usually in their capital city. They have established special corporations to bid for and facilitate such events. The chapter, through economic analysis, shows that the importance of events has increased to a stage where interstate rivalry to attract events has led to the establishment of an Events Corporation or Commission to coordinate the ever-increasing involvement of state governments. The transition from Expo '88 to South Bank Parklands in Brisbane is used as a case study, showing how the event was the catalyst to the establishment of the Queensland Events Corporation, changes in urban form and urban lifestyles.

Introduction

The role of special events in tourism attraction and promotion has assumed such importance that it is the topic of textbooks (Getz, 1991, 1997), and has its own journal (*Festival Management and Event Tourism*). While events are used in this way by small towns and villages, the really large events, such as the Olympic Games, World Cup, Formula One, etc., are generally city phenomena because of the need for infrastructure, such as accommodation and transport, which can only be supplied on an appropriate scale by cities. There are exceptions to this, such as Opera in the Outback in Australia, where the attraction for tourists is often the unusual nature of the venue.

Until the early 1980s in Australia, most sporting and cultural events were organised and managed by enthusiastic volunteers who were primarily motivated by the enjoyment of the sport or culture. Community and government attitudes seemed to

Managing Tourism in Cities. Edited by D. Tyler, Y. Guerrier and M. Robertson.
Copyright © 1998 John Wiley & Sons Ltd.

change around 1982–6 during which time Australian cities hosted the Commonwealth Games (Brisbane, 1982), Formula One Grand Prix motor racing (Adelaide,
1985), and the America's Cup Defence (Perth, 1986–7).

These events were all subject to scrutiny by academic researchers who drew
attention to the economic impact which the events had on their host cities via the
spending of visitors who came for the event. Studies such as Lynch and Jensen
(1984) on the Commonwealth Games, Burns, Hatch and Mules (1986) on Formula
One, and Centre for Applied and Business Research (1986) on the America's Cup
all drew attention to the business boost that occurred in the host city via tourist
expenditure. Burns, Hatch and Mules (1986) made a particular impact on the
thinking of government policy makers by pointing out that the extra local income
generated by the event (Formula One) exceeded the cost to the state government
of staging the event. (This event was run by a government-owned company using
public funds.)

Over the decade from 1986 to 1996 there was strong and growing recognition in
Australia of the importance of major events to the host economy. However, many
of the impact studies of events showed that the overwhelming majority of the
visitors were from other parts of Australia, with a small minority comprising international visitors. The expenditure boost which the events gave to their host economy was therefore a result of Australians switching their expenditure around their
own country. What the host city gained, the origin region lost.

This characteristic has clearly detracted from the national economic significance
of events, except for the Olympics, which is expected to attract 200 000 international visitors to Sydney in 2000. However, Australia has a federal system of states
and there are six state governments which, to a greater or lesser extent, have shown
a keen appreciation of the commercial and political value of hosting special events.

In political terms, the inaugural 1985 Formula One Grand Prix in Adelaide was
seen by Burns, Hatch and Mules (1986) as being a factor in the re-election of the
Labor government in the state of South Australia in early 1986. They comment
(p.27) 'it is interesting to conjecture what part the success of the Grand Prix played
in the re-election of the State Government'.

The Grand Prix was held annually in Adelaide on a city-street circuit adjoining
the central business district. It was an integral part of the city's calendar and
landscape until 1994 when the government of the neighbouring state of Victoria
outbid South Australia in a deal with the Formual One Constructors Association.
The event moved to Victoria's capital city, Melbourne, in 1996 following a good
deal of public angst in South Australia at the loss of an event which had become
something of an icon for the city of Adelaide.

This episode illustrates the intense interstate rivalry over special event hosting
that developed in Australia over the period 1986 to 1996. State governments began
to make it a feature of their economic policy to attract major events to their capital
cities in recognition of their commercial and political benefits. Indeed the Victorian
government set out to make Melbourne into Australia's special event city,
especially in relation to sporting events.

This chapter will explain the involvement of governments, especially state governments, in event tourism in Australia. It will follow the establishment of special
government agencies and companies formed for the explicit purpose of attracting

events which have potential for economic impacts via tourism attraction. Special consideration is given to the state of Queensland, where a special event (World Expo '88) was not only a major tourist attraction but was used as a catalyst for renewal of a neglected inner-city area.

Definition of a special event

Every year there are thousands of festivals, sporting carnivals, fairs, shows, and exhibitions held around Australia. The various state government tourism agencies compile annual diaries of such events and, according to Jago and Shaw (1995), their intention in doing so appears to be more informational than promotional. In other words, the vast majority of such events are run for their cultural and sporting influence rather than their economic potential.

That is not to say that many such events do not have a short-term economic impact on their host region, and do not receive some measure of government funding. The important distinction between these events and a hallmark or special event is clearly size. Ritchie (1984) uses the word 'major' in his definition, while other writers, such as Getz (1989) and Hall (1989), use words like 'unique' and 'status' in an attempt to differentiate between a special event and an ordinary one.

In their study of the inaugural Adelaide Formula One Grand Prix, Burns, Hatch, and Mules (1986) settled for a definition in terms of economics. That is, the event had to generate economic activity in other industries such as accommodation, transport, entertainment, retailing, etc. in order to be regarded as special or hall-mark. While most events will have this impact upon their regional economy, they will not all be noticeable in their impact on their national economy. Thus an event might be major to its host region but minor to the nation as a whole. For example, a regional sporting carnival might fill all the local motels, but this would be insignifi-cant to the nation as a whole, and indeed may result in nothing more than shifting expenditure around the nation.

Hall (1989) clearly discounts the regional, and even the large annual national events from consideration because they are not 'unique'. Such events are important from an economic and tourism perspective, especially as they appear to be part of tourism and economic development policy of various levels of government.

Whatever the definition, the Sydney Olympics clearly stands out as a hallmark event. In tourism and economic terms the various motor racing and motor cycling Grand Prix, the World Cup soccer, the Commonwealth Games, and various arts festivals such as the biennial Adelaide Festival all qualify. These types of events are all large enough to attract visitors who generate economic activity by their expendi-ture. They are also large enough to create media interest and so raise awareness about the host region as a potential tourism destination.

The list of events that qualify to be regarded as special by an economic and tourism definition would be shorter than the state tourism departments' diaries of all events, but it would still be quite extensive and is likely to be getting longer as people show a greater tendency to travel for such events.

For example, in the mid-1980s Test cricket matches were large events but did not attract significant numbers of people from outside of the host region. In the 1990s this has changed and we now see media coverage of numbers of British tourists who travel to Australia specifically to watch cricket, although to our knowledge the size of this phenomenon has not been documented.

Thus events such as the Melbourne Cup, the Australian Football League Grand Final, the Sydney Gay and Lesbian Mardi Gras may all now be regarded as major events in the sense that they attract enough visitors to raise the occupancy rates in the local accommodation sector, and they gain media attention which aids in promoting the host city as a tourism destination.

The case for government involvement

Some special events are funded, organised, and run by government organisations, some are run by sporting and cultural organisations and some by private promoters for profit. Many events that involve government are run at a loss. This is because the commercial structure of many major events is such that they can never make a profit for their operator. The Adelaide Grand Prix lost A\$2.6 million in its inaugural year (Thomson, 1986), and A\$3.97 million in 1992 (Price Waterhouse, 1993), and the Eastern Creek motor cycle Grand Prix lost A\$4.76 million in 1991 (Reark Research, 1991).

The sources of revenue to the government from such events are ticket sales, sponsorships, and corporate box sales. The costs include wages and materials involved in operations, royalty payments to the copyright holders for the event (e.g. the Formula One Constructors Association), and overheads such as depreciation of equipment. International television royalties frequently are paid to the copyright holders who, in cases such as Formula One, are not based in Australia.

It seems unlikely that private operators would be willing to take on the running of such events because of their low chance of breaking even, let alone turning a profit. Why, then, are state governments fighting with each other for the right to host such events and losing taxpayers money in the process? The answer lies in spillover effects or externalities.

When a tourist operator, say a hotel or a major tourist attraction, spends money promoting their business, they are indirectly promoting their area of operation as a tourism destination. When tourists respond to this promotion, they are likely to spend money with other businesses as well as at the hotel doing the promotion. Other businesses therefore receive a spillover benefit as a result of this single operator's actions and, in this sense, they (i.e. the other businesses) are parasitic (called free-riders in economics).

Because individual operators are unable to acquire or 'capture' all the benefits of their promotion expenditure, they are discouraged from investing in promotional activities to the extent that is optimum in terms of economic viability of the industry. This problem is often solved by local tourism businesses cooperating in a Tourism Promotion Association. Each business pays a levy to the Association which pools the funds and undertakes promotion expenditure on behalf of the whole region. At the broader state and national levels, government-funded tourism agencies perform a similar role in coordinating tourism marketing (Faulkner, 1994; Gilbert, 1990).

A similar rationale underlies state government involvement in running special events, despite the losses these events incur. If such events are seen as a way of raising awareness about a state or its capital city as a tourist destination, then spending money on the event is justifiable in terms of getting the right amount of promotion activity.

The argument is similar to the pollution argument. Each polluter does not bear the full impact of their pollution, yet they would each gain by cooperatively agreeing to reduce pollution. If the costs involved in getting the agents together and getting them to agree is greater than the benefits then they will not do so. There is then a case for the government to intervene, unless the cost of government action exceeds the benefits.

Since not all taxpayers will benefit from increased tourism, it could be argued that the event should be financed by a levy on those who stand to benefit – namely the tourism providers, such as hotel and casino owners. However, the economic benefits may be more widespread. For example, if the event attracts many visitors every year, and their expenditure, this expenditure raises general economic activity which benefits many sectors of the economy. Note that this expenditure is equivalent to new exports which would not have occurred without the event. In this case, it could be argued that the general community receives higher income (generated by the exports) because of the event and it is therefore legitimate to use taxpayers' money in funding the event.

In their study of the 1985 Adelaide Grand Prix, Burns, Hatch and Mules (1986) estimate that the event attracted visitor expenditure of A$8.274 million, plus staging and construction expenditure of another A$11.132 million to A$12.082 million. These expenditures would not have reached South Australia without the attraction of the event. The event ran at a loss to the state government of A$2.616 million. Overall the loss appears to be justified in terms of direct economic benefits.

A similar study of the 1994 IndyCar Grand Prix on the Gold Coast by consultants Ernst and Young (1994) found that the loss of A$10.5 million to Queensland taxpayers resulted in a gain of A$20 million in direct visitor expenditure which was attributable to the event. From a straight cost–benefit point of view, Indy looks to be worth while to Queensland, even before taking account of the tourism attraction effect which the event may have because of its international media exposure.

The interpretation of this has been challenged by Black (1994) who argues that if taxpayers have lost A$10.5 million on running the Indy event, it is only worth while if taxpayers' share of the economic benefits exceed the A$10.5 million, i.e. if the government gets back increased taxes of more than A$10.5 million as a result of the economic activity generated by the visitor expenditure. However, this overlooks the fact that taxpayers are also income earners and the benefits to them as a group includes the incomes generated by the event.

It could be argued that government expenditure on promoting any export can be shown to generate the same impacts as spending on tourism promotion. Why does the government promote tourism but not coal? The answer lies in the nature of the goods: coal is homogeneous, as are all of Australia's commodity exports, and would not benefit from promotion. Tourism is a differentiated product and as such will benefit from promotion.

This is particularly relevant to state governments in states which do not have a high tourism profile in the domestic tourism market. Because of their lack of icons like the Sydney Harbor, or a climate such as Queensland's, it could be argued that Victoria and South Australia fall into this category.

The benefits of an event in terms of tourism promotion and raising awareness in a way that may stimulate other commercial activities are not readily measurable. However, it does seem that Melbourne is deliberately positioning itself as the 'sporting capital of Australia' and that this is aimed at both the media and the sports-conscious public. Melbourne hosts annually both the Formula One Grand Prix and motorcycle Grand Prix, the Australian Tennis Open, the Melbourne Cup, and the Australian Football Grand Final. It has the largest sports stadium in the country at the Melbourne Cricket Ground.

Melbourne has less natural tourism appeal in terms of climate and attractions than, say, Sydney, the Gold Coast, or the Northern Territory. These latter destinations already have high tourism profiles and high awareness as destinations, both domestically and internationally. The marginal *awareness* benefit for them is likely to be less than it is for Melbourne, in terms of spending money to host an event. This may explain why Melbourne is keen to collect a brace of such events.

This is not to say that other regions are not keen to do so, just that Melbourne may have more to gain and may therefore be willing to spend more. For regions which already have a high tourism awareness, the economic value to them from special events may come more from the effect of encouraging the current flow of visitors to stay longer than from attracting a larger visitor flow.

Evolution of government involvement

The development of a deliberate government focus on special events can be traced to the 1980s when Australia played host to the Formula One Grand Prix (Adelaide, 1985), the the America's Cup Defence (Perth, 1986–7), Expo (1988, Brisbane) and the Bicentennial (1988, Sydney). The ability of these events to attract tourists and to focus attention on the host economy prompted some state governments to establish special units/organisations whose mission was to seek out events from around the world and attract them to the state.

Prior to this time, the funding, support and management of events was largely in the hands of the state government Departments of Sport, or Arts, as appropriate. Events were organised and funded mainly on the basis of their cultural or sporting impact. No particular attention was paid to their ability to attract tourists, or the economic impact of that tourism.

The first state in Australia to establish a special events unit was Western Australia where Eventscorp (WA) was established in 1985. The organisation is a government-owned company which aims to attract events to Western Australia which will draw visitors, or promote the state to visitors via media exposure of the event.

The strong emphasis on tourism and the business boost that special events can bring stems from the America's Cup Defence held in Perth in 1986–7 which was perceived by the community to have stimulated business and tourism. Soutar and McLeod (1989) found that the residents of the Fremantle region, where the event took place, 'felt that the America's Cup had increased job opportunities'.

There was a change of government in Western Australia in 1993 following numerous scandals in which the previous government had lost large amounts of money in business deals that went wrong. In such a political climate, Eventscorp could easily have been closed down by the incoming government but the widespread community satisfaction with the impacts of the America's Cup may be seen as a factor in the corporation's survival.

There are numerous advantages of an Eventscorp type of approach to event attraction over the pre-existing *ad hoc* committee approach. These include continuity of operation, accumulation of skills and knowledge, and maintenance of contacts in international sporting bodies. In addition, there is the advantage of establishing ongoing links with 'global marketing groups' which are helpful in guiding bids for events.

Eventscorp (WA) both bids for events which it stages, and assists other groups to bid for and manage events. The assistance may be both by way of funding, or help with negotiation and management. Over the period 1986 to 1996 the agency lists 66 events in which it has been involved, some four of which are annual events. Some of the better known internationally include the Heineken Golf Classic, the annual Hopman Cup of tennis, and the 1991 World Swimming Championships.

In 1988 the Queensland government established the Queensland Events Corporation (QEC) which took over the role of attracting events to Queensland, funding them, carrying out research into their impacts on the state, and in some cases organising them. The QEC comes under the umbrella of the Department of Tourism, Sport and Youth, thereby firmly acknowledging the tourism aspect of special events. The QEC is an independent corporation with a board of directors and a separate budget, but its strategies are firmly in terms of tourism attraction, and the economic benefits to Queensland of that tourism.

In the year of the establishment of QEC (1988), Brisbane hosted a World Exposition known as Expo '88. Although QEC was not involved in Expo '88, the event was a big success in attracting tourists to Brisbane, and in changing the landscape of the city. Public support for the establishment of QEC was no doubt partly attributable to the success of Expo. There is a more detailed examination of Expo '88 later in this chapter.

The QEC states its mission to be 'to develop and support events that are capable of generating substantial economic activity and that lift the profile of Queensland both within Australia and overseas'. Over the period 1991 to 1995 it has supported or assisted 39 events, including the 1994 World Masters Games and the 1994 World Gymnastics Championships.

The largest event in which QEC is involved is the annual IndyCar Grand Prix which is not run in the capital city of Brisbane, but on Queensland's Gold Coast, some 90 kilometres to the south. The region is a tourism mecca, featuring glorious beaches, benign weather and substantial tourism infrastructure. The event costs around A$8 million each year of taxpayers' money, and since 1991 has cost a total of A$86 million (Fredline, 1996 : 4). However, visitor surveys have been conducted every year, and they reveal a high level of interstate visitation, with visitor expenditure in Queensland amounting to over A$28 million in 1996 (KPMG, 1996).

Victoria, and more recently South Australia, have followed the lead of Western Australia and Queensland in setting up special corporations to attract and finance special events. However, the aims, activities, and outcomes for each state have been very different.

In Victoria, the new state government of premier Jeff Kennett established the Melbourne Major Events Company in 1991. The company's stated objective is to 'selectively target and aggressively pursue large events which bring significant economic, cultural and social benefits to Victoria'. The placing of economic benefits first in this list is an indication of the criterion used by the company in deciding which events to target. The company defines a major event as 'one which has the capacity to create enormous economic return, employment opportunity and international media exposure that increases tourism to the state'.

Its most controversial and noteworthy success was in winning the annual Formula One Grand Prix race away from South Australia in 1994. However, it has other notable successes to its credit, including the 500cc motorcycle Grand Prix, the Three Tenors Concert in 1997, and the 1997 Bledisloe Cup. The last of these is a rugby union competition between Australia and New Zealand, which is noteworthy because rugby union is possibly the fourth popular football code in Victoria, following Australian football, soccer, and rugby league.

Running in parallel with Melbourne Major Events Company, the state of Victoria has a Major Events Unit housed within the State Tourism Department. The unit was formed in 1992 and concentrates on attracting events, and assisting sporting and cultural organisations to prepare bids for events to be held in Melbourne and elsewhere in the state of Victoria. The company appears to focus on 'mega' events, leaving the unit to take responsibility for what might be regarded as second-tier events. The two organisations work closely together in order to prevent confusion.

The strong emphasis on attracting events within the state government of Victoria has seen it notch up a number of 'wins', including enticing events away from other states. Interstate rivalry, especially between Victoria and New South Wales, has added a touch of spice to these developments. Sydney has the biggest event of them all in the 2000 Olympics, but Melbourne has enticed other events away from Sydney, including the 500cc motorcycle Grand Prix, the Bledisloe Cup, and the Australian Athletics championship.

One unfortunate aspect of this interstate rivalry is the propensity for states to engage in a bidding war with each other, offering promoters higher and higher fees for the right to host the particular event. This process was very evident when Melbourne persuaded the Formula One Grand Prix promoter to move the event to Melbourne from Adelaide where it had been very successful for ten years. The sums of money involved have never been made public, but there is a clear danger of the nation as a whole being the loser if international operators are able to play one state off against another in this way.

Attempts by national administrators to forge cooperative arrangements between the states have thus far foundered on the rocks of interstate competition. This leaves the events-bidding process in Australia still very open to exploitation by clever promoters.

Since September 1993, when Sydney was announced as being the host city for the 2000 Olympics, the New South Wales government has tended to be preoccupied with that event. This is not to say that the government of premier Bob Carr has not been interested in attracting other events and has taken pleasure in announcing successful bids, such as the 18 January 1996 announcement of both the 1999 World Marching Band championships and the December 1997 visit of competitors in the Whitbread Round-the-World yacht race.

However, the New South Wales government has not seen fit to maintain a special company dedicated to winning events. In 1993 it formed a company called Special Events NSW Ltd under the then NSW Tourism Commission. The company's mission was to 'help to attract more events like the the International Motor Cycle Grand Prix, Sydney to Hobart Yacht Race, World Youth Cup Soccer, Tamworth Country Music Festival and others, which are proven to generate millions of dollars for the state's economy in tourist spending' (press release by the New South Wales Minister for Tourism, 22 July 1993).

Despite being somewhat hamstrung by lack of funding, and never having true independence from the State Tourism Commission, the company managed to produce calendars of events and a database on the events industry. It assisted a number of organisations in bidding for events and advised on marketing and management of several existing regular events. Over the period 1993 to 1995 it was involved in over 60 events with only a skeleton staff.

There was a new government elected in 1995, and the decision was made to disband the company. It was formally wound up in 1996 to be replaced by a Special Events Unit housed within the tourism ministry. A press release issued by the Minister for Tourism on 14 November 1996 states that the unit will bring 'special events promotion into the mainstream of the State's tourism marketing activities'.

While this statement might appear, on the face of it, to place tourism rather than economic benefits at the forefront of the events policy, the two goals can be coincident, and the new unit's strategy statement lists as one of its objectives to 'maximise the economic, social and cultural benefits of events to the government and the State of New South Wales' (Tourism NSW, 1996). However, the statement makes a number of references to cultural and tourism effects which places it apart from the Melbourne Major Events Company's emphasis on large events and economic impact.

In South Australia the government established the Australian Major Events Company (AME) in 1995 following the loss of the Formula One Grand Prix to Victoria. The company's charter was to attract events to the state which would replace the lost tourism and economic benefits of the Grand Prix. Its charter included the promotion of 'the benefit of major events to all South Australians'. However, it was not as focused on large events as the Melbourne Major Events Company, and has enjoyed some success in attracting a number of smaller events which nevertheless are higher yielding in terms of tourism expenditure.

AME's main period of activity was the year 1996 during which it supported 49 events, including the Adelaide Festival of Arts, Opera in the Outback, World Cup Cycling and Australia Cup Gymnastics. At the end of this period the state government of South Australia decided to focus the company on the tourism aspects of events and it was amalgamated with the state's Tourism Commission in late 1996. It should be noted that during some of this period a unit within the Department of Recreation and Sport was also in operation trying to win sporting events which would capture economic benefits and enhance the state's profile in tourism.

This episode illustrates the policy decision which governments must make about how to administer the whole area of special events attraction and management.

While Western Australia, Queensland, and to some extent Victoria rely on the independent corporation run along business lines, New South Wales, South Australia and Tasmania rely on traditional civil service structures. Research is needed to establish the relative effectiveness of the two approaches in terms of achieving economic benefits from hosting events.

Economic evaluation

Through the 1980s there was a growing awareness that the economic impacts of a special event on its host region were likely to exceed the cost to government of supporting the event. This awareness possibly began with the 1982 Commonwealth Games in Brisbane, and prompted a number of studies into events through the 1980s and into the 1990s. Some of the events that have been studied are shown in Table 11.1, along with the reference to the study.

The general framework for evaluating the economic impact laid out in Burns, Hatch and Mules (1986, Chapter 1) is in terms of the expenditure that occurs in the host region that is attributable to the event. There are a number of traps for the unwary here, most of which were categorised by Faulkner (1993) as expenditure 'switching':

- Visitors may switch their expenditure in time, i.e. they had planned a trip to the region regardless and had simply arranged the timing of their visit to coincide with the event. Their expenditure cannot be attributed to the event.
- Visitors may switch their expenditure in terms of location within a state. For example, during World Expo '88 in Brisbane, visitor numbers showed a marked

Table 11.1 A selection of economic studies of major events

Event	Reference
1982 Brisbane Commonwealth Games	Lynch and Jensen (1984)
1985 Adelaide Grand Prix	Burns, Hatch and Mules (1986)
1985 World Cup Athletics, Canberra	Department of Sport, Recreation and Tourism (1986)
1986–7 America's Cup Defence, Perth	Centre for Applied and Business Research (1986)
1989 Motor Cycle Grand Prix, Phillip Island	National Institute of Economic and Industry Research (1989)
1990 Australian Tennis Open, Melbourne	National Institute of Economic and Industry Research (1990)
1990 Adelaide Festival	McDonald (1990)
1991 Eastern Creek Motor Cycle Grand Prix	Reark Research (1991)
1994 IndyCar Race, Gold Coast	Ernst and Young (1994)
1996 IndyCar Race, Gold Coast	KPMG Management Consulting (1996)

increase in the south-east corner of Queensland, but a significant reduction in the far north of the state. The net gain in expenditure to the state was clearly less than the expenditure in the south-east corner by the amount that was switched.

- Governments may switch public expenditure from other public works to constructing facilities for the event. Robbing Peter to pay Paul is only an expenditure gain if they are in different states, and the viewpoint is the state. For example, if Victoria is the viewpoint, any Commonwealth funds spent on facilities may be considered a gain to Victoria as long as other Commonwealth expenditure in Victoria is not reduced.
- Local residents attending the event may be diverting expenditure from other activities in order to pay for admission to the event. There is no net gain to the local economy. However, if some residents decide to cancel a trip away in order to stay home and attend the event, their expenditure would have occurred outside of their home region but for the event. Their expenditure on the event is now a gain to the local economy.

In relation to government spending on facilities, Faulkner (1993) makes the point that the smaller the region of interest, the greater the probability that such expenditure is from a higher level of government and hence a net gain to the region. For example, Queensland government expenditure on facilities for the IndyCar race is neutral as far as Queenslanders go, being switched from elsewhere in Queensland, but it is a gain to the Gold Coast region, that is, unless the government makes compensating changes elsewhere in its budget that result in fewer funds being allocated to the Gold Coast in other areas of expenditure such as schools, roads and hospitals. Also, it is more likely that net gains from visitor expenditure will be increasingly eroded by leakages as we proceed from the national to the state and regional levels owing to greater dependence on imported goods and services.

Expenditure on such facilities may have a side-benefit in terms of future attraction for visitors. For example, the construction of the QEII stadium in Brisbane for the 1982 Commonwealth Games provided Brisbane with a first-class facility for staging other events, as well as a venue for local sporting competition. Sometimes the extra funds that become available, either from sponsors or higher levels of government, enable a region to achieve a standard of facilities it would not otherwise enjoy.

Most of the economic studies referred to in Table 11.1 use some kind of economic model to estimate the flow-on or multiplier effects on the rest of the economy arising from visitor expenditure and other expenditure attributable to the event. There is some debate among economists about the merit of this exercise. Some argue that the leakage of such expenditure to imports from outside of the region in question, and the 'crowding out' effects of such expenditure on other expenditure in the region may mean that the multiplier is very low and, indeed, lower than that estimated by many simple models.

Burns, Hatch and Mules (1986) estimated the multiplier for GSP for South Australia for the Grand Prix at only 1.192. In their study of the Eastern Creek motor cycle event's economic impact on New South Wales, Reark Research (1991) used national multipliers to derive an overall implied GSP multiplier of 2.47. There are a wide range of possible multiplier measures (see Burgan and Mules, 1992) and they can easily be misinterpreted by the uninformed. Because of the unreliability of multiplier measures, Melbourne Major Events Unit and the AME Corporation from Adelaide are tending to place more emphasis on the economic benefits arising from direct expenditure by visitors, and any gains in sponsorship and other revenue, rather than rely on justifying an event in terms of its multiplier effects.

Table 11.2 shows the financial cost to government and the estimated economic impact of a selection of special events. The table is not an exhaustive list of all major events or even of all those for which economic impacts have been estimated by researchers. However, it illustrates the general principle of the events returning more to their host region's economy than the cost of running them. It also suggests that some events have a higher yield than others, for example events such as Arts Festivals, or Masters Games attract an older, more affluent visitor who stays longer and spends more.

It could be argued that even where an event returns more in GSP than the government expenditure on running it, this begs the question of whether any other use of public funds would have yielded a greater return. However, to require this would place more stringent tests on tourism spending than spending on any other activity of government. A highway proposal is not required to justify itself against all other possible present and future uses of government funds. It is required to have a benefit–cost ratio in excess of one. As such it may be ranked by Treasury officials with other projects, but it is not the role of the events or tourism planner to carry out such a ranking.

The growth in Australia over the past decade in the number and size of Special Event Corporations, as agencies of state government policy, is testimony to the faith that such governments have in the ability of special events to generate economic and political benefits.

One such event was the World Exposition of 1988 (Expo '88) held in Brisbane, Queensland. This event actually predated the formation of the Queensland Events Corporation (QEC), but was regarded so favourably by the community because of its economic benefits that it was a major catalyst for the creation of the QEC. In the next section, Expo '88 is used as a case study of how large-scale government involvement is needed for such an event, and how the event achieved significant economic impacts, including tourism attraction, promotion of the host region for future tourism, and altered urban use and community perceptions.

Expo '88 involved the state government in an outlay of over A\$230 million, but was judged to be so successful in generating the tourism impacts refered to above that it could be seen as not only the catalyst for the formation of the QEC but also of similar corporations in other states of Australia.

Table 11.2   Financial costs and economic impact of various events

Event	Financial loss (A\$ million)	Impact on GSP (A\$ million)
1985 Adelaide Grand Prix	2.6	23.6
1992 Adelaide Grand Prix	4.0	37.4
1990 Adelaide Arts Festival	1.9	10.1
1991 Eastern Creek Motor Cycle Grand Prix	4.8	13.6
1994 Brisbane World Masters Games	2.8	50.6
1996 IndyCar	7.9	35.0

Case study – from special event to special place

Introduction

In 1988 the city of Brisbane, Australia, played host to an international exposition – Expo '88. The event coincided with the celebration of 200 years since European colonisation of Australia, the Bicentennial Celebration. The latter was centred largely on Sydney, where the first Europeans had arrived, but Expo '88 turned out to be a major part of the year of commemoration. Expo '88 ran from 30 April to 31 October and attracted 16.5 million visitors (including multiple visits), 23% of whom came from interstate and 5% of whom came from overseas, with New Zealand visitors making up almost half of the overseas contingent.[1]

The event focused much national attention on Brisbane, as had the hosting of the Commonwealth Games in Brisbane in 1982. Both events also acted as catalysts for redevelopment of the city of Brisbane, a city which had lagged behind the urbanisation of other Australian cities through the 1960s and 1970s. The modernisation of Brisbane, which had begun with the Commonwealth Games in 1982, accelerated under the influence of Expo '88.

The site on which Expo '88 was held was the south bank of the Brisbane River. This waterway winds its way through suburbs, past the central business district, past wharves and industrial areas, and eventually into the sea adjacent to Brisbane International Airport. The river is very much part of the city, and the south bank where Expo '88 was held is directly across the water from the shining towers of the Central Business District (CBD).

Prior to its use as the site for Expo '88, the south bank was a run-down area featuring mixed-use, old buildings, railway stations, and warehouses. In the late 1970s the Queensland state government began the transition of the area into a recreation and tourist precinct by siting the new Queensland Performing Arts Complex, the Queensland Art Gallery and Museum, and the State Library along a strip of river bank at the western end of the zone. Despite these developments, much of the central and eastern end of the area continued to be semi-industrial in its use. Expo '88 was used as the 'big bang' to convert the whole area into modern urban living and recreational space. The rest of this chapter describes the way in which Expo '88 was the catalyst and inspiration for the redevelopment of the whole area which is now known as South Bank.

The history of Brisbane's South Bank

Brisbane is the largest city, and state capital of the state of Queensland. The population of the city is 1.5 million, with a further 0.5 million living within a radius of 100 kilometres.

---

[1] Data on the visitation and impacts of Expo '88 have been obtained from 'EXPO '88 IMPACT – The Impact of World Expo '88 on Queensland's Tourism Industry', Queensland Tourist and Travel Corporation, October 1989.

The city was established in 1824 as part of the push north by the early colonists in Sydney. Initially, the new colony was a penal settlement for prisoners convicted of wrongdoing in Sydney, which itself was originally a penal settlement for prisoners convicted of wrongdoing in England!

Eventually land was opened up for farming in the inland, and by 1841 the south bank of the Brisbane river was a staging point for farm produce, particularly wool, on its way to Sydney via steamships which sailed up the river to tie up opposite the south bank. In the first quarter of 1842 some 1800 bales of wool were ferried across the river to the main wharf opposite for shipping to Sydney.[2] The area featured storehouses, wharves, ferries, inns of dubious repute, and a scattering of houses.

In 1897 a bridge was built connecting the south bank with the commercial and administrative centre of Brisbane on the north side. The bridge gave impetus to development and by the 1940s the area was flourishing as an entertainment precinct for troops on leave during the Second World War. Theatres, clubs and hotels thrived in the area in this period.

After the war, the area gradually decayed. Businesses were closed, theatres and nightclubs were replaced by warehouses, car yards, and light industry, which gave the area an image which was not compatible with leisure and recreation. The hub of entertainment in the city had moved north, and south bank fast became a 'derelict site' (Craik, 1992).

In preparation for the Commonwealth Games in 1982, the civic authorities modernised and upgraded much of the social infrastructure on the north side of the river. The passenger facilities at Brisbane Airport were substantially improved, roads were straightened and widened, and streets and parks were 'beautified'. The orientation for the Commonwealth Games was to the north and east, with the main stadium being well away from the centre of the city to the south-east.

Against all this development the south bank stood out as being in need of upgrading and redevelopment. The proximity to the CBD, and the crowd-pulling feature of an annual spring festival in the area were suggestive of potential for development based around leisure , tourism, and special events. Craik (1992) wrote that 'the rundown South Brisbane site' was 'directly opposite the CBD' and visible from the office windows of business and civic leaders who were proponents of Expo '88 as a catalyst.

However, the process began earlier with a state government decision to construct a Cultural Centre at the western end of the area. The Centre was to comprise an Art Gallery, a Performing Arts Complex, a Museum, and a State Library. Later refinements have added a Convention Centre, and private investors have been involved via the development of an international class hotel.

Initial planning for this Centre actually predated the Commonwealth Games, and the first stage of the Centre was the Queensland Art Gallery which opened in 1982, the same year as the Games. Land along the south bank adjoining the Cultural Centre was acquired by the state government for A\$15 million in 1984. This followed Brisbane being granted the right to host an exposition on the site to coincide with the Australian Bicentennial celebrations of 1988.

---

[2] This and other historical information reported here are contained in *South Bank – An Historical Perspective*, published by the State Library of Queensland, 1992.

The original Expo '88 site took up some 16 hectares, but the scope of the re-development of the area was increased to 42 hectares, of which the original 16 has become the South Bank Parklands. The remainder consists of the Brisbane Convention and Exhibition Centre, Rydges Hotel, and various mooted commercial and residential developments.

Expo '88

Originally conceived in 1974 as a centrepiece for Australia's bicentennial celebrations of 1988, Expo '88 ran into a number of early difficulties:

- The federal government would not provide any direct funding.
- The Australian Bicentennial Authority (ABA) was funded by the federal government, and despite being supportive, did not want to spend its funds on an exposition.
- The Bureau of International Expositions (BIE) had already awarded France the right to hold a universal 'A' class exposition in 1989 to mark the centenary of the French exposition – only one such exposition is usually allowed per decade.
- The governments of other states of Australia were reluctant to be involved, some out of pettiness, others due to lack of confidence in the organisers.

In the end, the Queensland proposal was for a 'B' class exposition on the site. The BIE rejected Queensland's proposal to make tourism the theme on the grounds that an exposition is not supposed to be a trade fair but rather is meant to be a showcase for the achievements of humanity. Eventually the theme which was agreed to after much wrangling was 'leisure in the age of technology', and the intention was to involve a high degree of private enterprise in funding and displays. In fact IBM was a major exhibitor, thus blurring the distinction between an exposition and a trade fair.

According to Craik (1992), the Queensland state government established the Brisbane Exposition South Bank Redevelopment Authority (BESBRA) to run Expo. The authority was also responsible for land acquisition, construction, management, and redevelopment of the site. The latter responsibility was the prime objective of Expo. In order to redevelop the site as a major tourist and leisure centre, the perceptions which the residents of Brisbane held about the area had to be changed from thinking of it as a degraded, semi-industrial district to thinking of it as an open, friendly, and relaxing place to visit. Expo '88 was the event which changed the landscape of South Bank and changed the people's perceptions of the site. A similar use of a special event to change public perceptions of a site marked for redevelopment is documented in Mules (1993), where a water-based festival was used to promote the transformation of a disused wharf area into a leisure and housing precinct.

The organising and financing of Expo '88 was riddled with intrigue as the various private industry and public sector parties manouevred for position. Reluctance by the private sector to underake any significant funding led to the state governement funding the event at a cost of A$238 million (Craik, 1992), although when costs borne by arms of government other than the South Bank authority were taken into account, for example the Police Department, the costs have been estimated at between A$400 million and A$600 million (Donohue, 1988).

In 1989 the Queensland Tourist and Travel Corporation (QTTC) published a report by the National Centre for Studies in Travel and Tourism (NCSTT) into the tourism and economic impact of Expo '88 (NCSTT, 1989). The report made no mention of the cost, concentrating instead on the tourism effects. Indeed, one could argue that since the ultimate objective was redevelopment of the site, the costs of Expo should not be set wholly against its economic impacts, but in some measure against the longer term impacts of the redevelopment.

Expo '88 resulted in 11.8 million additional visitor-nights in Queensland (NCSTT,1989), of which 7.7 million were by Australians from other states and 2.3 million were from overseas visitors. Total expenditure by these additional visitors amounted to A$555 million of which A$490.6 million was spent in the Brisbane region, with a further A$64.4 million being spent in other regions of Queensland. The latter occurred because of visitors using their trip to Expo as an opportunity to visit other tourism destinations in the state.

The Expo organisers took full advantage of its riverfront location and the layout of the site was in a ribbon style along the course of the river. The focal point was a water's-edge boardwalk – a broad promenade from which the CBD could be seen across the other side of the water, and on which continuous street entertainments occurred. The boardwalk also featured restaurants and mooring points for various craft, including tour operators. The boardwalk was extremely popular with visitors and residents alike, so much so that it has been retained and improved upon in the redevelopment of the area into the South Bank Parklands.

Other features besides the exhibition pavilions of the exhibiting countries were a fun park, monorail, various river-based entertainments, and a floating nautical museum. The provision of entertainment on the site was very popular with residents of Brisbane who averaged 7.8 visits each (Craik, 1992). The general upswelling of community enthusiasm for the event and the popular local use of the site prompted the State Library to declare in its official history of South Bank that 'the spirit of Expo refused to die' (Longhurst, 1992 : 89).

South Bank redevelopment

Expo '88 concluded in November of that year without a clear strategy in place for the site's future use. However, it was clear that the success of Expo in attracting crowds bent upon leisure and entertainment had cemented the notion of recreation and life-style in future planning for the area. In May of the following year the state government formed the South Bank Corporation (SBC) to replace BESBRA and to proceed with concept planning for the Expo site. SBC is a wholly government-owned and funded company with full protection of the crown. It was established with a board of five members drawn from state government (2 members), local government (2 members), with an independent chairperson.

In late 1989 the board appointed a firm of architects and a project management firm to devise a Development Plan for the site. The basic concept was for open space and public access with a park/gardens theme. A process of extensive public consultation resulted in substantial changes to the initial plan in order to maximise the area of park, and to place proposed high-rise developments a greater distance from the river. The architects' concept was for a park emphasising water and open green spaces, incorporating low-rise buildings near the river, with more intensity of built environment and greater height of buildings further away from the river. In April 1990 the revised Development Plan incorporating this concept was approved by the state government.

While it has not been stated explicitly in either the Development Plan or the SBC's Annual Reports, it seems that the strategy was for public investment in redevelopment, with private developers stepping in with commercial buildings such as hotels, apartment blocks and offices. The public investment has resulted in a park with a great deal of open space, including gardens, promenades, a waterway, and a massive lagoon incorporating a safe swimming beach complete with sand which had to be brought in. The beach and the promenades overlook the river and further to the skyline of the CBD on the opposite bank. Grey Street runs through the area and continues to carry through-traffic, including buses. This has emerged as a difficulty for the park, as fast-moving traffic detracts from the image of leisure and relaxation in a park setting and confuses the image of the whole area. It has also detracted from the attractiveness of the proposed development of residential and retail buildings on the non-river side of Grey Street. In January 1996, the SBC announced a proposal to realign Grey Street to take it the other side (west) of the development proposals, thereby integrating them more into the park and distancing the traffic further from the public focal points within the park. At the time of writing this plan had been withdrawn and new proposals were being drawn up.

These problems should not be overemphasised, as the park has attracted over 5 million visitors per year since opening in 1992 (South Bank Corporation Newsletter, January 1996). Some of the significant development events since opening have been:

1993   Construction commenced for Park Lane apartments
1994   Construction commenced on South Bank Convention Hotel
1995   Park Lane apartments opened, Brisbane Convention and Exhibition Centre opened
1996   South Bank Convention Hotel (Rydges) opened.

Over this period, a large number of events and festivals have been held in the park and on the adjoining stretch of the Brisbane River. Each New Year's Eve a fireworks display on a barge floating on the river next to the park draws thousands of spectators. On 26 January 1995 the Australia Day fireworks display attracted an estimated 120 000 people.

Other events which have been held at South Bank Parklands, as it is now commonly known, include:

September 1993   Spring Festival attracted 100 000 people.
March 1994   Chinese state acrobats performed at the Piazza
May 1994   Osaka-Tenjin Festival
December 1994   Christmas Lantern Festival attracted 230 000 people.
February 1995   Women's Beach Volleyball – Australian round of World Championships.

The redevelopment of the initial 16-hectare area of Expo into the South Bank Parklands has continued to evolve since its official opening in 1992. However, the major focus of the SBC for the future is the planning for the remainder of the 42-hectare space which is within its domain. This region is important as it adjoins the park and therefore will have an impact on the future success of the park as a public recreation area. It is also close to the CBD and will therefore come under development pressure for a variety of commercial uses.

In 1996 the SBC began a process of concept development for the remainder of the area. The emphasis in the concept is on residential, retail and commercial land use in order to keep the life-style image of the South Bank area. This continues the transformation of the land use of the whole area from one of decaying buildings, manufacturing industry, transport and storage, to one which emphasises modern urban life and leisure. The process which began with Expo '88 continues with the same theme of leisure and modern living.

Conclusions

Special events have become a major part of the policy landscape in Australian states. Such events are valued not only for their tourism attraction but also for the economic impacts that flow from the tourist expenditure. Events have thus become part of the economic development policy arena, as well as part of tourism policy. The benefits from such events can be so great as to justify considerable government expenditure on staging and promoting them.

The process and form of government involvement has become increasingly formalised since the days of Expo '88. Most state governments have established corporations or commissions to bid for, promote, and organise special events. Expo '88 showed that such events require large-scale government involvement in order to reap the considerable changes in tourism and lifestyle.

It is clear from the Australian experience that special-event tourism has become an industry or economic activity, and as such has moved away from purely sporting or cultural aims and impacts. As in any other industry, the participants find themselves in commercial competition, the rivals are other states and cities bidding for similar events, and for tourist expenditure. This competitive commercial environment is one that has implications for the economic welfare of the broader community, and as such is likely to experience increasing levels of government involvement as the rivals attempt to maximise the tourist flows to their own regions.

References

Black, T. (1994) 'The Queensland IndyCar Grand Prix: Assessing the costs and benefits', *Agenda*, 1, 259–61.

Burgan, B. and Mules, T.J. (1992) 'The economic impact of sporting events', *Annals of Tourism Research*, 19, 700–10.

Burns, J.P.A., Hatch, J.H. and Mules, T.J. (1986) *The Adelaide Grand Prix: The Impact of a Special Event*, Centre for South Australian Economic Studies, University of Adelaide.

Centre for Applied and Business Research (1986) *America's Cup: Economic Impact*, University of Western Australia.

Craik, J. (1992) 'Expo '88: fashions of sight and politics of Site', in A. Bennett, P. Buckridge, D. Carter and C. Mercer (eds), *Celebrating the Nation – A Critical Study of Australia's Bicentenary*, Sydney: Allen & Unwin.

Department of Sport, Recreation and Tourism (1986) *Economic Impact of the World Cup of Athletics, Canberra, 1985*, Commonwealth of Australia, Canberra.

Donohue, K. (1988) 'An economic and financial analysis of Expo '88', paper given to Expo '88 Seminar, School of Management, Queensland Institute of Technology, Brisbane.

Ernst and Young (1994) 'The economic impact of the 1994 Australian FAI IndyCar Grand Prix', report to the Queensland Events Corporation, Brisbane.

Faulkner, W. (1993) 'Evaluating the tourism impact of hallmark events', Occasional Paper No. 16, Bureau of Tourism Research, Canberra.

Faulkner, W. (1994) 'Towards a strategic approach to tourism development: the Australian experience', in W. Theobold (ed.), *Global Tourism: The Next Decade*, Oxford: Butterworth-Heinemann, 231–45.

Fredline, E. (1996) *Resident Perceptions of the Gold Coast Indy, an Exploratory Study*, unpublished dissertation for the Honours degree in Hotel Management, Griffith University, Gold Coast Campus.

Getz, D. (1989) 'Special events: defining the product', *Tourism Management*, 10, 125–37.

Getz, D. (1991) *Festivals, Special Events and Tourism*, New York: Van Nostrand Reinhold

Getz, D. (1997) *Event Management and Event Tourism*, New York: Cognizant Communication Company.

Gilbert, D. (1990) 'Tourism marketing: its emergence and establishment', in C. Cooper (ed.), *Progress in Tourism, Recreation and Hospitality Management, 3*, University of Surrey, 77–90.

Hall, C.M. (1989) 'The definition and analysis of hallmark events', *Geojournal*, 19, 263–68.

Jago, L.K. and Shaw, R. (1995) 'Special event calendars: conceptual and research issues', in *Proceedings of the National Tourism and Hospitality Conference, 1995*, Canberra: Bureau of Tourism Research.

KPMG Management Consulting (1996) 'Business, economic and social review of the 1996 IndyCar event', report to Queensland Events Corporation, Brisbane.

Longhurst, R.L. (1992) *South Bank – An Historical Perspective – From then Until Now*, State Library of Queensland.

Lynch, P. and Jensen, R.C. (1984) 'The economic impact of the XII Commonwealth Games on the Brisbane region', *Urban Policy and Research*, 2, 3, 11–14.

McDonald, S. (1990) 'The 1990 Adelaide Festival economic impact', Report to Tourism SA, Adelaide.

Mules, T. (1993) 'A special event as part of an urban renewal strategy', *Festival Management and Event Tourism*, 1, 2, 65–7.

National Centre for Studies in Travel and Tourism (1989) 'Expo '88 Impact – the Impact of World Expo '88 on Queensland's tourism industry', Tourist and Travel Corporation.

National Institute of Economic and Industry Research (1990) 'The 1990 Ford Australian Open in Melbourne', Report to Tennis Australia, Melbourne.

Price Waterhouse Economic Studies and Strategies Unit (1993) '1992 Formula One Grand Prix: economic evaluation', Report to Australian Formula One Corporation, Adelaide.

Reark Research (1991) 'Evaluation of the impact of the Toohey's Australian Motor Cycle Grand Prix at Eastern Creek, New South Wales', Report to New South Wales Tourism Commission, Sydney.

Ritchie, B. (1984) 'Assessing the impact of hallmark events: conceptual and research issues', *Journal of Travel Research*, 23, 1, 2–11.

Soutar, G.N. and McLeod, P. (1989) 'The impact of the America's Cup on Fremantle residents: some empirical evidence', in G. Syme, J.B. Shaw, D.M. Fenton and W.S. Mueller (eds), *The Planning and Evaluation of Hallmark Events*, Aldershot: Avebury.

South Bank Corporation (1996) *Newsletter*, Brisbane.

Thomson, N. (1986) 'Financial impacts upon the public sector', in J.P.A. Burns, J.H. Hatch and T.J. Mules (eds), *The Adelaide Grand Prix: the Impact of a Special Event*, Centre for South Australian Economic Studies, University of Adelaide.

Tourism NSW (1996) 'Events strategy', paper prepared by Manager, Special Events, Tourism NSW, 4.

12 Events as entrepreneurial displays: Seville, Barcelona and Madrid

MARTIN ROBERTSON and YVONNE GUERRIER

CHAPTER SUMMARY

This chapter looks at the mega-event trilogy, the Barcelona Olympics, the Madrid European Year of Culture and the Seville Expo, that took place in Spain in 1992. These events were seen as a way of changing the image of the cities and of Spanish tourism, which has traditionally been associated only with 'sun and sea' holidays. Large hallmark events are one way that cities can create an image internationally and attract internal investment with the aim of promoting long-term growth. If cities are to achieve long-term social and economic benefits from these events, it is argued that they need to cement good public–private partnerships, difficult in Spain which has a large traditional public sector unused to working in this way, and develop strategies which look beyond the event itself. The chapter demonstrates that all three mega-events were high-quality products and in the long term Barcelona and, to a lesser extent, Madrid have benefited through infrastructure enhancement and a higher international profile, although Seville has failed to exploit the success of the Expo. However, the chapter points out the essential contradictions in a global economic system that increasingly requires cities to act as entrepreneurs and compete with each other intranationally on the world stage to host ever more spectacular events. The market will always favour some cities over others and less successful cities will be unable to compete. Even in the successful cities, this type of competition will tend to increase inequality rather than facilitate social redistribution.

Introduction

The end of the Second World War was marked not only by global relief but also by fervent rematching and renewing of Europe's urban mosaics. Cities were seen as

Managing Tourism in Cities. Edited by D. Tyler, Y. Guerrier and M. Robertson.
Copyright © 1998 John Wiley & Sons Ltd.

symbols of all that was good in a country's society and therefore they needed to be re-established as quickly as possible. Neil Smith (1996) describes this movement as the 'European gentrification' of central urban and inner-city areas. In Spain it was the ending of Franco's tyranny that marked the movement back to both order and calm. Within this, Madrid was the first Spanish city to be 'gentrified'. The message was clear, Spain (like the rest of Europe) was going back to work.

In the 1990s, cities have once again become the panacea for national ailments. They are less now just symbols of power but more symbols of attraction for visitors and thus, it is hoped, business investment. The economic multiplier effect of urban tourism is reverentially cited in all urban development plans. Large-scale events, as one type of urban development, are seen as 'short-term events with long-term consequences for the cities that stage them' (Roche, 1994 : 1). Moreover, as Hall (1992 : 44) opines, 'events are generally seen in a positive light by government and private industry because of the perceived economical, commercial and promotional benefits in the hosting of such events'.

In 1992 three mega-events were staged in Spanish cities: the Barcelona Olympics, the Madrid European Year of Culture and the Seville Expo. This chapter will consider how this Spanish event trilogy attempted to change the image both of these cities and of Spanish tourism and assess its success in achieving this.

The development of Spanish tourism

Spain has 'become identified as the major holiday site for western European tourists' (Bote Gómez and Sinclair, 1996 : 65). The scale of tourism into Spain is massive: in 1990, 52 million international tourists and 13 million Spaniards took their holidays in Spain (Bote Gómez and Sinclair, 1996). The tourism sector is vital to the Spanish economy, representing 8.09% of GDP and 11.2% of employment in 1990 (González and Moral, 1996). However, tourism is strongly concentrated in the eastern and southern seaboard and islands – the costas – which together provide about 75% of the available accommodation (Barke and Towner, 1996).There is an increasing awareness among Spain's tourism planners of the fragility of the traditional 'sun and sea' holiday market, with which Spain has become synonymous; a recognition brought home by the recession of the late 1980s and early 1990s that saw the first drop in overseas visitor numbers. Planners recognised that the market for 'sun and sea' holidays is stagnating with the shift away from the 'grand' summer vacation and that Spain faces strong competition from other Mediterranean destinations as well as increasingly from long-haul destinations, for example in the Far East, that are perceived as more exotic (Ministerio de Comercio y Turismo, 1993). Furthermore the traditional market of low-cost, low value-added, seasonal and coastal tourism hardly maximises the contribution that tourism can make to the Spanish economy. In this context Spain has sought to change its market identity and develop new tourism products as well as to improve the quality of the 'sun and sea' offering.

Mass tourism in Spain has its origins in the early 1950s when Franco's regime promoted tourism both as an economic tool to reduce the public deficit in the balance of payments (Newton, 1996) and as a propaganda mechanism which would give legitimacy to the regime by sending foreign visitors home with a positive view of the country (Pi-Sunyer, 1996). In 1951 a Ministry of Information and Tourism was created, significant because it was one of the first examples of a ministry with tourism in the title (Newton, 1996) and also because it linked tourism with propaganda (Pi-Sunyer, 1996).

The devaluation of the peseta in 1959 and the 1959 Stabilisation Plan, which pragmatically espoused liberal economic policies encouraging foreign investment and foreign trade, led to a boom in mass tourism through the 1960s. The focus was on growth fuelled by private sector speculation; there was a disregard of aesthetic or environmental factors and the potential for regional development and the development of tourism in Spain's interior was ignored. Apart from some fluctuations due to the oil crises in the 1970s, tourist arrivals continued to grow during the 1970s and 1980s (Bote Gómez and Sinclair, 1996). However, post-Franco, there was a move away from state centralism and towards more regional control of tourism planning and a recognition of the need for more government intervention and control of tourism. There was also more awareness of environmental issues and the quality of the tourist product (Aguilo, 1996; Santos Arrebola, 1995).

Fayos (quoted in Aguilo, 1996) argues that the 1990s have seen another shift of focus to a third generation of tourism policies in Spain, represented in the Plan to Improve the Competitiveness of Spanish Tourism drawn up by the Ministry of Industry, Commerce and Tourism in 1993 (Ministerio de Comercio y Turismo, 1993). This approach sees competitiveness as the key to tourism development, is consumer driven and focuses on increasing segmentation of the tourist sector. However, despite such initiatives, the traditional image of Spanish tourism as fundamentally mass tourism in resorts and beaches is hard to change. As Robinson (1996 : 41a) argues:

> The Spanish tourist industry is a prisoner of its own rapid success, fastened within a historical pattern from which it will find it almost impossible and economically undesirable to break free.

Compared with resort-based tourism, the scale of urban tourism in Spain is small. However, the three main cities of Madrid, Barcelona and Seville presented an opportunity for Spain to develop an alternative to its traditional tourism offering. These cities have very different characters. Madrid has always been the major urban destination in Spain, ranking among the top ten of world cities for visitor numbers albeit competing for this position with other major European cities such as Brussels, Vienna, Rome, Copenhagen and Munich (Barke and Towner, 1996; Ashworth and Tunbridge, 1992). Barcelona, prior to 1992, was essentially a business and commercial centre (Priestley, 1996). It seemed to have everything that was necessary for an aspiring tourist city but was nevertheless a problem to position as a destination in its own right rather than as a stop-over en route to the resorts of the Costa Brava (Pi-Sunyer, 1996). Finally, Seville is a small historic city with strong Moorish influences situated in Andalucia, one of the least developed regions in Spain. The development of tourism there would help redress some of the economic imbalance between the north and south of Spain.

Urban tourism and the world economy

The realisation of the significance of large or 'hallmark' events (Hall, 1992) and the frequency of their performance is a direct response to the Europe-wide economic and political transformations of the last two decades. The world market has become more significant in economic and political terms for all nations in the European Union (as well as all the other members of the worldwide economy). Thus most countries' national governments have either partially or wholly turned their attention away from managing internal national markets and towards the international one. This has precipitated competition at an intra-national level among many cities and regions, finding themselves vying for a share of the global economy while receiving less favourable fiscal support from national governments.

Ever more this has prompted cities, urban regions and emerging conurbations to take two paths. One is to divest themselves of many of their previous public provision roles, transferring them instead, where possible, to the private sector; and, second, to seek further inward capital investment. This inward capital investment is sought by projecting themselves onto a global platform: to attract both private investment and European Commission funding. For both of these sources a civic image has to be created, and created in such a way as to make the city an attractive investment. A current tool in generating that civic image, civic pride, and thereafter inward investment, is the hosting of a large-scale event. This event may run any number of days. It is likely to be either a one-off event or a series of one-off infrequent events. The event serves to financially boost the city, i.e. to give an initial show of vitality to convince prospective investors of the city's focus and its worth. Thus cities compete to build conference centres, host sporting events etc., because they 'feel that investment in prestige projects, cultural spectacles or international events will help foster a positive image' (Jewson and Mac-Gregor, 1997 : 29), and thus ensure long-term growth. Put more simply, the argument is that a city that has the essence of all that is good in civil life, i.e. art, culture, and general quality of the social milieu, will be attractive to external investors.

The image of the event, its appeal and its likely financial outcome, viewed either over a short or long timespan, for investors is dependent on the structure and strategy of the event. It is also dependent on the objective of any given investor. Figure 12.1 illustrates the two different investment perspectives – 'short term' and 'long term' – and indicates how a long-term strategy and extensive interaction between the host event organising committee and investors is required for long-term investment opportunities to arise from the event.

The role and control of 'image'

The re-imaging of Spain's cities aimed to promote these cities as new and vibrant: economic, political and cultural dynamos. The re-imaging process also sought to actively involve the private sector, forming public–private partnerships that could pursue the international markets that Spain requires. The images utilised had to have international appeal and indeed, as will be discussed below, they have been

1

2

@
Short term
(spectacle)
opportunity

Minimum
investment

ⓑ
Substantial
plan of long-
term strategy

Invitation to
invest in 'booster'
event infrastructures

Continual
'host' development
committee

Idea of event

Counselling

Supports
and interacts
with committee
in city (region)
investment

Long-term
investment
opportunities

Leaves
event

Operates
and takes
profits

4

3

○ = Key points of event management process

@ = Short-term investment perspective

ⓑ = Long-term investment perspective

= Long-term investment process

⟶ = Host committee guidance

Figure 12.1   Four stages of short- and long-term investor viewpoints

much admired internationally for their sense of style. However, they have also been criticised for their shallowness.

The criticism, first heard by city residents but more recently echoed by planners and theorists, is that the image ignores the long-term internal needs of the city; these needs are outweighed by the forces of international marketing (Pi-Sunyer, 1996). Furthermore, it has been argued that the public–private partnerships have moved out of the control of the public authorities that set them up in the first place.

Public–private event management partnerships (taking the form of committees) are inherently complicated and diffuse. Their coordination requires a government agency capable of managing all the financial, administrative, construction, social

ıat are likely to arise from the event. Often, public sector
ərience of dealing with these projects which require, as

rganisational intelligence and new mechanisms of organ-
:o-ordination . . . which display market features but also
ıance quality assessment and accountability.

r from having mixed and ill-defined objectives. As Pad-

> Public organisations lack the clearly defined objective of profit-making, par-
> ticularly those local development agencies engaged in the kinds of task associ-
> ated with city marketing, co-ordinating and facilitating between a wide range of
> implementing bodies.

The history of Spain over the last forty years is of a public sector which has not
encouraged accountability and motivated quick action and which has not been
successful in controlling and gaining the full benefit from the tourist industry.
Approximately 18% of all Spanish employment was in public government administration during the year of the three events (Allard and Bolorinos, 1996). Here the
culture of 'a job for life' persists and short term contracts of employment are hardly
known. A sense of tradition is ubiquitous. These factors and 'the division of functions along horizontal rather than vertical lines of responsibility' (Dawson,
1994 : 187) in Spain tends to encourage 'short-termism'. Emphasis is put on short-
term projects likely to engender emphatic political victories. (President González's
zealous support of the 1992 events was claimed in Spain's newspapers to have been
not unrelated to the forthcoming elections of 1993.) Changing the public sector
structure and emphasising the need for accountability and efficiency is a tall order
when government employees and their families may control as many as 8 million
votes.

Although the Socialist government elected in 1982 signalled its intention to focus
on the quality of urban development, the danger is that 'quality' is determined
solely by the needs of the international market and what international investors and
guests expect and less by the needs of the host community who have to live in the
city in the run-up to, during and after the event. The impact of major and 'spectacular' events can easily camouflage the civic (i.e. legitimate) purpose of the event. The
event as a product is judged on its 'quality' but the event as a social and economic
tool is not. Furthermore, the areas of cities which are regenerated as a result of the
event attain property values which exclude those people who were originally intended to benefit (Hall, 1997). For example, flats in Barcelona's Olympic village,
built as a conversion project in a working-class area and intended to be resold at
low prices, were actually being sold for prices of up to £200 000 (sterling equivalent)
(Pilger, 1992).

There are examples from other cities where this process of 'imagineering' a city
as a component of a city 'entrepreneurial' race (Jewson and MacGregor, 1997,
Harding, 1994; see also Chapter 1 in this volume) is claimed to have failed to benefit
the host community. The process of 'imagineering' is imported from the United

States where it has been claimed that it has only served to polarise economic and geographic disadvantage still further. Rutheiser (1996 : 287) reflecting on the experience of the Atlanta games claimed that the image creators 'Inadvertently confused the city with the words (and images) they have used to describe it' and that 'boosters have avoided acknowledging those aspects of the city, and its population, that do not fit'.

In the next part of this chapter we will look in detail at the design of image, its deployment and its pre- and post-event symbolism in relation to the Spanish event trilogy. We also consider the extent to which the image helped regeneration and indeed whether it was engineered to be sustainable at all. We will compare and contrast the cities rather than providing three separate case studies while remembering that the three cities we are focusing on bridge very separate cultural identities, being part of very different regions of Spain.

The design of image

> Now he [sic] wants to behold something sacred; now something informative, to broaden him, now something beautiful, to lift him and make him finer; and now something different, because he's bored (Feifer, 1985 : 269).
>
> We live in an age of niche markets, in which customers have become accustomed to high quality and extensive choice (Osbourne and Gaebler, 1992 : 15)

Consumers have become increasingly more demanding and their product loyalty has become more transient. The evolution of global information media has allowed the expectations of people to widen to an extent that would not have been dreamed of twenty years ago. To meet consumer needs the design of a product has to be clear, attractive, testing enough to induce interest but not so testing as to induce a search for something more easily clarified.

The design of an event, as a product, has to meet these criteria but equally has to appeal to both potential visitors and the potential investor. It is both a creative and a strategic enterprise. As Echtner and Ritchie (1993 : 3) point out, 'creating and managing an appropriate destination image are critical to effective positioning and marketing strategy'. Image creation is not incidental to overall development, it is a catalyst for other changes.

Felipe González, the then Spanish prime minister, gave voice to the image requirements of Expo '92 as follows:

> . . . our particular concept of development: to reconcile the cultural heritage of the past and the modern advances and harmonise economic expansion with the quality of the environment, within a perspective of global solidarity (González, 1993 : 11).

The theme of the Expo was the 'age of discoveries'. Opened on 20 April 1992 by King Juan Carlos, it generated the enthusiasm of all Spanish fiestas, displayed architecture of breathtaking stature and was recorded as having had 40 million visits, some 4 million more than was necessary, according to the organisers, to break even.

The rhetoric associated with the Olympic Games equally included the themes of modernisation, building on the cultural heritage and reaching out internationally. Juan Antonio Samaranch, the president of the International Olympic Committee in 1992 (and the first president to preside over the Games in his home city), said:

> The Games represent a fresh start for Catalonia, they are fundamental in the regeneration of the region and the city. The games are a great opportunity to modernise the city, to promote the region, and to provide investment in facilities which the city will use after 1992 (Stevens, 1992 : 24).

Pasqual Maragall, mayor of Barcelona, talked in 1990 about the way in which the event was embedded in the long-term strategy expressed in the Barcelona 2000 Social and Economic Strategic Plan. The aim was:

> . . . to consolidate Barcelona as an Enterprising Metropolis with an influence over the macro region in which it is geographically situated, and to provide a modern, socially balanced standard of living deeply rooted in Mediterranean culture (Maragall, quoted in Clavell, 1991).

It should be remembered that prior to the Olympic build-up Barcelona had been seen essentially as a commercial and business centre in which hoteliers had tended to view their market almost solely in that way. They believed that business demand alone for rooms would surpass supply (Priestley, 1996).

For Madrid, as the Cultural Capital of Europe in 1992, the prime motive for hosting the year was to amplify the image of Madrid as a 'City of Arts'. There was not a need to re-image and create a new product as in Seville. The city already housed a great number of art galleries, museums, theatres and fine architectural buildings. Although a point of contention, it also possessed the transport and accommodation infrastructure needed to sustain visitor numbers. Accordingly, the city already owned its identity and wanted instead to enhance it and expand its tourist market. While Madrid, as the political, financial and administrative capital of Spain, might have been expected to be largely impervious to national market fluctuations, a dip in demand from the domestic market preceeding 1992 encouraged this path.

The deployment of the image

Pasqual Maragall, mayor of Barcelona, speaking at the debate 'Preparing for the 21st Century: London's Future' in 1996, responded to the question 'how do the population commit themselves to the process of reimaging their city?' with the answer 'the politicians have to be trusted, firstly at local level'. Maragall argued that by analysing the culture and qualities of a city, working out where it should go in the future and then engendering support from the populace, civic pride would follow. Certainly, while his and his city's endeavours were hardly easy, Maragall has achieved most of his plans for Barcelona and his obvious passion for the project and role as its figurehead must have played a part in this success.

Building for the Olympic Games started in 1986 and the sporting facilities were only a small part of the physical re-imaging. Barcelona received a new airport terminal and major refurbishment of the waterfront/beach a̶ toration of the quays (as part of what was called the Port 2 construction of an Olympic village for the athletes and the creation o̶ and plazas (Barke and Towner, 1996), a new convention centre and an u̶ the telecommunications system further served to redraw the city.

Barcelona is now the European city with the highest population growth. It h̶ much stronger international identity as a result of the changes of 1992. The artists̶ Antonio Gaudí (whose architecture has come to be identified with Barcelona) and Joán Miró (whose images were used, in giant puppet form, during the Games) have become synonymous with the city. Consequently, Madrid has found a city competitor of style and vitality and, while Madrid remains the financial and political capital of Spain, its hegemony is not as complete as ten years ago.

Madrid's physical re-imaging was never as substantial as that of Barcelona. Prior to 1992, while there are records of a tourism strategy, plans were not ambitious and did not emanate in any clear way from the hosting of the European Year of Culture, which Barke and Towner (1996) claim was aimed, in many senses, more at *madrileños* than at foreign tourists. It is only since 1994 that a new strategy for inner-city development and investment has really taken place. This includes substantial upgrading of the inner-city railway line and improvement to the airport. It was recognised in 1992 that Madrid Barajas Airport was not equipped to handle the extra visitors for the Expo and the Summer Olympics (Pincheson, 1992) as, despite being one of the busiest airports in Europe, it did not have an advanced traffic-control system or the facilities required to deal with large numbers of visitors (shops, hotels, adequate catering provision and car-parking provision).

During the 1980s Seville had the highest level of tertiary-based employment in any of Spain's cities, estimated at about 60% of all employment. However, as Expo '92 approached, industrial investment in Andalucia increased markedly. It was recognised that the transport and communication infrastructure were below standard and particularly inadequate for the international market. Accordingly the Expo was used as a lever to extract support from the government (Municipality, Regional and Central), the EU and limited private sources. These resulted in a motorway linking Seville and Madrid, new roadworks around the city, a modern railway system, an extended airport and the building of a high-speed rail link between Seville and Madrid (although there were complaints that the rail link did not extend beyond Madrid into France to become a truly international link). From this, Seville gained an image of accessibility it had never had before.

Seville also benefited from the introduction of an advanced telecommunications system. This as well as the resources on the Isla de la Catuja where the Expo was sited and which had previously been wasteland were expected to provide the basis for economic growth after the event (Dawson, 1994).

The island itself was home to some of the most outstanding installations ever seen. These represented different countries of the world and allowed each visitor to pursue his or her own 'discovery'. However, only an estimated 40% of the structures were retained after the event. This was in contrast to Barcelona, where the re-use of the facilities constructed for the Games for social benefit was planned from the outset (Abad, 1988). Fundamentally elements of consistency and

i the product image is to stay in people's
as difficult to exploit for long-term benefit.
ısm there was even talk of 'Andalucia being
not have been a helpful image conducive to

223

ʒh-quality tourist product at the time of staging.
ʔaintain the image associated with the high quality
ʔent. Despite plans to turn Cartuja into a technologi-
ʔentre, little has happened. Plans were put forward in
1997, ⌐   ʔpo, to engineer these developments. But there are
currently legaɪ ⌐   n relation to the financial management of the event,
questioning the propriety ⌐ both government and selected police chiefs. Doubtless,
this will dampen enthusiasm for development.

Furthermore, plans, developed in 1995, to build technological centres at either or
both Las Rozas and Villalba, 20 and 30 kilometres, respectively, north of Madrid
seem nearer fruition than those at Seville. The completion of either of these will
generate a large number of jobs in what is already a booming sector of employment
in Madrid. Seville seems to have missed out on the opportunity to be the high-tech
centre of Spain.

So in terms of sustainability, the Seville Expo has not been a success. Its revenues
have been plundered by gross inefficiency, by a government whose plans were
definitely misdirected and possibly, pending the results of the legal investigations,
corrupt. An investment of Pta 800 000 million in Seville and Andalucia has not
helped to correct the north–south divide in Spain but instead has hardened the
preconceptions of each side of the other. Seville's image has suffered from the
speculative rather than the strategic approach taken to the Expo.

Barcelona has rehoused many of its population and added a substantial travel
and communication infrastructure. It is unclear whether a 'trickle down' of investment benefit in the city centre and port area has reached other parts of the city.
Further, it may be questioned whether the Olympics provided Barcelona with a
clear, overarching identity (Pi-Sunyer, 1996). Regardless, Barcelona is now more
popular than it has ever been.

Events are market-driven but, by their very nature, which is dependent on orig-
inality and short-term spectacle, suffer from a short product life cycle. Each event
needs to be sufficiently more interesting than the previous one. The immense
logistical complexities of ensuring that the image is interesting enough to satisfy the
'public gaze' and that this matches the rational objectives of ensuring that it attracts
the market segments appropriate to the stage of growth, while also meeting the
desires of all the event stakeholders, means that a mega-event is always a risk.
Although events can enhance the image of a city internationally these benefits will
quickly decay unless there is an on-going process of image boosting (Echtner and
Ritchie, 1993). It will be fascinating to observe what happens the next time Barcelona (or Madrid or Seville) hosts a hallmark event.

City events and national image

To what extent have the 1992 trio of events helped Spain as a whole to diversify its tourism product? Interest in convention and other forms of business tourism has been growing but business tourism has only had a marked success in Madrid, Barcelona and, to a lesser extent, in Valencia (Priestley, 1996). These cities have historically been given prominence by business. They also already had some of the physical infrastructure and attractions in place before the event in order to justify their ability to stage the event in the first place. The expensive and long-term alterations that are required to turn around their image are beyond the means of other cities. That is not to say that those cities which use a different form of 'boosterism', such as Bilbao, will not be successful. But they will find it harder to attract national and international attention for lesser events and therefore it is uncertain whether their drive for internal or external investment will be successful.

The General Secretariat for Tourism (Turespaña) adopted Joán Miró's art work as the marque of Spain. The images of this Catalonian artist had also been used by Barcelona (see above). Simultaneously, but independently and unplanned, Miró's images were adopted by Viva Air and La Caixa Bank, among others. This helped to project an image of leisure opportunity in Spain internationally, while marketing experts comment that more could have been made of its potential (Aldersley-Williams, 1994): it could have been an abiding image for Spain. The longevity and ubiquity of the images had more to do with coincidence than strategy.

Conclusion

In terms of selective enhancements the event-based re-images are immensely valuable. As national promotion narratives, they are cohesive. However, as intercity competitors, the imagineered cities, like any other product, are governed by the rules of the 'product life cycle'. Accordingly, they face the risk of saturation and thus demise. If the decentralising of power is not correctly administered then, as Jessop (1997) states, the value of comparative competition as a regulator of intranational regeneration is lost to selective competitive advantage. This is to say that a national strategy set to improve the image of the national product (primarily and essentially the tourism product) is instead lost to the international successes of the principal cities. It is true, all cities can gain short-term successes in the hosting of events. With good planning, the right image and incisive marketing and promotion, an event can reap a substantial intake of visitors. However, as a national strategy, for the whole nation, it is doubtful. Only for a few cities will this drive long-term success.

The fact remains that the immense infrastructure demands required by any hallmark event necessitate huge international investment. This is undoubtedly going to create some international leakage. Figure 12.2 delineates the flow of finances and indicates how difficult it is to retain investment within the city economy rather than allowing many of the benefits to flow outside. However, if managed properly, if event and urban development plans are concise and both long term and holistic, take account of all skills needed, and the lines of responsibility are clear, then the benefits can outweigh the leakages. This was the case in Barcelona. In this way the 'image' can be seen as successful. Otherwise, it is easy for the residents (who have lived through it), the nation (who have inspected it through the media, day by day, or else visited it) and the international consumers (who have enjoyed or disliked it) to think of it as no more than an ephemeral (sometimes invasive) and opportunistic entertainment.

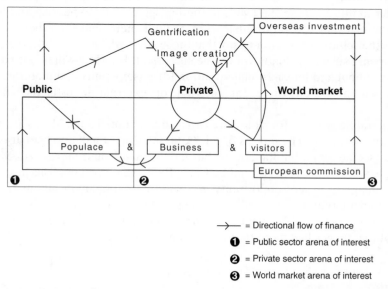

Figure 12.2   The entrepreneurial balance

To this final point, it should be added that various models of accountability and quality strategy can be utilised to amend inequalities. However, their advantage, their ability to rectify quintessentially administrative mistakes, does not alter the fact that cities are competing with other cities. This state of urban entrepreneurship has to accept the heritage of previous investment and previous historic development: '. . . that the market will continue to favour some cities more than others' (Harding, 1994 : 201). Moreover, this advantage, an 'imagineered' advantage, by its own design unshackles the chains of control which allow recourse to correct the inequalities for those that cannot compete in the long term (and who often catastrophically deplete their resources in trying to). This highlights, rather than reverses, their economic weakness.

    One thus must ask whether the clamber to market cities, through events or other form of 'entrepreneurial display', can really hope to address social inequalities, or produce citywide, not to mention nationwide, solutions. Economically, and thus, it would seem, socially, it is going to foster an increasing number of spatial gaps. Economic boosterism, set in a geo-economic and political structure that currently views intranational competition as more viable than redistributive social policies, is not a mode to which the long-term strategic quality models, such as those of Hall (1992), Getz (1991) and Ritchie (1984, 1991), can be easily applied.

Of course, models of strategic event management can be utilised in order to make the best of the event for the city and thus beat competitors. Yet this risks saturating a market already viscous with entrepreneurial city activity. Alternatively, it is suggested that the image of the successful cities (e.g. Barcelona, Madrid and – arguably – Seville) could be honed on the basis that they are collaborators contributing to the national economy, rather than intranational competitors in an international market. Competition is vital, but a worldwide battle waged through exercises in entrepreneurial display at the cost of unsuccessful cities is simply irrational.

However, for Spain, weighted against change by an increasingly ageing population, largely dependent on state support, and by an estimated fifth of all Spanish employment located in public government administration, it is easy to comprehend the resistance to reform. The drive towards efficiency is not an easy one. In the meantime, the entrepreneurial battle continues in Spain, as elsewhere.

Acknowledgements

Many thanks to Rafa Estebanez, European Officer, London Borough of Southwark District Council for his invaluable advice and information. Also thanks go to Nikki Barton at Nykis Digital Design, London for reproducing the diagrams.

References

Abad, J. M. (1988) 'Intervencion de Josep Miquel Abad', *Journades Internationales de turismo en el Mediterraneo*, Chamber of Commerce, Industry and Navigation of Barcelona.

Aguilo, E. (1996) 'Research into policies on tourism', *The Tourist Review*, 1/1996, 12–17.

Aldersley-Williams, H. (1994) 'Cities bid to make their marque', *Management Today*, August, 30–33.

Allard, G. and Bolorinos, J. (1996) *Spain to 2005: making room for the private sector*, London: The Economic Intelligence Unit.

Ashworth, G.J and Tunbridge, J. (1992) *The Tourist–Historic City*, London: Belhaven.

Barke, M. and Towner, J. (1996) 'Urban tourism in Spain', in M. Barke, J. Towner and M. Newton (eds), *Tourism in Spain: Critical Issues*, Wallingford: CAB International, 343–74.

Bote Gómez, V. and Sinclair, T. (1996) 'Tourism demand and supply in Spain', in M. Barke, J. Towner and J. Newton (eds) *Tourism in Spain: Critical Issues*, Wallingford: CAB International, 65–88.

Clavell, V (1991) *The Repercussions which hosting the 1992 Olympic Games will have on Development of Tourism in the City of Barcelona*, MSc thesis, University of Surrey.

Dawson, J. (1994) 'Seville', in A. Harding, J. Dawson, R. Evans and M. Parkinson (eds), *European Cities towards 2000: Profiles, policies and prospects*, Manchester: Manchester University Press, 179–193.

Echtner, C.M. and Ritchie, J.R.B. (1993), 'The measurement of destination image: an empirical assessment', *Journal of Travel Research*, 31(4), 3–13.

Feifer, M. (1985) *Going Places*, London: Macmillan.

Fosler, R.S (1992) 'State economic policy: the emerging paradigm', *Economic Development Quarterly*, 6(1), 3–13.

Getz, D. (1991) 'Assessing the economic impacts of festivals and events: research issues', *Journal of Applied Recreation Research*, 16(1), 61–77.

González, F. (1993) 'Foreword', in P. Rispa, C. Alonso de los Rios and M. José Aguaza (eds), *Expo '92 Seville Architecture and Design*, Sociedad Estatal para la Exposición Universal, Electa, Milan.

González, P. and Moral, P. (1996) 'Analysis of tourism trends in Spain', *Annals of Tourism Research*, 23(4), 739–54.

Hall, C. M. (1992) *Hallmark Tourist Events: Impacts, Management and Planning*, London: Belhaven Press.

Hall, C.M.(1997) 'Mega events and their legacies', in P.E. Murphy (ed.), *Quality Management in Urban Tourism*, Chichester: John Wiley, 75–87.

Harding, A. (1994) 'Conclusion: towards the entrepreneurial European city?', in A. Harding, J. Dawson, R. Evans and M. Parkinson (eds), *European Cities towards 2000: Profiles, policies and prospects*, Manchester: Manchester University Press, 195–206

Jessop, B. (1997) 'The entrepreneurial city: reimaging localities, redesigning economic governance, or restructuring capital', in J. Jewson and S. MacGregor (eds), *Transforming Cities: contested governance and new spatial divisions*, London: Routledge.

Jewson, J. and MacGregor, S. (eds) (1997) *Transforming Cities: contested governance and new spatial divisions*, London: Routledge.

Ministerio de Comercio y Turismo (1993) *Futures; Plan Marco de Competitividad del Turismo Español*, Secretaría General de Turismo, Turespaña, Subdirección General de Medios de Promoción.

Newton M. (1996) 'Tourism and public administration in Spain', in M. Barke, J. Towner and J. Newton (eds), *Tourism in Spain: Critical Issues*, Wallingford: CAB International, 137–66.

Osbourne, D. and Gaebler, T. (1992) *Reinventing Government*, New York: Plume.

Paddison, R. (1993) 'City marketing, image reconstruction and urban regeneration', *Urban Studies*, 30(2), 339–50.

Pi-Sunyer, O. (1996) 'Tourism in Catalonia', in M. Barke, J. Towner and M. Newton (eds), *Tourism in Spain: Critical Issues*, Wallingford: CAB International, 231–64.

Pilger, J. (1992) 'The power and the glory; John Pilger on the meaning of the Olympic Games', *New Statesman*, 7 August.

Pincheson, E. (1992) *Madrid in the 1990s: A European Investment Region*, The Economist Intelligence Unit, Special Report No M608, London: Business International Ltd.

Priestley, G. K. (1996) 'City tourism in Spain: a recently discovered potential', in C.M. Law (ed.), *Tourism in Major Cities*, London: International Thomson Business Press.

Ritchie, J.R.B. (1984) 'Assessing the impact of hallmark events: conceptual and research issues', *Journal of Travel Research*, 23(1), 2–11.

Ritchie, J.R.B. (1991) 'The impact of a mega-event on a host region awareness: a longitudinal study', *Journal of Travel Research*, 30(1), 3–10.

Robinson, M. (1996) 'Sustainable tourism for Spain: principles, prospects and problems', in M. Barke, J. Towner and M. Newton (eds), *Tourism in Spain: Critical Issues*, Wallingford: CAB International, 401–26.

Roche, M. (1994) 'Mega events and urban policy', *Annals of Tourism Research*, 21, 1–19.

Rutheiser, C. (1996) *Imagineering Atlanta: The Policy of Place in the City of Dreams*, London: Verso.

Santos Arrebola, J.L. (1995) 'Spanish tourist resorts: new initiatives', *The Tourist Review*, 3/1995, 40–43.

Smith, N. (1996) *The New Urban Frontier: Gentrification and the Revanchist City*, London: Routledge.

Stevens, T. (1992) 'Juan Antonio Samaranch', *Leisure Management*, 12(3), 24–27.

13 Conclusion: urban tourism – the politics and processes of change

DUNCAN TYLER and YVONNE GUERRIER

Introduction

This book was produced as a contribution to the emerging field of urban tourism, aiming to move the debate beyond the descriptive towards a more conceptual understanding of the processes involved in the development and management of tourism in cities. Although Hughes (1997) calls for 'something approaching a paradigm' for urban tourism research, we do not suggest that we have reached this point here. However, in this concluding chapter, we wish to attempt a synthesis of some of the themes identified in the Introduction and to suggest some ways forward for future research.

This book has demonstrated that the study of urban tourism should not just be about the demand and supply of the tourism product. Instead, tourism development should be viewed in terms of the management of change of cities and their functions and the decision-making processes that leads to that change. We see urban tourism as a social and political response to the major post-Fordist changes that have manifest themselves in our cities in the late twentieth century.

The urban tourism process

The study of urban tourism is inevitably the study of change: change in the economic base of cities, change in the use of urban spaces, change in the cultural life of residents. Some of the changes that tourism produces may be predicted, some may be unexpected. Changes may be desirable for some stakeholders and against the interests of others and so inevitably the change process becomes political. For those involved in the business of developing tourism the issues are how to manage the change successfully and the people affected by that change and how to judge what type of change is correct and ensure benefits accrue to appropriate stakeholders. Usually there is a particular concern, at least by those in the public sector, to benefit those people who have suffered most from the decline in traditional urban functions.

Managing Tourism in Cities. Edited by D. Tyler, Y. Guerrier and M. Robertson.
Copyright © 1998 John Wiley & Sons Ltd.

Urban tourism, therefore, is about the social processes of change and the political decision-making processes that dictate the nature of that change and identify the winners and losers. We shall first examine the politics of decision making and then the way in which change affects social processes within the city.

Politics of decision making

The aims of urban tourism

From the case studies presented in this book, it is clear that there are many different motivations for developing urban tourism. These range from the need to manage the inevitability of urban tourism (Evans, Shackley, Tyler), to the planned regeneration of economies (Akehurst, Dodson and Kilian), enhancing local and national prestige (Robertson and Guerrier, Hall, Mules, Tunbridge), and improving the quality of life of resident populations (Tyler, Khan, van der Borg). These aims are not mutually exclusive but addressing them is a political issue involving, as it does, the subjective assessment of what is good for the future of the city and the various stakeholders and interest groups within it, and the approaches taken to urban land and economic development.

Any decision, especially where real estate is concerned, is sure to be influenced by various interest groups. The mobilisation of bias is inevitable and if managed well can build on areas of common interest and mould partnership or collaborative arrangements. If poorly managed it can lead to dissonance among groups within the city. Dodson and Kilian, for example, show that the Muslim and black sectors of the community felt excluded from the consumerist Victoria and Alfred Waterfront Development, and Tunbridge demonstrates the inherent risks of interpreting history through the eyes of one interest group only. On the other hand, Tyler and Akehurst show how urban policy instruments can be used to pursue common aims and bring together various actors in the pursuance of an agreed way forward.

Evans and Hall discuss issues about the level of decision making. At what administrative level do you pitch the development? Should the redevelopment of docks be a state and national issue rather than a local one? Should World Heritage Sites really mean that the social welfare of the neighbouring suburbs become a secondary issue to tourism management?

There is no answer to these questions. However, in reality, decisions as to the type and nature of development have to be made, no matter how long one tries to put them off. This means that decisions as to who wins and who loses have to be made. These decisions are necessarily reflected in the aims of the urban tourism programmes adopted.

Inclusion, exclusion and resistance

Developing the aims of urban tourism, therefore, can lead either to the inclusion of interest groups through the establishment of partnership arrangements which extend beyond mere consultation to inclusive, collaborative planning or to exclusion and pent-up hostility. The cases presented of fast-track or élite planning suggest that perhaps this is not the most harmonious of routes to follow.

Research into urban interest group behaviour and influence would help to identify potential areas for concern for decision makers to address at early stages of planning. Allied to this would be a study of mechanisms of resistance adopted by excluded groups and the impact of exclusion on local communities in terms of both their perceptions of tourism from which they have been excluded and their tactics to end their exclusion and become long-term positive contributors to the urban tourism scene.

Scale and pace

Urban tourism, especially in the larger, well-known national and international cities, can suffer from a lack of focus as to why tourism is being developed. Tyler discusses the problems that Southwark Council in London had of coming to terms with the tourism industry in what was once the main commodity trading and distribution centre for Britain. Hall shows quite clearly how the politicians of Sydney and New South Wales saw the Darling Harbour development as being of statewide and national importance, and similar pictures are painted by Mules, Robertson and Guerrier, Khan and Tunbridge.

Clearly there is some schizophrenia here as to the role of tourism in the city economy. The main dissonance appears to be that between national or state prestige and overcoming local economic and social welfare issues. There seems to be an issue of scale and pace. Tourism developed in a top-down manner, seeking prestige, often seems to forget the fact that the real problem to be addressed is local-level deprivation. Fast-track, master-planned developments rarely, if ever, seem able to address this local deprivation issue, largely perhaps because the glamour and prestige that goes with mega-events and mega-developments is dominated by an élite – an élite that has rarely taken an interest in the areas in question until the opportunity arises for political or economic advantage. However, as Tyler and Akehurst show, a slower, more locally sensitive approach that builds in the local ownership of ideas and plans is surely more likely to consider the issues of local economic deprivation that urban tourism often tries to address.

Research into the relative success of fast-track and more pragmatic development approaches would be useful. Issues such as local ownership of ideas, local employment take-up rates, political prestige and economic viability of individual projects should be addressed.

Appropriateness of change

It is also clear from the case studies that successful urban tourism development is 'appropriate'. By this we mean that it offers opportunities to the local communities, both business and residents, that they are capable of taking up, given the appropriate amount and level of training and support and advice.

Tourism still faces the hurdle of overcoming the image of it providing jobs that are not considered 'real' by those who are used to work in manufacturing or distribution. Tyler discusses resistance from the GLC and London boroughs to tourism for this reason through the 1970s and 1980s. It still seems true that during times of economic boom tourism has trouble recruiting and retaining staff. Khan, in fact, discusses the problems caused by labour shortages on the Singapore tourism industry, and other problems arise when labour is imported to overcome these shortages. These are issues that face the tourism sector in cities around the world.

The question is, however, not just about the quality of new jobs but access to them. How many of the right skills are available in the local community, and to what extent can the mismatch be corrected? Should training and education be primarily a government initiative, a responsibility of the private sector or a part-nership between the sectors? Akehurst mentions educational institutions and on-the-job training in Kalisz to fill skills gaps. Also if the training agencies can respond, can the industry back this up with well-paid and interesting opportunities that provide a career?

Again we have to look at the politics of the issues. Who should pay for and undertake the training? How far should the industry be regulated on the matters of minimum wages, training standards and use of illegal, often imported, labour?

Research into these areas should be undertaken in order to help tourism become fully integrated into a city's economy and play a full part in the post-Fordist struc-ture. These issues also link into those previously mentioned of scale and pace. Locally sensitive development schemes also require locally sensitive training and employment opportunities. If this is possible then perhaps exclusion will be reduced by spreading the benefits of development to the local and traditional communities.

Politics of change and power of interest groups

Much of the above discussion involves the mobilisation of interests. This is often in a formalised way through national and state government machinery, but rarely are these unbiased and the influencing tactics of developers, residents groups, local authorities and indeed professional bodies all play their part in shaping the nature of the urban tourism product. Often those worth the most resources in terms of money, access to decision makers, negotiation and PR skills will win over those with lesser skills in these areas. Akehurst, Tyler, Hall and Khan all mention such influ-ence to a greater or lesser extent, and Mules discusses interstate rivalry for large events that ended in poaching.

There is potentially a rich vein of research into these areas, looking at the relative importance of players and exploring the development process and structures, and indeed some of the chapters in this book examine these topics. Hall discusses the politics of top-down planning in Australia, Tyler the importance of partnerships structures in London and Akehurst the wariness towards central planning and outside influence in Poland. Evans also considers the relative impotence of local communities in the face of management plans developed for the World Heritage Sites at Giza.

Allied to these influences on decision makers are those in power themselves. The importance of leadership is seen in the chapters by Tyler, Hall, Khan and Akehurst. Leadership and the urban governance, the administrative structures and policy tools play a major part in shaping the nature of urban development, and urban tourism is no exception to this.

Social processes of change

Image

This book has shown how, for tourism to develop in a city, the image of that city must be attractive to the professional classes as a place in which to live and to visit. Cities with the 'wrong' image or without a clear image at all need to 're-image'; mega-events (Robertson and Guerrier) or spectacular new developments (Dodson and Kilian, Hall) can play their part in that process.

This process of 'imaging' and 're-imaging' turns the city into a commodity; a product competing with other products in the marketplace (see Robertson and Guerrier), a place to be consumed (Urry 1995, also Dodson and Kilian) with the tourist as consumer. Gabriel and Lang (1995 : 71) argue that one metaphor that may be used to understand the modern consumer is the consumer as explorer: '. . . today's Western consumer is constantly exhorted to savour new tastes, to discover new pleasures, to explore new worlds.'

However, there is a tension here:

> Surely one of the defining paradoxes of modern consumption is the consumer's need to mix the familiar with the unfamiliar, the simultaneous travel to exotic places with patronage of McDonald's and Holiday Inns (logo: 'No surprises'), the simultaneous capitulation to the comfort of habit and the pursuit of adventure (Gabriel and Lang, 1995 : 79).

The successful urban tourist space is, therefore, one which offers excitement, spectacle and stimulation at the same time as safety, security and familiarity. This need to provide a safe playground for the global middle class may result in a sanitisation of traditional urban areas. The paradox is that at some point this process may make the area less attractive to precisely those people it is trying to attract.

What effects does this commodification of the city have on social processes within the city? As Urry (1995) points out, one sense of the word 'consume' is to devour, to eat up. We have seen in this book the example of Venice (van der Borg), a city so in danger of being 'eaten up' by tourism that it must consider issuing tickets for entry. However, consumerism is also about choice. What happens when tourists no longer choose to visit? Hong Kong, at the time of writing, is facing a dramatic fall in tourist numbers, especially from the Asian market. While this is in part due to the current economic problems in the region, there is also a perception, in some markets, that the city is less interesting and less safe after the ultimate mega-event, the handback to China. It has become just another Chinese city. A final issue is about what happens when a city fails to live up to its 'image'. As Robertson and Guerrier show, image makers may conveniently forget about those aspects of real city life that do not fit with the carefully constructed image; tourists can be only too aware that the reality of the city is not as expected when they actually visit.

Use of space

All tourists change the nature of the space that they occupy (Hughes, this volume, and Dietvorst and Ashworth, 1995) both materially by their presence and symbolically by designating a space a 'tourist area'. Drawing on MacCannell (1976), a tourist city becomes a patchwork of 'front areas' where the residents (hosts) perform for the benefit of the tourists and 'back areas' where the residents go about their everyday business. As the 'front areas' take over the centre of the city so the 'back areas' are crowded out to the periphery.

But tourist areas are not fixed. The book has provided many examples of attempts to move tourists into new parts of the city, both to reduce the pressure on already overcrowded attractions and to spread the economic and social benefits of tourism. The attempts to encourage tourists from the North Bank to the South Bank of the Thames, described by Tyler, is a prime example of this.

Carrying-capacity assessment is, as van der Borg argues, a central theme running through much research on urban tourism. Carrying capacity essentially looks at the use of urban space starting from a theoretical framework different from that of sociologists such as Urry and Hughes. Even taking into account that carrying capacity is not merely seen in physical terms, the number of tourists who can possibly be packed into St Mark's Square, but also in socio-economic and socio-anthropical terms, it is a nebulous and problematic concept. This is not to argue that we should not attempt to measure the impact of tourists on a space, merely, to state the obvious, that this is not a straightforward process.

Ownership of space

The discussion above raised the issue that, as tourism develops in cities, parts of the city become effectively 'owned' by the tourists rather than the residents, in that their needs are considered paramount in planning the amenities in the area and their presence defines the character of the area. The paradox is that, as was discussed earlier, the impetus for developing tourism in the first place was often to benefit those residents who may feel dispossessed by it.

However, as this book has shown, the picture is not as simple as a conflict between tourist and resident. There may equally be a diversity of interests between residents and residents, particularly between the traditional residents of inner city areas and the 'new' inhabitants in gentrified areas, who, in their desire for an attractive urban leisure environment, may have more in common with the tourists (see, for example, Dodson and Kilian). Equally, tourists are not a homogenous group; Western heritage tourists 'use' cities such as Cairo and Damascus in a very different way from tourists from other parts of the Middle East (Evans, Shackley).

We have discussed above the ways in which the planning process may empower or disenfranchise different interest groups who lay claim to an urban space. However, it is important to remember that the appropriation of a space by a group of tourists is not always the result of a planned tourism policy, as Hughes has shown in his discussion of gay tourism in Amsterdam.

Multi-cultural fluxes

The social heritage in a city, the distinctive customs and way of life that make a city different, is often as attractive to the visitor as the physical heritage. It has long been recognised that an influx of tourists to a destination challenges the local culture and customs both because these customs are crowded out or so adapted to make them acceptable to the visitors that they cease to have any meaning for the inhabitants and because tourists may import or promote the development of what may be regarded as undesirable practices (vice, gambling, drugs, etc.). While it may be obvious that rural and small communities can suffer in these ways from the development of tourism, the arguments are less clear-cut when urban tourism is considered since cities are, by their nature, both places of change and places of possibility.

Many of the cities discussed in this book are by their nature multicultural, cosmopolitan places that have always been open to influences from all around the world. Furthermore, the residents in one city are the tourists in others: cultural change also comes from residents bringing back ideas from abroad. Residents may resist living in a cultural museum as much as they may resist their physical environment being turned into a museum: modern Londoners, for example, may not wish to spend *all* their leisure time in pubs drinking warm beer and speaking Cockney rhyming slang! Nevertheless, in cities as in other tourist destinations, locals can feel their cultural heritage is under threat from tourism: the problems are arguably greater in smaller cities where it is harder to get away from the tourists (Venice being an obvious example), more mono-cultural cities or those which are newly opening up to outside influences (e.g. cities in the former Eastern bloc).

Researching the politics and processes of change

This final chapter has focused on both the political processes surrounding the development of tourism in cities and on the social changes that result from tourism development. None of the areas of research we have identified above are new, and all have their body of literature. What has not happened to date, however, is the application of them to the field of urban tourism. Perhaps in urban areas more than any other, issues of interest group politics, political decision making, territoriality and management of change of economies is at its most complex given the social, cultural and interest diversity that exists in most towns and cities.

It is this diversity, borne out of the urban location and nature of urban population that makes urban tourism a field of study in its own right. Deeper understanding of the field would, we believe, come from the investigation of it through a multi-disciplined approach that concentrates on the social and political processes of the management of change, decision making, urban governance and influence.

Further reading

We have recommended that the study of urban tourism should embrace a multi-disciplined approach focusing on the management of change and the political nature of decision making and policy development. Here we set out some reading that may help those interested in this approach to explore these issues further, and in turn relate them to the tourism sector.

Mabey and Mayon-White (1993) bring together a series of readings on the management of change in organisations. The book covers such issues as power, politics, team building and managing mess – all applicable to the field of urban tourism and the management of the broader extra-organisational change seen in our cities. Guerrier *et al.* (1995) consider the way that people think about their environment, and include a chapter on urban areas. They look at issues to do with managing conflict, interest groups, and policy dilemmas from a range of philosophical, psychological, economic and sociological perspectives. Gabriel and Lang (1995) offer a wide-ranging discussion of the way that consumers are regarded within modern society. As cities are increasingly places of consumption rather than production this approach may offer new insights into tourist behaviour and management.

On the policy-making front Hall (1994) presents an overview of the impact of politics on tourism development. Chapters 6 and 7 are particularly relevant, addressing issues of the local state and tourism's position in capitalist society. In particular he considers the empowerment of the citizen in urban redevelopment. Hall and Jenkins (1995) present the basic theories of policy and decision making in the tourism context. As a broad introduction it fills the gap between the tourism literature and the pure political science material of Lindblom and Woodhouse (1993) and Ham and Hill (1993). Both of these latter authors discuss the role and behaviour of governments and interest groups in the state's decision-making process, putting it firmly in the context of late twentieth-century capitalism, which, as we have seen, has been transforming our cities. The role of interest groups and lobbies in policy making is reflected strongly in the policy network theories of Rhodes and Marsh (1992) who see policy making dominated not by democratic process but by organised networks of groups manipulating the policy agenda to fit their own interests. This is what Dowding (1995) calls the 'dominant paradigm of the policy-making process in British political sciences'.

It is hoped that through this and further reading in such subjects the field of urban tourism can become a dynamic area of research reflecting the changes now taking place in cities around the world.

References

Dietvorst, A. and Ashworth, G. (1995) *Tourism and Spatial Transformations*, Wallingford: CAB International.

Dowding, K. (1995) 'Model or metaphor? A critical look at the policy network approach', *Political Studies*, 43, 1, 136–58.

Gabriel, Y. and Lang, T. (1995) *The Unmanageable Consumer*, London: Sage.

Guerrier, Y., Alexander, N., Chase, J. and O'Brien, M. (eds) (1995) *Values and The Environment*, Chichester: Wiley.

Hall, C.M. (1994) *Tourism and Politics: Policy, Power and Place*, Chichester: Wiley.

Hall, C.M. and Jenkins, J.M. (1995) *Tourism and Public Policy*, London: Routledge.

Ham, C. and Hill, M. (1993) *The Policy Making Process in the Modern Capitalist State* (2nd edn), Hemel Hempstead: Harvester Wheatsheaf.

Hughes, H. (1997) 'Book review: Tourism in Major Cities, Law, C (ed.)', *Journal of Vacation Marketing*, 3, 2, 180.

Lindblom, C.E. and Woodhouse, E.J. (1993) *The Policy Making Process*, Englewood Cliffs, NJ: Prentice Hall.

Mabey, C. and Mayon-White, B. (eds) (1993) *Managing Change* (2nd edn), London: Paul Chapman.

MacCannell, D. (1976) *The Tourist: a New Theory of the Leisure Class*, London: Macmillan.

Rhodes, R.A.W. and Marsh, D. (1992) *Policy Networks In British Government*, London: Clarendon Press.

Urry, J. (1995) *Consuming Places: A Review Of New Studies*, London: Routledge.

Appendix: Papers presented to The Urban Environment: Tourism Conference, South Bank University, September 1995

Belfast: Tourism and open space management.
Acheson, A.

Metropolitan Bilbao: A revitalisation process through knowledge, culture and art.
Atxutegi, I.

The practicalities of tourism planning and implementation in a Polish city.
Akehurst, A., Walters, J. and Whitehead, A.

From drawing board to drawing crowds: Constructing the image of the city.
Bates, S.

Valuing the locations of accommodation in cities: Relating the tourism market to urban policy.
Bull, A.

Repositioning tourism within a traditional city destination, to maximise direct and indirect benefits to the community.
Carter, R.

Destination culture: place specifics – conservation and tourism in the developing world.
Crookston, M.

A framework for tourism in urban development
Crouch, S.

From model to simulation: Scale in the architecture of tourism.
Davies, P.

Planning for tourism in London: World City, whose city? A critique of local development plans and tourism policy in London.
Evans, G. and McNulty, A.

Pyramids, mosques and museums – resolving issues of resource management in Cairo.
Evans, K.

The utilisation of ethnic minority cultures as an urban tourism product.
Feeney, C.

War and cultural tourism in Berlin and London.
Foley, M. and Lennon, J.

The Castlefield Management Company: A case study in urban tourism management and tourism planning.
Gibson, C. and Hardman, D.

An exploratory examination of urban tourism impact, with reference to residents attitudes, in the cities of Canterbury and Guildford.
Gilbert, D. and Clark, M.

Heritage based tourism as a catalyst for urban regeneration.
Haynes, G.

The tourist as streetwalker: gaze or daze?
Holloway, C.

The urban–cultural alliance in perspective.
Hughes, H.

Local plans: the contribution towards sustainable tourism.
Human, B.

The visitor industry in Bristol and Bath: Complementary or competitive destinations?
Jackson, M.

City tourism – a positive force for economic regeneration, the environment and the quality of life of the local population.
Jeffreys, E.

Creating the urban tourism product.
Law, C.

PATHS towards PEACE: A stakeholder-benefits approach to city centre tourism mangement in Canterbury.
Le Pelley, B. and Laws, E.

Urban tourism: A Latin American perspective.
Lumsdon, L. and Swift, J.

The architect's role in city tourism.
McKeith, G. and Campbell, S.

Tourism prospects in south London.
Millman, R.

Urban tourism and the small independent museum.
Parker, D.

Tourism and urban regeneration: the application of place image as a policy analysis instrument.
Selby, M.

Tourism in Glasgow: tourism as a factor in the regeneration of declining industrial cities.
Sneddon, G.

Sports stadia and arena: Realising their full potential in the urban environment.
Stevens, T.

The importance of an European airport in the development of urban tourism: The impact of the TGV Junction at Lyon.
Tesse, P.

A monumental task; Sustaining Prague for, and from, tourism.
Thompson, C. and Heap, T.

Reconstruction from discovery: An urban design masterplan for Cutty Sark Gardens, Greenwich.
Timpson, M.

Arts and tourism in flagship regeneration.
Voase, R.

Destination culture: Developing the arts.
Wason, G.

Integrating a destination into a city product.
Wray, S.

A future for urban tourism: A synthesis.
van der Borg, J.

Author index

Subject index